EDUCATING
THE IMAGINATION

Educating the Imagination

Essays and Ideas
for Teachers and Writers

Volume 2

Edited by Christopher Edgar & Ron Padgett

Teachers & Writers Collaborative

New York

Educating the Imagination, Volume 2

Teachers & Writers Collaborative
5 Union Square West
New York, N.Y. 10003-3306

Library of Congress Cataloging-in-Publication Data

Educating the imagination / edited by Christopher Edgar & Ron Padgett.
—1st ed.
    p. cm.
    Contents: v. 1. Writing poetry. Writing fiction. Inventing language. Bilingual / Cross-cultural. Evaluation. Reading. First & last. A look back.— v. 2. Letting go. Writing poetry. Writing plays. Writing across the curriculum. Parody & humor. Reading. On language. My high school English teacher. Exemplary models.
    ISBN 0-915924-42-0 (v. 1 : acid-free). — ISBN 0-915924-43-9 (v. 2 : acid-free)
1. English language—Rhetoric—Study and teaching.   I. Edgar, Christopher, 1961– .   II. Padgett, Ron.
PE1404.E29 1994
808'.042—dc20   94-1182
                                                                            CIP

Printed by Philmark Lithographics, New York, N.Y.
Design: Christopher Edgar
Cover drawing of pansies: Joe Brainard

Acknowledgments

Teachers & Writers Collaborative is supported in part by grants from the New York State Council on the Arts and the National Endowment for the Arts.

T&W programs and publications are also made possible by funding from The Bingham Trust, American Stock Exchange, The Bydale Foundation, The Witter Bynner Foundation for Poetry, Chemical Bank, Consolidated Edison, Aaron Diamond Foundation, New York Community Trust, New York Times Company Foundation, Henry Nias Foundation, Helena Rubinstein Foundation, The Scherman Foundation, and the Lila Wallace-Reader's Digest Fund.

Gratitude is also due to New Directions Publishing Corp. for permission to reprint "This is just to say . . ." and "As the cat . . ." by William Carlos Williams, from *Collected Poems: 1909–1939. Vol. I.* Copyright © 1938 by New Directions Publishing Corp.

T&W regrets any omissions and will gladly rectify them in future printings of this volume.

Table of Contents

Preface to Volume 2

by Christopher Edgar and Ron Padgett

Like the first volume of *Educating the Imagination*, this second volume is comprised of articles from the past seventeen years of *Teachers & Writers*, the bi-monthly magazine of Teachers & Writers Collaborative. Most of the articles are by teaching writers and creative teachers. Our initial idea was simply to pick those pieces that might qualify as "greatest hits," but having done so, we found that together they were more than that. They resonated among one another, exemplifying the myriad approaches to teaching imaginative writing that might be termed (very loosely) the Teachers & Writers approach. Shortly after the birth of Teachers & Writers Collaborative, the poets, fiction writers, playwrights, and other artists working in its program realized that there is no one way to teach writing; that different people teach different ways; that different students learn differently; and that to reduce the teaching of writing to a codified method was to falsify (ossify) the entire process.

Of course this is not to say that there aren't many wonderful and useful techniques for teaching writing. In fact, the essays here are mostly practical—many are for immediate adaptation and use in classrooms at all levels—but at the same time there is always a "theoretical" side that comes through, not to mention a "human" side. One thing the authors have in common is a great faith in and respect for their students as writers and as thinkers. Perhaps the ultimate beauty of this book is that it reminds us that it's hard *not* to get inspired by students' imaginations; in a number of ways, the students are the real stars of these two volumes.

Volume 2 opens with Anne Martin's discussion of the writing process movement—and what it may miss aesthetically and developmentally. Julie Patton's "Deep Song" chronicles her struggles and successes with issues at the heart of writing, education, and childhood.

Beginning the section on poetry writing, Jim Berger's two articles focus on using repetition and line-length as ways for students to begin to understand and write poetry. Nan Fry explores using the riddle in a similar fashion: as a means to get students inside an object, image, and poem. Jane Avrich silences those who doubt fifth graders can write wonderful and powerful sonnets, and Dave Morice's "Poetry Poker" provides a playful and surprising entrée into poetry writing. Achille Chavée shows how one of his poems grew out of his collaborating with a bartender.

Next, Daniel Judah Sklar demonstrates how to establish an understanding of theater and an atmosphere of cooperation in "Playmaking." Herbert Kohl examines the joys of mounting adaptations of existing plays with younger students.

Much of T&W's work in recent years has involved using imaginative writing with other disciplines; we include a selection of pieces here under the "writing-across-the-curriculum" rubric. Margot Fortunato Galt's "The Story in History" presents three exercises to get students writing using American history as an inspiration. Elizabeth Radin Simons has her students explore the folklore of names, childhood games, and pranks (including telephone pranks). Ron Padgett provides insights into the physical qualities of grammar and its relation to dance. Rosalind Pace and Marcia Simon's "Image-Making" documents an in-depth bookmaking workshop, delving into the nexus of visual art, design, and writing. Finally, Bernadette Mayer gives a number of unusual science writing exercises.

Parody is a terrific way to have students learn both about literature and themselves as writers. Robert Hershon, Marvin Hoffman, and Joyce Dyer provide three inventive and humorous ways to do this.

Frances Reinehr's "Storytelling" discusses the importance of stories and myths in children's literature, education, and personal lives.

Next comes a group of pieces about language by poets, which we included just because they are fun to read. These are followed by selections from a special issue of our magazine devoted to memories of "My High School English Teacher," by Allen Ginsberg, Anne Waldman, Bob Holman, David Unger, Arthur Dorros, William Kennedy, Jessica Hagedorn, Steve Katz, and Elmore Leonard.

Finally, we round out this volume with three wonderful essays that we could not classify. Christian McEwen's "Four Women" profiles four of the initial writers in the T&W program: June Jordan, Anne Sexton, Muriel Rukeyser, and Grace Paley. Sheryl Noethe gives us a spirited account of her spirited residency as poet-in-the-schools in Salmon, Idaho (pop. 3,306). And the late Flora Arnstein plans a city with her students, showing how large a classroom can be when we take an open approach, and have, as Arnstein says, "the courage to follow where it leads."

Anne Martin

Allowing the Unconventional

If there has been one positive change in elementary education within the last decade, it is the renewed interest in children's writing. There are many strands in this minor revolution, including the whole language movement, the influence of new language teaching programs in New Zealand and Australia communicated to Americans by pioneers such as Don Holdaway and Marie Clay, the National Writing Project, the Bread Loaf Writing Program, Teachers & Writers Collaborative, and, perhaps most widespread, the work of Donald Graves and his associates in New Hampshire. The rekindled enthusiasm for children's writing is all to the good, but, as with many other reforms that have swept through schools (such as the short-lived "open classroom" movement), these new practices tend to be over-simplified and misused.

"Process writing" has become a catch-all phrase for a variety of writing programs. Though on the surface these programs may seem alike because they use similar routines and vocabulary, they sometimes have quite disparate assumptions and results. Often, new writing programs are introduced to teachers with insufficient initial training, and, once launched, with insufficient follow-up sessions and assistance. Teachers rarely have the chance to meet with colleagues on a regular basis over a long term for discussion of issues, questioning of philosophy or practice, and exchanging experiences and thoughtful reflection on what is happening in the whole classroom and to individual children. In the absence of built-in exchanges, teachers are often left to their own devices to develop their own teaching. It is not surprising that in many classrooms of teachers newly converted to "the writing process" the suggestions and recommendations gleaned hastily from workshops and books are followed to the letter with excessive zeal and punctiliousness, far beyond what was intended originally by the pioneers in the field. The result can be a reformed program just as rigid as the one discarded, though presented with currently approved language and trappings that give the appearance of enlightened change.

The danger of a new orthodoxy was clear to Donald Graves himself several years ago:

> The writing process movement has been responsible for a new vitality in both writing and education. But orthodoxies are creeping in that may lead to premature old age. They are a natural part of any aging process. Some are the result of early problems in research (my own included); others come from people who try to take shortcuts with very complex processes. These orthodoxies are substitutes for thinking. They clog our ears. We cease to listen to each other, clouding the issues with jargon in place of simple, direct prose about actual children.[1]

However, it seems to me that even where orthodoxy is consciously avoided and a teacher thoughtfully adapts "process writing" (do we really need to use the word "process" every time we speak of writing, which *refers* to a process anyway?) to a particular classroom setting, age level, and school, other vexing questions may arise. I feel almost churlish to raise objections when there are so many good things that are developing in classroom writing programs—the validation of each child's subject matter; teacher and peer assistance in writing; cooperation among children; open, clear discussion of writing problems; a new role for teachers as consultants, learners, and researchers; joyful enthusiasm for the written word—but in many descriptions of writing programs or actual classrooms, I find myself troubled by the seeming absence of, or at least casual disregard for, the darker and mysterious aspects of writing. In all the happy activity of first drafts, "conferencing" revision, final drafts, filing papers into writing folders, publishing, celebrating authorship, and public readings, what happens to the offbeat writing that evades a clear beginning, middle, and end, that makes no sense to teachers or other children, that does not lend itself to revision based on other people's questions, that has no clear logic, no details, no showing-instead-of-telling, that is not first "rehearsed" and then tried out with different "leads"? Is it subtly rejected or cajoled into other forms that lend themselves better to classroom expectations?

Theoretically, as thoughtful, tolerant teachers, we try to accept wide divergence in children's thinking, but actually we are often torn between the strong conviction that children's individual expression is basic to education and the simultaneous guilt that we are not sufficiently doing our duty of training children in writing skills. Once we have worked past the beginning problems of how to get children started writing—when and how to make technical corrections, and how to encourage a lively writing program—we are faced with more subtle questions of content and form, adult expectations, and children's responses. This was not a problem for me when I was teaching very young children. The non sequiturs and seemingly random jumps in their stories could be justified as both charming and significant in their own terms, as in this dictated story by four-year-old Marilyn:

> Once upon a time when my mommy did something, every time she picked the flowers she didn't know they were flowers. She picked more of them, and she didn't want the flowers. And she went home. Once my baby didn't want to go in the crib. She cried and yelled, yelled and yelled. And my mommy cried and cried and cried all day. And I just watched television.

But what to make of this story by nine-year-old Nancy?

> Once a little girl was in the kitchen and drank some milk and started to throw up all over the butter and jam. Her mother didn't have breakfast and her mother had toast and used the butter and jam and the girl was okay and the mother. And the mother was allergic to it too and throw upped and they lived happily ever after.

While Nancy's narrative comes through despite its unusual subject, there is much ambiguity both in the sentences and the meaning. By the middle elementary grades, there is the strong expectation that stories should have a beginning, middle, and end; that they should be more than a few sentences long; that they should contain detail, maybe dialogue, description, a logical sequence, and sentence variation; and that they should meet various other reasonable criteria for writing, along with more or less correct mechanics. As someone who values good writing, I don't object to these general aims. It's just that they are not always applicable to the stories that nine- and ten-year-olds write. Take, for instance, Martha's story about an imaginary vacation:

> I went to Las Vegas and won $200,000 and I bought a yacht for $6,000 and a fur for my mother and she loved it! I hired some police to guard all of us with all that money! So one of the police was really a burglar so he held me up and I said, "Stop playing jokes!" He said, "Okay," and he fired his gun. He missed me and all of a sudden my father sat on him and he died!

Unlike Nancy's story, this one has a well-defined plot, characters, logical sequence, dialogue, drama, and a surprise ending. Yet there is bound to be some uneasiness about it, partly because it is so short. In this story, we get the feeling that a lot is missing. But for the author it says precisely what was meant, as Martha informed me in no uncertain terms when I cautiously asked some questions to fill in the gaps. In other instances, I might have tried to persuade the author to work on expanding the story. The chances are that the revision would be an improvement. Again, on principle I am in favor of rewriting or reworking material. But in practice I have often found it counterproductive with primary grade children, and also with older children who are still working out a particular bit of subject matter and are not yet ready to produce a polished piece of work.

In Lucy Calkins's *Lessons from a Child*, the author gives many examples of first and final drafts to illustrate the progress children make when they go through revisions of their writing. Yet the approved final versions are often jarring because they seem so much weaker than the original drafts. Here is a section of a long story by Susie written in the fourth grade. First draft: "I ran to my grandmother and just hugged her. We were both so happy to see each other. My grandmother laughed and cried at the same time." After her teacher challenged her to lengthen the story because her writing was usually the same length, Susie (clearly an outstandingly able and conscientious writer) revised the passage to this: "'Hi, Babydoll!' my grandmother said. I gave her a kiss. My grandmother's eyes were filled with tears but she was laughing. We were so happy."[2] The first version is touching because of its directness and simplicity. The final one seems forced and less deeply felt.

Stories such as Martha's imaginary vacation in Las Vegas are rarely cited by writing process proponents unless they have undergone many conferences and revisions and have "before" and "after" versions that show improvement. Yet these stories are rather typical in the early grades, and perhaps a necessary stage in the development of narrative. Stories like Nancy's are never cited, probably because they are too oddball. Whereas abstract, experimental visual art is allowed and approved, even beyond primary grades, writing is generally expected to conform to achievement standards that include acceptable form and content, just as much as improved writing mechanics.

What is acceptable is often narrowly defined in terms of conventional expectations. By fourth grade, with stimulation, practice, motivation, and encouragement, most children can produce at least a few examples of what are considered creditable models of writing at their grade level. But those aberrant pieces of writing that tend to pop up more frequently in classrooms that honor individuality in other creative areas may be pivotal work for their authors, though neither they nor we understand why. In fact, it may be crucial to encourage some of this offbeat quality in all of us. I believe that the sources of writing within us have to be activated first, before we can impose standards of form. The first challenge is to get at the material that needs to be written.

Children themselves, by the middle grades or even earlier, tend to scorn their "weird" thoughts, and are reluctant to play with language in writing. Teachers also are uneasy with material that does not lend itself to routine questioning or revision. It is no accident that poetry was largely ignored early on by the Graves writing process followers, and even fiction writing was approached with much apprehension for fear of the TV-inspired junk writing that would probably emerge. It is true that many children's early attempts at fiction may be imitative and modeled on action shows they admire, which creates problems for teachers who struggle to respond positively and yet productively. But it is equally true that cutting off children's potential for "crazy" writing may cut out the expression of some of their deepest thoughts and feelings, those that are not understood consciously by their authors and can be communicated only in symbolic fragments.

Through various poetry exercises and games, older children will let themselves write ostensibly meaningless stream-of-consciousness pieces that often give them much pleasure. Out of these abstract "poems" may come one or two powerful lines, images, or thoughts, as in this exercise by Sally (age nine):

> I can see you with my words
> Can you see my words of the world?
> Daddy and Mommy see my words of the world
> cats and dogs girls and boys will cry
> so you can cry but you will not.
> So be very sweet.
> Cookies need more cement and so will you
> Mommy can cry and Daddy can cry too.

After a lot of exercises of this kind, some children will attempt to make use of their own crazy thoughts in a more controlled fashion, such as in this parody of a fairy tale opening by a fourth grader:

> In the thick tangled vines of the jungle, there was a castle with golden towers. In it there lived a princess. Her name was Leonora. She had hair as orange as an orange. Her skin was the color of a peach. Her lips the color of an apple. She was a perfect fruit bowl.

However, it takes a great deal of time and effort to learn to release thoughts and feelings, and then learn to organize them in written form.

Not all children can do this in the course of the year, and when I was teaching fourth graders I was perpetually in self-doubt, trying to justify my shaky faith that the children were working towards writing effectively even though I was maintaining my guilty resistance to grammar exercises, English worksheets, and checklists of "skills mastered." Are the children really learning? Would they do better with more conventional approaches? These are not rhetorical questions. Every minor or major decision in the classroom depends on basic values, whether articulated or not, and unless there is strong school support for your convictions, there is bound to be destructive self-doubt if you go counter to currently accepted practice.

In the case of Nancy, who wrote the breakfast story, I had special reasons for worry. As soon as she felt comfortable in the room, she decided to set me up as her enemy. She told me she planned to do everything bad that she could, and then said sweetly, "Don't worry, it's just a phase!" Unfortunately, the phase lasted the year, except for occasions when she would forget and talk to me in a friendly way until she caught herself and went back to defying me at every turn. This was a new experience for me. I had always considered myself the children's advocate, but Nancy put me in the role of enemy of the people. It wasn't much of a comfort to know that there were family problems, and that the previous year Nancy had spent much of her school time in the nurse's office with stomach aches. I still had to deal with Nancy's daily behavior and the ripple effect it caused.

I am providing this background only because it illustrates something that surprised me. I had always assumed that a trusting relationship between a child and a teacher was essential to real learning. But in spite of my evident failure with this child, something curious happened to Nancy's writing. She went through an evolution from rambling, seemingly pointless stories to concise, clear narratives from her own life.

At the beginning, story writing was one of the few things Nancy liked to do. She hated reading and feared math. I always approved of her writing, though she was amazed that I could like the breakfast story that had such indelicate subject matter. As she threw herself into her battle against me, Nancy virtually stopped writing, and handed in only the bare minimum of assignments. Her mood, both at home and school, was expressed in one poem:

> I am mad
> mad is angry
> angry is fresh
> fresh is go to your room

go to your room is mad
and I am MAD

While I insisted on her fulfilling daily classroom assignments, I accepted short pieces and tried to avoid making an issue of her resistance. Then one day in April, she wrote another story that closely paralleled the one she had written in October:

> Once upon a time I went to the frigerator and drank some sour milk and then I threw up on the butter and cheese and my mother's toast and my mom used the butter for the toast and then we were dead.

Nancy didn't give any sign of recognizing this previous theme. I accepted the story casually without questions or comments. Within a few weeks, Nancy began to write again. She voluntarily spent a whole day with another child writing several pages of a story about a "Goody Two-Shoes" girl. And then suddenly she began to write about her own family and her concerns. One story depicted graphically how her father seemed to neglect her in favor of his new wife and babies. Another was a projection into the future in which her parents were too busy to come to her college graduation. It ended:

> I asked why they weren't at my graduation party. They said, "Daddy had to go to Denver for another business meeting. And I had to work overtime." I said to my dad, "Denver is more important than me. Mom, working overtime is more important than me. I just have two lousy parents." Then they explained they would of losted their jobs if they didn't miss my graduation. I said, "I must of been not quite a mature adult."

This story was so important to Nancy that she spent hours copying it onto a stencil for the class magazine, starting over each time she made a mistake until she finally did it to her satisfaction.

It seemed to me that something significant had happened to Nancy through her writing. Whatever the strange breakfast stories meant to her, they needed to be written and accepted as part of a long-term struggle which led her from obscure, confusing, symbolic stories to explicit, well-written accounts of what was on her mind. This didn't come through conferences, editing, corrections, workbook exercises, or skill lists. Nor did it come from positive relationships with other children or the teacher. Nancy's need to express ideas and feelings in writing was strong enough to impose its own laws and necessities, given an environment where writing was valued, shared, accorded time and respect, and expected of everyone.

This experience suggests to me that mere acceptance of oddball work is important enough to make a significant difference in a child's capacity to learn, even when mutual sympathy and understanding are missing. While it is undoubtedly better to have a good working relationship, there may be some value merely in the faith in children's capacity to learn the skills they need, though their routes may appear unnecessarily circuitous and downright peculiar.

Some material may be so unclear to the author that even well-meant help can interfere with and destroy a difficult and fragile new theme. If we impose too many questions or suggestions in conferences with peers or the teacher, we may lose some of the most original and deeply felt writing that children are groping towards. A "first draft" may consist of odd fragments, such as we might find in adult writers' notebooks and journals, to be worked through gradually over time, re-worked in other forms, or perhaps discarded altogether if they serve no more purpose for the author. Writing, like all creative acts, is complex and mysterious and no matter how happily we take on the enlightened attitudes of the process writing movement, there will be perplexing questions, great individual differences, and work that is unclear and yet valuable.

In the last analysis, there is no foolproof way to teach writing (or anything else), and too much reliance on method—rather than the underlying purposes and spirit of a writing program—can be as harmful in a process writing or whole language approach as it can in traditional lessons. Let us maintain our respect for the complexity of children's thoughts and feelings, and the ambiguity that remains at the heart of any creative work. We need to give children space and time in which to experiment freely with writing, to produce unrevised "throw-aways" as well as undeveloped sketches. Though our job is to teach, sometimes it is most productive to refrain from tampering too early with children's work. Most of all, I think teachers need to keep talking with each other and exchanging ideas and experiences. We all need help from others to remain open to the wide variations in children's writing, to strengthen our faith in their own drive to master language, and to keep us in awe of the power of the written word that is reflected in the work of children.

Notes

1. Donald Graves, *A Researcher Learns to Write* (Portsmouth, N.H.: Heinemann, 1984), p. 18.

2. Lucy Calkins, *Lessons from a Child* (Portsmouth, N.H.: Heinemann, 1983), p. 94.

Julie Patton

Deep Song

> *Once the fairies have created the right atmosphere, two rhythms are needed, the physical rhythm of the cradle or chair and the intellectual rhythm of the melody. The mother fits together these rhythms, one for the body and one for hearing, using various measures and silences. She blends them till she finds the very tone capable of enchanting the child.*
>
> —Federico García Lorca, *Deep Song*

The following paragraphs in italics are excerpts from my teaching diary, alternated with excerpts from a poem by Octavio Paz:

With the lights off, I turned the pages of Octavio Paz's book of poems to "San Ildefonso Nocturne," quietly briefing my students about free association. Then I began to read . . .

In my window, night
                                        invents another night,
another space:
                                carnival convulsed
in a square yard of blackness. . . .

. . . slowly tugging on the words and my memory of nursery school to merge them with the breath in the room, the late afternoon light on the smooth, polished floor of an old mansion. The room became an instrument for daydreams, soft voices, as the music quieted us toward sleep.

But I seldom fell asleep. In nursery school, I was always meditating on the sounds coming from a cello the length of the man who played it. There was something human about the cello's form and voice, the way it became an extension of the player-musician. The cello was a black woman with hands on her hips, a large doll humming a lullaby, the body of a headless woman with the face of the young man leaning over it, his arms alternatingly holding it, pulling sound through the warm body of wood, that of the instrument itself and the drawing room swaying with light-colored leaves through leaded glass windows. I know how rooms change shape, swell with the sounds within them, how inanimate things walk and talk, and words and sounds connect time and space.

Sign–seeds:
                    the night shoots them off
they rise,
     bursting above,
                              fall
still burning
          in a cone of shadow,
                                        reappear,
rambling sparks,
                    syllable–clusters,
spinning flames
               that scatter,
                         smithereens once more.
The city invents and erases them.
I am at the entrance to a tunnel.
These phrases puncture time.
Perhaps I am that which waits at the end of the tunnel.
I speak with eyes closed.
                         Someone
has planted
          a forest of magnetic needles
          in my eyelids,
someone guides the thread of these words.

For me, the light in the classroom and the sounds of the poem became a single wave, a four-dimensional conversation between Octavio Paz, the students, myself, and my past. One of my fourth grade students, Michael Spann, was inspired to write this poem:

Dark night, bright moon
Brightening stars
Little dipper, big dipper
Dark spilling stars
Different stars form a picture and
Love notes high up in the sky
Comets and meteors bursting through and
Around the moon
Dancing far off on Venus
The bright heated sun beats hot
The stars come to the open window while
I swiftly twist and turn
I'm knocked out

talking and walking in my sleep
I'm outside hungry and the night
wants me in bed
Cats and dogs look for food at midnight
While the homeless children
make a newspaper bed
I'm freezing in the cold
I'm drifting through and crashing into walls
Paper and plastic flying in my face
Schools are closed, germs in my stomach
My head's beating fast
dreaming of the snow blizzard that happened last week
The snow forty feet high
while the red bullseye faces north
My footsteps take me to a sunny place
I'm confused. It opens my mind.
I look at my shadow
My blood is in love
It's flowing lights
I read a book
It was just me, myself and the grass
the wind blew wild and scattered the water
I got wet so I walked in front of
a mountain that was behind me,
the wild wild wind and the washing water

Teaching poetry *is* a poetic activity. It invites research, experimentation, creative play, and adventure. I constantly revise new goals, and set new tasks. No exercise or approach is ever chiseled in stone; and at the end of each school year my enthusiasm for a job well done is often cut short by the changing demands and expectations that I place on myself, usually as the result of reviewing the anthologies my students produce. In fact, all it seems to take is the act of passing out an anthology that I recently slaved over to have my head swimming with new resolutions for the coming school year.

Teaching poetry is a highly contextualized act that depends on our ability to maintain an open dialogue between the world and ourselves as writing teachers and to project ourselves into the work so that the writing workshops suit the specific needs of each learning environment as an extension of our poetic consciousness and the interests of the children. My most effective workshops have involved a sympathetic understanding and approach to my own childhood, not adult formulas or models. Although sometimes I have brought poems into the classroom to show the rich possibilities of poetic language, I was self-conscious about overwhelming my students with too much adult chatter. More importantly, I was concerned about the danger of students' imitating poems as still-life models removed from the students' own lives.

I wanted to focus on the art of teaching poetry as it relates to ideas, wonder, astonishment, and discovery—and to encourage the students to explore their own ideas, write from their bodies, their centers, and to communicate their sense of intimacy and familiarity with the world. Besides, poetry is more than the printed word, and one doesn't have to depend on poems in order to inspire kids. Poetry, like science, is inquiry, a search for "truth," taking in the full measure of the world and naming or categorizing the things within it. All art is this quest, this questioning. The key thing is to ignite the children's curiosity. I had another motive as well: I wanted to get close to their creativity to explore the world as they articulate it. As Thoreau noted, our childhood dreams vanish from our memory because we fail to learn their language.

"How is it possible not to feel that there is communication between our solitude as dreamers and the solitudes of childhood?" asked the French philosopher Gaston Bachelard. Solitude is a word on horseback riding into the distant sunset while everything else races toward the twenty-first century. It's the lifejacket poets use to float in or dwell in their streams of consciousness.

What is solitude, and how does one find sufficient space for it among thirty-five students in the middle of the buzzing afternoon? The word *solitude* conjures up images of seclusion, isolation, and a nostalgia for the past. To me, it also evokes the seemingly anachronistic concerns of nineteenth-century writers mourning the loss of idyllic space to the industrial world. For Bachelard, the concept of solitude is the conquest or suspension of time, and more specifically, the writer's potential to abolish the distances between dreams, to compress or extend the literary imagination while retaining and preserving one's childhood as a deepening life resource. Rilke, too, inquired how we could imagine our lives to be anything more than we were able to imagine in a single childhood. Both Bachelard and Rilke draw attention to the possibilities of childhood as a source of wonder, and the need to grant it its true potential.

Childhood still has and needs its sacred and secret spaces. How can the poet/teacher create the space in the classroom for his or her students to weave together the real and the imaginary so that, in

Bachelard's words, "the child knows the happiness of dreaming which will later be the happiness of the poet"?

This is not a pretentious goal if you consider that the poet is first of all committed to the gathering of language as an ongoing process that cannot be measured by time or static words on a page. Language is much more than the saying of things, it is how we project and *mark* our being in the world.

Perhaps the ability to manipulate boundaries really belongs to the Greek goddess of memory, Mnemosyne, and her three daughters, the muses Aoede (song), Medete (meditation), and Mneme (memory). These figures provide the perfect backdrop on which to hang my thoughts and concerns about an approach to writing that enabled me to use poetry in the classroom in a fresh and exciting way.

One recent year, I stared at the pages of one of my student anthologies long enough to hear the energy of the classroom, the cacophony of voice, movement, and the light from expectant gazes swirling around and away from the inertia of the words on the pages, to realize that my students had not really let go. Somewhere in their hands and limbs loosening up for summer flight was the verve, the run, the gesture of their own deep songs. Yet despite my ardent appeals to let go, some of the students had been afraid to celebrate the dash and dare of their true verbal sophistication. I had not yet found a way to communicate to them that poetry is music. I had to find a more effective means to project my students past the walls that seem to separate the making of an image from the sound that props it up and intensifies its meaning, and to submerge them in . . .

Aoede.

Anyone who has spent five minutes with children can observe how they play with the poetic function, take pleasure in exploring sound by inventing words, repeating rhymes and raps for street play, doing double dutch, and even talking to dolls. The problem for me was how to communicate this same feeling of spontaneity and ease with language, a similar sense of poetry as activity, gesture, and light, and the notion that both words and sounds carry poetic meaning. For instance, I felt that I could fascinate them with the fact that the rain rains, a house houses—these are things they can engage their senses and curiosity in. The river rivering in Langston Hughes's poem "I've Known Rivers" calls attention to the flowing wave of the refrain with a breathlessness that obscures specific words, but not the idea that a river is a phenomenon we can all immerse ourselves in—in speaking like water we "absorb the lesson of the stream." This is what I had to bring them to understand.

Although I often avoided using adult poems for reasons mentioned earlier in this essay, my thoughts were constantly focused on the memory of rooms that are still filled with the love of being read to. I became a writer in those rooms. The umbilicus of my writing hand is tied to those talking books and the impulse of reading. I can still hear the words that transported me through time and space, informing me that the world itself is a book.

When I did read adult poems to my students, I would read only parts of them, as sound bites. I'd go through all kinds of linguistic gymnastics to blur the edges in order to leave as little of an aftertaste lingering in the air as possible. Kids are the real "quicker-picker-uppers": they can grab a sentence in mid-air and remind you of it days later ("But Ms. Patton, you said . . ."). Reading poems or parts of them as sound bites sets a certain mood and sends the students floating.

The following excerpt from my diary illustrates these concerns:

January, 1990. *In my own work, either visual or written, I usually begin by responding to an aural stimulus; it might be music, the sound of wind tempting tornadoes on a lake, or the sound of horseshoes on stone. I used to revel in the funereal march of tired limbs on their way to bed. . . . Surely the tentative gathering of limbs against the body before settling them down was one of the great pauses that informed the lyric voice of the nineteenth century. No wonder they lamented the anonymous whir of the "horseless carriage," there was no breath to it, no rhythmic inhale or exhale.*

The inner ear holds things. We make reference to the ear as "having picked something up" or "catching" things as low to the ground as footsteps. It's almost as if the head has hands that it clasps to its sides like a catcher's mitt, either that or it doesn't have enough folds to store the world's secrets, so they spill to the point of overflowing, forcing the hand to deliver or the mouth to speak. The question is not just to stretch and fill the students' ears, but to compel them to sing.

They have to search for silence in a modern world hip-hopping to video games, the sound of broken bottles, even the name "tags" shouting for recognition from concrete walls—whatever, it's their world, and the flight of pigeons over rooftops and the slow drag of buses still count for something even if it's only their rhythm that moves words onto paper.

Rhythm is expectation. One wave follows another. We anticipate the lull between two seesawing notions of time, the tick and the tock. Cradling is the place of repose between two rockers swinging back and forth. We are caressed, soothed, calmed toward our interior selves. Words sing, and the love of being read to is part of a primordial urge that connects us to deeper, more abiding rhythms—including the ocean rocking inside of us, the loud breathing and ticktocking shoes of nannies drawing us toward sleep. . . .

Medete . . .

is the nanny, the muse turning out the lights so that we can retreat from the clamor and chaos of the world and the classroom.

On the one hand, meditation implies contemplation, reflection, concentration, focusing; on the other, release, dispersal, letting go. Both invite us to dwell. Medete's gesture provides dwelling space for eyes, ears, and the dreaming self at risk under glaring, harsh lights.

Denise Levertov asked, "Can I distinguish between dreams and writing—that is, between dream images and those that come into being when I am in a poem-making state?" The problem is how to accomplish this in a situation where the measuring stick is about how well one sits and pays attention. One can either meditate *on* something or *in* something. Poetry is meditation that blurs the edges into quiet openings, a locus that enables us to dwell on things and in things. It's about intervals, extending the lull, and the openings between consciousness, and drawing curtains so words can dream and reveal themselves.

It's the same solitude that Bachelard says poets bear witness to— "an aspiration to cross the line, go against the current, to rediscover the great calm lake where time rests from its flowing. And this lake is within us, like a primitive water, like the environment in which an immobile childhood continues to reside."

We recognize things because they exist within us, are a part of our being. Remembering is the act of pausing and re-collecting. To remember is also to dwell:

Mneme . . .

is spinning threads in the center of the classroom. These threads are rays of light seeking anchor in the corners as a human voice vibrates across the smooth tops of desks, encouraging the children to pick up the beat with their pencils. Perhaps this one, two, three P.M. light has been distilled into the quick of all children who sat and still sit, collecting thoughts or escape routes home.

April, 1990. *Lately I've realized that light is one of the most powerful catalysts for evoking personal memory. I found myself trying to still everything in its immense silence, until I realized that light is kin to music. It too carries the*

*rhythm of the world it encloses—the movement of the clouds, punctuating sun
or moon, and boom! the deep pause between thunder and lightning. As the
clock measured off the seconds between noon and the untangling of limbs from
the metal bars of chairs and desks, we digested more than food and information, we took in the light and dwelled on it as it marched across the room
dragging its colors through the windows, open or closed. We waited for it to fall
full-face and lull us into daydreams. Sometimes in that atmosphere of hushed
and restrained voices, it was the only rhythm that counted.*

Mneme makes memories with a cradle of light and song that sets
us into deeper grooves. This particular cradle is a chisel-like tool rocking to and fro over a metal plate, preparing a ground for inking.

I was reminded of this as I sat in the back of a classroom listening
to visiting writer Quincy Troupe talk a blue streak and raise black-
consciousness poems from a remote past. It was history, but the
language, like their own, was laced with familiar sounds. Stirred by his
tongue, the children got on waves of light and sound and rode—
straight into the fluorescent sixties.

Quincy was Mneme, a griot, transmitting words of the past until
the students merged their voices with his, mirroring his rhythm and
energy in return. The repetition was the perfect mnemonic device and
at his suggestion they turned to him, his persona, lingo, and style, and
the lingering sounds of sixties poems for the day's writing subject:

Quincy Troupe Soul Man of Cool. Cool, Cool, too cool,
jazz musician cool with vines hanging over his Quincy
Troupe too-cool shades with his jazzy jazzed clothes
and his too-cool motherland too-cool shoes. With his
too-cool spirit, and his too-cool soul, too-cool
too-cool wherever he goes
writing out his feelings with paper and pen
he's the coolest of all the too-cool men

   —*Jenean Hamilton, third grade*

In the 1960s, the same decade that Don L. Lee penned "But He
Was Cool or He Even Stopped for Green Lights" (one of the poems
that inspired Jenean Hamilton's poem), Lee also sang the blues about
the increasing schism between "public schools or private schools in
the A.M. and street schools and home schools in the P.M." Several decades later, this clash of cultures and the cry for more relevancy and
better learning conditions has grown louder.

In the nineteenth century, some writers expressed a growing anxiety about the intensification of solitude in the din of the expanding

urban metropolis—the deafening roar of the crowd where there's no one to talk to but the machine. Nowadays, television sets, Walkmans, Nintendo, video games, and boom-boxes are among children's closest companions. They think, write, and study to their persistent rhythms. In poem after poem, my students rage about the condition of the world and the disappearance of safe space. They no longer have the luxury of playing in the streets. They are banished to their rooms with their electronic companions. All the more reason to find ways to broaden their horizons, to expand the space of the paper and the world around them.

Lincoln

It makes me think of Lincoln projects on a hot Saturday night
The sun is beaming down on a hot black girl
The bareness of the brain is darkening
The system of life
Thinking about life made an old lady cry
Fire!
Among the kids of the world
Laying in bed listening to LL Cool Jay, momma said, knock you out
Profanity hitting the street and backfiring and hitting the black youth
    jumping the trains, and jumping life
It's the tracks crying for your life
The heart is beating like the rhythm of a handshake
You're dying, you're killing
And now you're finished

   —*Lakesha Hawkins, sixth grade*

As a poet teaching in the schools, I have waged an ongoing struggle with the ugliness and mediocrity fencing in most "inner-city" kids. Knowing they lack the cool, airy relief of gilded concert halls and lilac-filled museums—as well as a strong awareness of their own cultural heritage—the presumptuous and intervening poet has to depend on the portability of the human tongue to create an environment for Aoede to sing in, Medete to suspend or focus awareness in, and Mneme to re-collect.

On its most basic level, Lakesha's poem—like Michael Spann's—was the result of being fed up. It was the last straw after the abandoned lot—the last offense in a succession of offenses that piled shoes on top of bottles, and years of indifference before entering the school door and climbing to a classroom that offered little aesthetic relief. I understand the importance of Beauty's rooms or what the *Book of Changes* calls grace—Art, the world of adornment and ideas. So I decided to read my way out of the room, carrying the kids on my tongue. Aesthetics can be a means of survival. Can't afford an instrument? With tongue and cheek create a symphony. Outnoise the noise, moon-walk, make shoelaces double-talk and walls cry your name. Anything to outwit the enemies, mark territory. Urge a toy truck along the floorboards with the throttle of your throat, or write.

January, 1990. *When they removed the tall rows of plane trees from my street, my eyes burned to replace them. A few years later, the neighborhood was set on fire. By the end of the third night on the streets (better watch for an ignited house than remain in one), I started making my way into other spaces— Beauty's room was a lesson in abstract expression burning crimson in the midnight sky. I was thirteen. Reading and writing were a struggle against silence. Books and my mother's paintings communicated the possibilities of projecting the world onto other spaces. How does someone teach a child to claim art—the right to do so as a manifesto for their dangerous and frightening tomorrows? Giving them pencils and pens is one way of communicating the openness of the creative act as a territory they can seize for their own personal freedom and sense of flight without adult intervention. It's like putting down crumbs so they can eventually make their way toward a more whole, less fractured self. They need a poetic license for their whole lives.*

One day, Wonderful Worthington, one of my sixth grade students at P.S. 157 in the South Bronx, came bouncing into the room proudly displaying a new badge. A hefty kid, he reminded me of the lion in *The Wizard of Oz* trumpeting his new badge of courage. The badge to behold was a "poetic license" that he'd been given by another visiting writer, and it did represent a kind of courage. The courage to make words bend to your will, stretch like Silly Putty or fit like Erector Set pieces. This is a principal skill that many creative writers draw on, one that enabled Wonderful Worthington to take risks and come up with startling images:

> When I wake up in the morning
> I walk to school
> Its sounds of terror bang on your wall
> When I look at the water
> The water kind of vanishes as the bird sings it back
> Summer arises in the country
> There are no sounds but yourself
> A dog cries in the night
> Then you find out the dangers of darkness
> When I look out the window before supper
> It's like a big black fat cat sleeping on my house

The night is a sound killer
When you wake up you feel like writing
But your fingers are froze
The paper is burning for words I take a nap
I've just come from La-La Land
I didn't know
I thought I saw my mom cooking eggs on the bed
But that was one of La-La Land's tricks

    —*Wonderful Worthington, sixth grade*

Freewriting and Free Association

> Art was a game, children assembled words that ended with the sound of a bell, then they shouted and wept their verses and put shoes on them. —From *The Dada Painters & Poets*

As in Wonderful's poem, writing is alchemy, and the elixir is words—words potent enough to summon up other words. The metamorphosis that occurs in creative writing is revealed to my students through the process of freewriting, stream of consciousness writing, and free association.

In particular, my using the "game" of free association grew out of my frustration with children's creating short pieces within minutes, as if they had run out of ideas, while still running their mouths like babbling brooks. I could find no real reason for their brief gestation periods and the finality of the class period's period. I wanted them to fill their papers with the same breathless energy that they talk with. Now, to explain the concept of freewriting, I exaggerate by drawing an extremely ridiculous face on the board with a wavy stream pouring from its head. The drawing is so elementary that the children get a kick out of assuming the "stream of consciousness" is really hair until I explain that it really represents their thinking, which, like water, seldom stops its natural flow and runs over and around things even in sleep, when we dream. The visual reference is useful, and they comprehend consciousness very clearly when it's linked with being "knocked unconscious," or losing or gaining consciousness. Sometimes I explain the different levels of consciousness by comparing them to the levels of a house—the basement being the "subconscious"—while I explain that this isn't the hierarchy that it appears to be, that in writing all levels flow into the same bubbling stream.

The key is to let them know it's okay to explore on paper the honest language of the speaking mind bouncing from one subject to another, and not to censor this process. This is where I take the opportunity to distinguish between creative writing and the rest of the writing they do all day, which is geared explicitly toward the two extreme poles of right and wrong. Freewriting, free association, and stream of consciousness writing reflect spontaneity, flight, abandon, the freedom to make dynamic connections, the dash of et cetera, the fact that we're more like flow-thru tea bags than individually wrapped lumps of clay. It's vital for children to feel comfortable exploring the richness of language, the magical, evocative, suggestive power of words—to feel literally rich with words and empowered by them, and at the same time exercise creative play with language.

Many avant-garde artists have been inspired by the work of children. The Dadaists and Surrealists invented techniques based on children's creative play. They drew words out of hats or cut them from newspapers and then arranged them according to their random fall. They stressed the occasional, circumstantial nature of poetry as "an activity of the mind," not its "immutable and static beauty," as Tristan Tzara put it.

The writing hand is not as fast as the mind. I implore the kids to "arrest" words that pop into their minds and put them on paper exactly as the words come to them. I tell them that each word is a "clue" to other words. Other times I tell them we're going to "meditate" on words, or go on an archeological dig.

Next I guide them through an exercise in free association. I ask them if their mother ever told them *not* to "associate" with a particular person or group. In my wilder moods—and depending on the time—I get rid of my Romper Room voice and have them do free association as a competition, quickly calling on someone, or a team of students, to see how fast they can come up with a word. When they discover that they have a real arsenal of words that they can cull from with confidence, they then battle it out and unearth the most intriguing associations.

I toss the first word off the top of my head and grab the first response. I accept all the different types of responses, just to illustrate that there is no right or wrong. I emphasize this point again and again. *Hat* might call up *head, black, sky, stars, man,* or *feet*—any connection is fine, the important thing is that they sense the connection and see it all in action. They understand that editing is usually a no-no, and try to seize their elusive first impressions.

After a few rounds, I begin to encourage sentences, full phrases, the possibilities of extending a word—"footsteps in the dark" might get "a man walking in a dark alley" or "a shadow on a wall."

This game has many variations. The archeological dig yields dreamy possibilities that enable them to keep hunting, digging to take apart a word. It's like peeling bark from plane trees. Certain images invite wonder—*window* extends the vision, so does *night* with its depth—these words function as archetypes or fundamental concepts that reveal the mystery and magic inherent in them. It also depends on how you pronounce the words. Some words demand a whisper, and this in itself functions as a sign; sound carries meaning. For me, this process of free association and freewriting is not an end in itself, but rather a warm-up to the writing exercise whose title, "Deep Song," underscores my intention to tow them under and get them to flow. The following example illustrates how one student in the Bronx has harnessed this free association skill to her advantage:

> Summer blues roll away as I comb my hair
> I feel like collecting seashells on a winter
> night, to be the earliest one to smell
> a rare flower to me is a gift,
> love the sound of a crackling fire, of a
> crackling marshmallow, of a cracking peanut,
> of a crackling star between the moon and sun.
> A book holds many ideas which I might never think of.
> I love to feel slivers and slivers of glue
> when I'm angry, cotton is in a way like snow,
> they're both soft and white, the candle burns
> the rope and I fall into a scrumptious cherry pie,
> the heart sticks out of my mouth and I hate it
> so I cut my neck and it's the end of me so
> I roam the earth in the body of a pale sad ghost
> and make it happy for having me.
>
> —*Cynthia Martinez, sixth grade*

Deep Song

Why not take advantage of students' ability to juggle words, images, and sounds at the same time? Motivated by my students' success with freewriting and mimicking sounds, along with my increased determination to allow my students to daydream, I found a more comfortable way to work with the deep song of poetry in the classroom. One particularly ugly day when the garbage outside was piled higher than usual, I began meditating on my own past while preparing the students for the unusual exercise of listening to me read while they freewrote and free-associated at the same time. I turned off the lights, and a hush settled over the room. My voice and the Octavio Paz poem threaded through the room (I had chosen the Paz poem deliberately for its abstraction, complexity, and space). I read quietly and softly. I told them that the exercise would not be that much different from doing homework while watching TV or listening to M. C. Hammer, making mouthnoises and rapping, and jazzing math at the same time. After all, the students were already wired for it. I also warned them that I was going to start off slow and then go faster but that they should still free-associate the sounds and the words even if they did not understand their meaning or the meaning of the poem, but that they should not write down the words directly from the poem—this would be like writing down whatever the TV says while they do their homework. I reminded them that their pieces should be their own visions, their responses, and that I just wanted to immerse them in the flow of words. I told them not to worry if my words became a blur and that forgetting my voice could even be a good sign. Let it become background music, something they could take off on. I told them "to get lost," and that it was fine to put their heads in the crook of their arms and rest. Deep Song is about the pleasure of sounds, of being read to in old Carnegie libraries on three-legged stools, about lullabies behind closed curtains. And with the slow deliberation of my breath anchored to a past memory, I read and they journeyed.

The important thing about Deep Song is tone: you need to understand what it is you wish to accomplish, what mood you want to project. If you want a poem about a river, your tone should reflect that. Intent has everything to do with the success of this exercise, as does the confidence the kids place in you and your voice. You have to feel your way through the poem as you read, sensing when and where students are having trouble.

I stop if necessary to see what's happening with the kids. I often let go of my text in mid-stream to urge them on: "Come on, flow with the words, the stream of consciousness, it's night, the poet said "night," what do *you* see, feel, think, or imagine? What images or sounds does the word invite? Put yourself into it and go with the flow. See through the poem!"

One of the best things about merging the oral transmission of poetry with the process of writing is that it gives me the opportunity to emphasize the poem as an open structure, as if it has no real beginning or end. Endings and beginnings depend on our breath and attention span. You can read and reread a poem and go backwards and forwards, giving the students the chance to intervene, see through words, and fill in the blanks. I don't perform the poem the same way each time. The only thing that is consistent is my insistence that they interact with the poem.

To inspire confidence, I move around the room, choose a few of the best pieces, and read a few lines to the class to show how these students express their particular vision and take liberties with words. I also do this to gauge the students' reactions. It's a very sensitive exercise that demands delicate response, a gentle classroom environment, and a flexible teacher. When I see that the students are responding, I continue reading. I repeat words and lines, pause, then continue, carefully pronouncing everything—even the intervals.

Deep Song reminds me of how the poet Vladimir Mayakovsky described the technique he used to compose poems. For him, rhythm was primordial, words secondary:

> I walk along gesticulating and muttering—there are almost no words, yet I slow my pace in order not to impede this muttering, or else I mutter more quickly, in the rhythm of my steps. Rhythm is the basis of any poetry and passes through it like a din. Gradually one is able to make out single words in this din. Where this fundamental rhythm-din comes from remains unknown. For me it is every repetition of a sound, a noise, a rocking or any repetition of phenomena which I mark with sounds.

Deep Song is also about the joys of speech, of reading aloud. I enunciate and feel the roundness of vowels, *u* like a cup, *o* like a soft round ball. Reading aloud is a very pleasurable sensation; you "cradle" and engrave not only words but the beauty and the pleasure of the poet's sound in the students' ears until it all becomes a part of them (Mneme!).

For me, this exercise was a major breakthrough. I felt that I had finally made the classroom *my* room. The kids felt equally comfortable, and responded with some incredible poems. No two poems were alike, and I found myself waking up in the middle of the night, reading and rereading them, and marveling over the leaps of imagination they made. Michael Spann's poem underscored Michel Foucault's notion that "to read and to journey are one and the same." Here is what I imagine Michael did in response to Paz's opening line ("In my window night invents another space"): he grabbed the word *night* and invented a whole universe. When we read a poem from a book, it is possible to go back and forth within the poem. When we hear it read, the sounds and lines quickly evaporate into thin air, and we compensate for our lapses in memory and understanding by filling in the blanks. When we write poetry—grouping sounds into words, words into lines, and lines into poems—we use what Roman Jakobson called "elliptical perception." One word is potent enough to conjure up an entire poem. Tracy Marshall understood (and visualized) the word *night* differently than Michael Spann or the other students:

> Like the silent nights are fun to listen to
> Listen. And how stars are twinkling
> And how fire flames on a warm night
> See how the drummers play the drums
> And people dance to music. Why
> am I sleeping? Wake me! I want to hear
> the beautiful African music
> Help me, someone, I am awake.
> Now it's time to tell my parents
> what a beautiful nightmare I had
> See how the waves are floating?
> I am a poet.

> —*Tracy Marshall, fourth grade*

According to Jakobson's concept of elliptical perception, "the expressive power of language is distinguished by the interchangeability and mobility of words. Although the listener penetrates and enters the poem, it remains intact, and through its powers of revelation a re-creation is produced, not a double." Bachelard seconds this idea in a different way: he defines the imaginative power of words as "inductive magic": "In poetry words regain their potential for dual meanings. They attract one another and create relations which reverse the real and figurative poles. Images are 'lived,' 'experienced,' 're-imagined' in an act of consciousness which restores at once their timelessness and newness."

Ironically, one of the side benefits of the Deep Song exercise is the opportunity it gives students to learn big, mysterious words. Paz's poem is full of words and phrases that they have to penetrate with their imaginations, or understand simply by sound or context. Once they don't feel intimidated, they enjoy being privy to adult language. My students liked the apparent "bigness" of *horizon* and *aquatic,* and hearing *geometries* in an unusual context.

Sometimes I stop and explain the word, depending on the appropriateness of breaking the rhythm, other times I can feed in the definition in such a way as to make it become a part of the reading. I've even casually thumbed through a dictionary while hesitating on a phrase, like a broken record, hammering the words into their subconsciouses. I encourage them to make use of the word, tell them it's theirs. To my surprise, the students remember and use the words weeks later, confidently claiming another word for their growing word bank. The quick comprehension is due to the fact that they hear the word in a context that intensifies its meaning. Sometimes the reverse happens and the students latch onto sounds in much the same way that Mayakovsky did and turn them into whatever word intuitively occurs to them—hence Katrina's odd use of "bonding" and "coup" in the poem below. I was so perplexed by these words' seemingly complicated presence in the midst of such a serene poem that I asked the author what she meant. All Katrina knew was that they occurred to her and felt right. I pointed to the word *coup,* and when I asked her to pronounce it, she uttered "cope," but I present it as she wrote it.

Shadows

I see brown, blue and purple birds on my wall in autumn
It is morning, the wind blows through my window
as it touches my foot
Across my window there are colors as the sun touches my hand
Down the block there's a yard with bonding children
as they coup
My apartment is shapeless, my bed is
red as the sky in morning at the break of dawn
There's one window, a girl in there
watching the moon and the stars
She's blind, she's only feeling
the moon and the stars

   —*Katrina, third grade*

The following poem by Ladia is interesting in the same way, although I had a feeling she was stuck on the letter *a:*

God is my ruler, he guides me every day
No matter where I stand
I'm having a good day
Along my way the trees are blossoming
I see light in my eyes
Every night at prayer my childish soul accepts his promises to me
I am abyssed on the solid ground
I let God accost my mind first
While I'm on the ground
God is in an acropolis in Heaven looking down
Whatever your problem, adduce it to God
The girl is coy, she doesn't know my God
God adds adornment to this earth
I toddle across.

No angels in America
God keeps them every day while a blaze
is with the devil
Choices are made by people, decisions by God
I can't wait to see the loud scenery of Heaven
The girl will be free when she's knocking on heaven's door

   —*Ladia Lindsay, fourth grade*

Ladia was a fascinating and eager writer who churned out strange, almost Nietzschean pieces whenever Chris Edgar and I encountered her, which was unfortunately only three times. Chris and I shared a residency at P.S. 157 in the Bronx, where he was also teaching Russian to a fourth grade class. We decided to put in an appearance in a new classroom. The first week I opened up the writing workshop with the free association/Deep Song exercise. The next week I returned with Chris without having informed him of what had taken place. He introduced a lesson by discussing the Chinese poet Li Po. After reading a poem or two, he was overwhelmed by a handful of students begging him to read their completed poems. They had been writing all the while he was talking, assuming that this was what we expected of them. One student borrowed the line "you will die of poems."

Cold night with blue moon and
a homeless person thinking about
his love, a bird flying in the sky
and can you come back?

A big tree in an empty space
and smile to an image
I cut ten bricks and can't succeed

I find a friend with a China hat
and tell him how he looks
and say he is skinny
and tell him
he will die of poems

   —*Tyson Joye, fourth grade*

☆   ☆   ☆

In his essay "How to Make Verse" Mayakovsky called for the "constant restocking of the storehouses, the granaries of your mind, with all kinds of words, necessary, expressive, rare, invented, manufactured and others." The warp and weave of language contains layers of voices, sounds, and meaning whose texture is built up through time. Consciously or not, the poet/teacher is involved with this fabric of memory—and its various associations with time and space—because of his or her concern with the act of releasing and intervening in what is latent. Memory is a thread we can unravel and wind. The poet/teacher encourages the child to make use of this reservoir, to recall, recollect, and remember. The poet/teacher is the demiurge, the conjurer, the midwife helping the child to deliver.

"Intervention" is the word that comes to mind when I think of the poet in the school. The poet intervenes—in the primary sense of the word—between teachers and students, inside and outside, using consonants and vowels as if they were small hands lifting the dingy green walls until the room rises to accommodate the students' new potential, wide as the books the poet has devoured and the other poets he or she speaks for. Then and only then can the child (and the child that persists in the poet) wander in and out of Imagination's rooms freely venting the clutter of feelings, sounds, and ideas circulating in a cloud of chalk dust, pencil shavings, and institutional air.

"Presumptuous" is the other word that comes to mind when I think about teaching poetry in the schools. The poet/teacher wants a part of himself or herself (or what he or she has to impart) to stay with the students forever—even if it's only to add the word *poetry* to their vocabularies, or impress them with Pablo Neruda, Mayakovsky, Li Po, Don L. Lee, or with a visit by a contemporary poet such as Quincy Troupe.

Despite the disorder and chaos of the world and some of our schools, it's possible to mesmerize a classroom. Erase it and replace it with poetry until the classroom sits in one's mouth and you row away with the rudder and oar of your tongue, until you arrive where the poet left off—a thousand words ago on an archipelago of motionless childhoods playing musical chairs with words. Aoede was there with her lyre, and so was Mnemosyne, mother of all lyric voices.

Mnemosyne is the mother of the muses romancing her children—all children—to sleep. The poet is the nanny, mother, wet nurse, or maid carrying on the tradition of the ballad, the song, or lullaby. She is the griot, the dark cello that I remember from my childhood. As Lorca said, "Let us not forget that the cradle song is invented by women whose children are a burden. Naturally the women can't help singing to them of their own . . . blues, love sonnets, the rain outside the window, and silent refrains."

Deep Song is more than a how-to exercise. It is also an acknowledgment of the possibilities of childhood and poetic solitude.

A soft melody sings in the voice
of my ear
I'm all by myself in a lonely room
The light touches the sight of my eyes
My feelings are shattered like a black hole that's left behind
The wind blows through the window, it surrounds me with its touch
as it dances with my hair
My heart whispers to me in a quiet voice
It said, "There's something in you that's blocking the sunlight
keep on holding to your strength, tight"
I did not have an answer to dread
My soul was crumbled like rice and bread
My soul is weak, my soul is weak

    —*Armead Moody, fifth grade*

        ★   ★   ★

Running body, my body, your body
a messed-up room in
a house as small as quarters
forever the room goes
like the silk dress
fingerprints in the rain
the wind lives with the women
Hot hands
A black hill
and some big and small trees
The hill goes and the tree stays
Stone rocks hit the girl
Don't worry
the wind goes
the people get cut
born to break a leaf
light eating
light raising me
light runs home
light is on time
time is light
I kiss light
kiss me

    —*Terence Martin, third grade*

Bibliography

Bachelard, Gaston. *On Poetic Imagination and Reverie*. Translated by Colette Gaudin. Dallas, Texas: Spring Publications, 1987.

Jakobson, Roman. *Verbal Art, Verbal Sign, Verbal Time*. Edited by Krystyna Pomorska and Stephen Rudy. Oxford: Basil Blackwell, 1985.

Lorca, Federico García. *Deep Song & Other Prose*. Translated by Christopher Maurer. New York: New Directions Publishing Corp., 1980.

Mayakovsky, Vladimir. "How to Make Verse," in *Modern Russian Poets on Poetry*. Edited by Carl R. Proffer. Ann Arbor, Mich.: Ardis, 1974.

Motherwell, Robert, ed. *The Dada Painters and Poets*. Cambridge, Mass.: Harvard Univ. Press, 1991.

Paz, Octavio. *Selected Poems*. Translated by Eliot Weinberger. New York: New Directions Publishing Corp., 1984.

Jim Berger

Repeating Lines

Poetic form is often the result of some sort of repetition that creates a pattern. Rhyme and alliteration use the repetition of sounds; syllabic poetry repeats the number of syllables per line; poetry in stanzas uses the stanza as the repeated unit; and often there are repeated lines, such as the refrains in ballads and songs. Even "open" poetry or free verse often contains repeated words or phrases, or has a consistency in the line lengths and the ways the lines are broken. In the broadest sense, you can even consider ordinary units of syntax to be forms of repetition. Think of the simple sentence: subject/verb/object. When this pattern is disturbed, the effect of the same words becomes completely different.

Repetition and pattern are part of what draws readers into and leads them through a poem, and the deliberate use of repetition can be used by teachers and beginning writers to create simple but quite effective poems.

Repetition creates a pattern, and an established pattern creates an expectation. The writer then has a choice: continue the pattern or break it; give readers what they expect (which is a pleasurable result), or throw in a surprise (which is equally or even more pleasurable). It's the same in sports. Let's say in basketball, you have the ball, you drive to the right and score. Next time you have the ball, you drive to the right again and score. You've established a pattern and created an expectation in the defender. So, the next time you get the ball, what do you do? Fake right and drive left. Of course, in basketball, it's no fun to be faked out, but in reading poetry it is. It may be that that moment of indeterminacy, when the pattern may or may not be broken, is one of poetry's greatest pleasures.

Many poems can illustrate this. The simplest are nursery rhymes:

London Bridge is falling down
Falling down
Falling down
London Bridge is falling down . . .

Okay, what next? Will it continue to repeat forever and ever? That would be pretty boring. Of course not: My fair lady! And notice that even the game children play to this song makes a distinction between the repetition and the break from the repetition. It's during the "My fair lady" line that the child gets captured in the bridge. An African lullaby of the Akan tribe has a similar effect:

> Someone would like to have you as her child
> but you are mine.
> Someone would like to rear you on a costly mat
> but you are mine.
> Someone would like to place you on a camel blanket
> but you are mine.

By now the pattern is clearly established. So now it changes.

> I have to rear you on a torn old mat.

It's a small but distinct change that definitely breaks the repetition. And this is a very important line for the meaning of the poem. It identifies the speaker and puts what's gone before in a new perspective. The poem then concludes by repeating the beginning, a soothing ending appropriate for a lullaby:

> Someone would like to have you as her child
> but you are mine.

It's important to realize that the use of repetition and change is not just a formal conceit. The line that breaks the repetition will often contain a critical shift of meaning as well. Generally, however, I present this idea to younger students as a matter of form; as they play with the form, the mutations of meaning seem to generate themselves.

I tried a variation on this form myself and it came out like this:

Modern Incantation

> Can't you be quiet even for a minute?
> You baby crying, water dripping,
> voice on the telephone,
> can't you be quiet even for a minute?
> You buzz of an electric appliance,
> you tapping of rain, you vibration,
> I'm going nuts! Can't you be
> quiet?

The form here is almost identical to that of the Akan lullaby. There are two instances of "Can't you be quiet even for a minute?," each followed by a list of three things that should be quiet. (You might notice that these noises become increasingly abstract and all-encompassing, progressing from a baby crying to a vibration.) Then the repetition is broken: "I'm going nuts!"—the emotional climax of the poem—functioning in the same way as the single non-repeated line in the Akan lullaby and in "London Bridge." My poem ends with a repetition of the first line, but only a half repetition—and with an unusual linebreak—because I didn't want the sort of soothing closure of the lullaby, but something more abrupt and in keeping with the hysterical tone of the poem.

Experimenting with form does not preclude writing meaningful poetry. The mind is always full of meaning and feeling, and these will inevitably break through into the poem. In fact, when you take your mind off the meaning a little bit and concentrate more on the game of the poem, sometimes, paradoxically, the meaning comes through even more strongly. Another poem that shows this simple pattern well is Federico García Lorca's "Silly Song" ("Canción Tonta"), translated by Harriet de Onis:

Mama
I wish I was silver

Son
You'd be very cold

Mama
I wish I was water

Son
You'd be very cold

Mama
Embroider me on your pillow

That, yes
Right away

Here, the breaking of the repetition ends the poem and creates that terribly eerie, unsettling, though also somewhat comic feeling. I also like to read this poem in Spanish to the students, even if none of them understands the language, to show that the pattern of repetition and surprise are apparent even in the (mostly) unintelligible sounds of a language you may not know:

Mama
Yo quiero ser de plata

Hijo
Tendras mucho frio

Mama
Yo quiero ser de agua

Hijo
Tendras mucho frio

Mama
Bordame en tu almohada

Eso si
Ahora mismo!

I've used these ideas and techniques as a student teacher of fourth grade students at the United Nations International School in New York; when I taught third grade at the International School Moshi in Moshi, Tanzania; and more recently to elementary and high school students at the Usdan Center for the Creative and Performing Arts in Huntington, N.Y., and at P.S. 29 and P.S. 31 in the Bronx as a member of the Teachers & Writers Collaborative artistic staff. During all these residencies I emphasized how repetition can be found in all sorts of areas: music, sports, painting, history, architecture, botany, you name it. I also stressed how the element of surprise, breaking the repetition, is important. After reading each example poem, we discussed which lines repeat (and which ones almost repeat), which do not repeat at all, and which create surprises in the poem. Of course, we also talked about what the poems meant—who the speakers were and what they were saying and feeling—and we tried to see how the break in the repetition related to the poem's emotional content.

And then the assignment: write a poem that uses repeating lines and that at some point breaks the repetition and creates a surprise. It's often easiest to first think up the line that will repeat; then you have something to go back to when you're stuck. The repeating line should, of course, be a good one: mysterious, funny, beautiful, terrifying, or all of these combined. It's very important to have a good repeating line. And a good surprise line. The subject? Whatever the writer wants. As the examples below illustrate, poems in this form can be on any subject. Students can do variations on the examples if they have trouble starting.

If the results seem too mechanical at first, a bit *too* repetitious, just let the students keep writing. At least they're picking up the form. It may be that the surprise isn't surprising enough or that the repetitions lack any internal variation or are being used too often—even within each repetition it's good to slip in small surprises. And if the student doesn't follow the form exactly, but comes up with a good poem, then all the better.

Here are some of my students' poems.

The Brain

The brain is made of squshy
mush with veins of intelligence
and veins of blood. It's
divided into three different
parts with intelligence of
every kind. The brain is made
of squshy mush connected
in the head. The brain is made
of squshy mush, but I warn you
if you are a doctor not
to fool around with it.

> —*Tom, age ten, U.N.I.S.*

★   ★   ★

Maybe

I love you, maybe,
or maybe not.
This is true life, maybe,
or maybe not.
You've hurt me, baby,
that's not a maybe.
We're "lovers," maybe,
or maybe not.
We're enemies maybe,
but I hope not.
You're Romeo, maybe,
or maybe not.
I'm Juliet, maybe,
but you know I'm not.
Get real, baby.
This ain't Camelot.
Are you my knight, baby?
I think not.
I love you, maybe,
or maybe not.

> —*Shannon, age fifteen, Usdan*

★　　★　　★

Discussions of a Class

Trees, she said.
Words, hair,
thought, she said.
Describe, she said,
short, starting, she said.
Talking, fighting, creature,
she said.
These all can be words of a
poem, she said.

They are all concentrating,
observing. It is all silent now.
Yet there seems to be a bit of
    confusion.

　　—*Rolinda, age thirteen, Usdan*

★　　★　　★

Me What Not

I not to eat a shark not in water
I not to sleep a dog not to bark
I not to ride a bike a paint with no color
I not to draw a tree without bark
I without chocolate pants that do not cover.

　　—*Josh, age nine, Usdan*

★　　★　　★

At the Beach

On the beach with the hot hot sun.
On the beach with the radio on.
On the beach running in the waves.
I will put suntan lotion on my legs.

　　—*Karen, age eight, P.S. 29*

★　　★　　★

Mom I am big as a cat.
Mom I am a zebra girl.
Mom I am a peach people, eat me, Mom.
Mom I am a bone, dogs eat me.

Mom I am a bow, girls wear me.
Mom I am a mule, I go to the zoo.
Mom I am a snake, I look like a plant.
Mom I am a clean mop.
Mom I am a school, the children come there.
Mom I am a bumpy girl.
Mom I am a frog, I live in the water.
Mom I am a tree.
Mom I am a hop hop frog.
Mom I am a letter, they put me in a box.
Mom I am a book writing.
Mom I am a rat cats eat.
Mom I am a lion.
Mom I am a movie screen.
Mom I am a feel world.
Mom I am a kiss girl.
Mom I am a girl of you.
Mom I am a library.

—*Yolanda, age eight, P.S. 31*

★   ★   ★

Daddy, do you want to play football?
No, son, I'm busy.
Daddy, do you want to play baseball?
No, son, I said I'm busy.
Daddy, do you want to study?
Yes, son.
Mommy, Daddy doesn't want to play with me.
Robert.
Yes, dear.
Play with Darryll.
Okay, dear.
Let's go play, son.
I don't want to play. I'm looking at TV.

—*Darryll, age nine, P.S. 31*

Jim Berger

Short Lines and Long Lines

When you're writing a story or an essay it doesn't matter where you end your lines. You just start at the left-hand margin and write until you get near the right-hand edge of the paper, then go down to the next line and do it again. Ordinary punctuation marks and syntax tell the reader where to pause, where the units of meaning begin and end, and so forth. But in poetry it's crucial where each line ends—with what word it ends and the next one begins—for the lengths of the lines and the choices of end words determine the flow and rhythm of the poem and give added emphasis to particular words. For the poet, line length is like an extra form of punctuation that further clarifies both the poem's sound and its meaning. It's partly this extra subtlety and detail in the organization of sound and meaning that make poetry what it is, and different from prose. A poem written in short lines, where the sentence is divided into smaller units, tends to have a quicker, choppier rhythm. The frequent jumps of the eye are repeated in the mind:

> Just try
> talking
> as if you were
> writing a
> short-
> line poem.

Short lines give a certain excitement, a newness, to what you're saying. A new rhythm makes you listen more carefully. Inherent in short-line poems are beautiful possibilities of music and dance, raindrops, machinery, gunfire, traffic jams, anxiety, speed, hesitation, and breathlessness.

Another thing about short lines is that they provide a continual series of small surprises. Each line contains a small, discrete chunk of information, and you cannot discover the next chunk until you jump down to the next line. I like to introduce students to this idea by writing a short-line poem on the board a single line at a time and asking the students to guess what will come in the next line. Certain William Carlos Williams poems, although widely used for other types of writing assignments, are perfect:

I have eaten
(Infinite possibilities: "the ice cream, the bread, the hamburger, the banana"—
the poem, of course, says:)
the plums
(What next? "They tasted good, they were sweet, they were juicy. . . ." No, sorry, not so fast; these short-line poems like to tell just a *little* bit at a time.)
that were in
(In what? "The store! the refrigerator! the car!"
Very close, very close.)
the icebox
(And I'll give you the next line:)
and which
("Were good! Were delicious!" Hold on, hold on; this poem goes along *very slowly*.)
you were probably
("Wanting to eat yourself!" Hey, good guess!)
saving
(See, he *still* won't tell you everything! "To eat yourself, to eat for lunch.")
for breakfast
(Hurray! At last, the end of the sentence—that was one sentence divided into all those lines.)
forgive me
("For eating your plums? I'll buy you new plums? I didn't know they were yours.")
they were delicious
("And wonderful! I loved them! Best plums I ever had. . . ."
Good ideas, but he still goes slowly:)
so sweet
(Okay, last line coming, make it a good one—
"And fantastic, and so juicy, thanks for your plums.")
and so cold
(!)

Although the rhythm is quick and choppy, the real joy of a short-line poem is actually in its infinitesimal hesitations, its slow drawing out, its gradual revelation. With every line, the poem creates expectations and delivers small surprises. The surprise in each line—even if it's just a small one—is what I try to emphasize to the students.

But there's another thing to notice. Certain words, placed at the end of a line, inevitably lead you immediately to the next one. For instance, all prepositions do this. A line ends with *to*. . . well, to what? to where? to whom? You've got to go to the next line to find out. It's the same with *in* or *for* or *toward*. The preposition will naturally seek its object. The articles *the* and *a* also lead you on to the next line. So do verbs. "She rode": rode where? rode what? Conjunctions also serve the same purpose, as do other sorts of words in different circumstances. At the end of a line, all these words impel you to proceed immediately to the completion of the statement. So, when you end a line with one of these "impelling" words, you give readers a slightly confusing, but delicious double message. The syntax instructs them to proceed, but the end of the line insists that they hesitate. The result is that what finally arrives in the following line receives additional emphasis because of that hesitation and tension.

There are other words that have the opposite effect at the ends of lines. They bring you to a stop, a culmination, a conclusion. Nouns do this well, especially as the objects of the verbs or prepositions that lead the reader to them:

> The monster opened
> the casket.

When a noun as the subject of the sentence ends the line, it will more likely propel you to the next one:

> The casket
> had been opened!

Adjectives and adverbs can be conclusive, although under other circumstances they can impel you forward, as in:

> The green
> leaves slowly,
> slowly changed.

And here a verb is the concluding word.

It's possible to see which end words impel and which conclude in the Williams poem about the plums. I go through this with the students line by line as before, this time trying to decide which lines lead you on to the next, and which bring you to a stop.

> **I have eaten**
> (Could be either; in this context, probably it pushes
> you along.)

the plums
(Definitely a conclusion, though the next line
shows it's not a dead stop.)
which were in
(Definitely impels you.)
the icebox
(Conclusion—stops you.)
and which
(Go on . . .)
you were probably
(Go on again . . .)
saving
(Still pushes you on, and with just a single word,
like a pivot.)
for breakfast
(Finally the conclusion.)
forgive me
(Stop.)
they were delicious
(Stop.)
so sweet
(Go on . . .)
and so cold
(The End.)

When you build and build and then at last conclude, you can create an incredible amount of tension in what appears on the surface to
be a very simple poem. And it comes from knowing how to handle
the short lines. A short-line poem like this is not, as some people may
still believe, just cut-up prose.

If there's time, and if I think the class' attention span can stand it,
I like to run through another short-line poem quickly, maybe another
one by Williams:

As the cat
climbed over
the top of

the jamcloset
first the right
forefoot

carefully
then the hind
stepped down

into the pit of
the empty
flowerpot.

What a beautiful, still moment this poem creates. The hesitations and impulsions of the poem perfectly mirror those of the cat.

When it's time for the students to start writing, I simply tell them to write a poem in short lines, about anything, and each line should contain a small surprise, and some lines should push you on to the next, while others should stop you.

★   ★   ★

Long lines are oceanic. They wash over you like waves, one after another, each of them full of shells and sand and fish and surfboards, pieces of wrecks and bodies of sailors. The long line is more conclusive and inclusive than the partial, subdivided short line. If short lines are like quick pants, long lines resemble great, deep breaths.

That's how I present long lines to students at first, as units of breath. I tell them, "Take a deep breath, then as you exhale, make up your line. When you take a new breath, start a new line." Sometimes the long line will resemble a long sentence; other times it may look like a short paragraph. I try to demonstrate this extemporaneously. I take a dramatic deep breath, then try to exhale some words that sound like poetry: "Outside it's raining and I suspect that the roof is leaking. Oh no! It's falling on that boy's head! Quick, get a towel!" I show by my voice and gesture that I've run out of breath, then I take a great new breath and resume. "There, that's better. Lightning and thunder! The chalkboard is a cradle for a whale and all the different pairs of shoes have lost their feet and are smearing the desks with mud." It's just an example to demonstrate the procedure.

Then I have the students make up a few of their own and write them down, since they may be too shy to compose lines spontaneously out loud. (However, it's great if you can get them to read the lines aloud. It can be a kind of game to see who can make up the longest line that can be read in a single breath.) It may be necessary to show students how to arrange long lines on the page. Since each line of the poem will very likely go beyond the physical line of the paper, tell students to continue their poetic lines on the next physical line by leaving a small indentation. This will show that it's still the same line being continued. The next new poetic line begins at the margin again. It helps to illustrate this on the chalkboard.

Teaching long-line poems doesn't require the same detailed examination that teaching short-line poems does, at least at the introductory level. Writing a poem with long lines takes a bit more patience and endurance, and requires more than just the inspiration to crystallize an instant: the writer has to have something to write about. So what I stress in long-line poems—after the breath unit—is the subject matter or genre. The two broad types that seem to fit best with long-line poems are the catalogue and the narrative.

Perhaps the greatest narratives in history are in long-line poems— Homer's *Iliad* and *Odyssey*—and we are fortunate to have excellent English translations of both, by Richmond Lattimore and by Robert Fitzgerald. I read a few lines aloud, perhaps from a battle scene in the *Iliad*. The action and gore usually get a lively response. I've found it best to paraphrase somewhat, especially with younger students. Here is my paraphrase from Fitzgerald's *Iliad,* Book 17:

> Then the son of Telamon, magnificent Ajax, whirled about and
> broke
> Into the group of Trojans that had circled the dead soldier Patroklus,
> Thinking now to drag the body away to their town and make the
> people proud of them.
> And the famous son of Lethos, named Hippothos, tying his swordbelt
> around Patroklus' ankles, pulled the body backward on the
> battlefield.
> But fate and death came to him, no one could stop it.
> Ajax leaped through the crowd and struck Hippothos' metal helmet
> with his spear,
> And the helmet crumbled, smashed by the great spear in the huge
> hand.
> His brains burst, all in blood, out of the wound. On the spot
> His life died out in him, and from his hands
> He let Patroklus' foot fall to the ground
> As he fell forward headfirst onto the body.
> And he would never be able to repay his parents for taking care of
> him
> Since his life was cut short by the spear of Ajax.

The expansiveness of the form lets the poet tell as much as he or she wants. The poet can go into the minutest detail, then suddenly move to something else, which is why long-line poems are a particularly good narrative form for writers who don't yet have a feel for the prose paragraph. Long lines also tend to generate a forward motion, so that the poems stretch out vertically as well as horizontally. The long lines give the sense of a procession or parade, which is another metaphor to use with the students: the floats, balloons, marching bands, clowns, and so on advancing with a steady pace but with great variety along an avenue. That could even be the subject for a long-line poem. Speed and excitement can erupt within the overall gradualness.

The other possibility for using long lines is the catalogue poem, which is basically a list—but a list with personality, with life. One type of catalogue poem focuses on a particular object—a friend, a car, an animal, for instance—and tells everything the poet knows, sees, and feels about that thing. One of the great poems of this sort is Christopher Smart's "Jubilate Agno," which shows wonderful perceptiveness and love for his cat Jeoffry, but then expands from the details about Jeoffry to a sense of God's presence in the world. Here is a short excerpt:

> For he will not do destruction if he is well fed, neither will he spit without provocation.
> For he purrs in thankfulness, when God tells him he's a good cat.
> For he is an instrument for the children to learn benevolence upon.
> For every house is incompleat without him & a blessing is lacking in the spirit.
> For the Lord commanded Moses concerning the cats at the departure of the Children of Israel from Egypt.
> For every family had one cat at least in the bag.
> For the English cats are the best in Europe.

For younger kids the language can be hard, but you can probably find a short passage that will make the point. Other good catalogue poems are African praise poems.

Another type of catalogue poem aims for a universal scope. Walt Whitman's "Song of Myself" is a good example. His narrator is a kind of supernatural being who sees everything, both outside and inside— "tenacious, acquisitive, tireless . . . and can never be shaken away." His powers of observation are infinite, and so is his power of sympathy. He not only sees, but emotionally enters what he sees.

For younger students, just a few lines, preferably written on the board, will serve as an example. Older students can digest a longer excerpt. Here are some lines from section 8:

> The little one sleeps in its cradle,
> I lift the gauze and look a long time, and silently brush away flies with my hand.
> The youngster and the redfaced girl turn aside up the bushy hill,
> I peeringly view them from the top.
> The suicide sprawls on the bloody floor of the bedroom,
> It is so. . . . I witnessed the corpse . . . there the pistol had fallen.

And so on. With older students, I recommend that you go over the entire passage. You can point out the variety and contrast in the things Whitman sees, and how he moves so quickly among them, like a movie or a ghost; how he tries to include a whole society in his poem, just giving a line or two for each thing, but how there's action in every line; and how he makes you see and hear every event.

John Ashbery's "Into the Dusk Charged Air" is a strange catalogue poem you might want to use. It is a four-page list of names of rivers, each with a small description. It begins:

> Far from the Rappahannock, the silent
> Danube moves along toward the sea.
> The brown and green Nile rolls slowly
> Like the Niagara's welling descent.
> Tractors stood on the green banks of the Loire
> Near where it joined the Cher.
> The St. Lawrence prods among black stones
> And mud. But the Arno is all stones.
> Wind ruffles the Hudson's
> surface. The Irrawaddy is overflowing.

It seems an impossible task to maintain enough variety, but Ashbery pulls it off. For one thing, the poem as a whole has a structure and variety. There are slow, stately sections and rapid, churning sections; clear sections and muddy sections; frozen sections and thawing sections. You can discuss these various structures with older students. For younger ones it's sufficient to think about a poem that lists and describes all the examples of a particular thing—a poem of cars, mountains, streets, highways, stores, buildings, or animals. What's important is to say something particular about each thing. This is a good type of poem to do as a group, with each student contributing a line. Also, when each student contributes a line (or two or three), you don't have to deal with writer's cramp, a problem with younger students writing at length in a single sitting.

A final point to be made about line lengths is that after having experimented with different lengths in these assignments, the students begin to get a feel for forms as both readers and writers. When reading poetry, they'll have a better idea of what the writer is doing, and even in prose they'll frequently come across the rhythms and techniques of short-line or long-line poetry. (Think of Hemingway's sentences set next to Henry James's.) In their own writing, they'll have another possibility for expression, both as conscious manipulation and as another avenue along which the unconscious can reveal itself.

I used the short-line poem technique at P.S. 29 and P.S. 31 in the Bronx. I used the long-line technique at P.S. 31 and at the Usdan Center in Huntington, New York. Below are some examples of the students' work.

Animals

Birds—free and spiritual, swooping down, going to the bathroom on
    your head.
Or a camel—slow and spitting on the ground; ignorant and lazy, an
    annoying movement.
Cats—constantly meowing and purring; graceful and with poise—
    they move like ballerinas.
These tigers seem to be laughing at you—Ha Ha—I may eat you
    up—They're truly crazy!
I love the giraffe—he's kind of towering over us—keeping an eye on
    the trees.
Oh, God, not the cow! What a pitiful sound—Moooooooo! Can't
    you think of anything better to say?
I think I'm paranoid! Ticks! Ticks! Ticks!
Don't come near me! I hate you!
What a cunning animal—that kangaroo! So close to its baby—always
    hopping around. Doesn't it ever get tired? Not like that
Rhinoceros—fat and slobbering—dragging its huge putrid body from
    place to place.
Ah! The adorable little prairie dog—I'm sure all little children would
    love to have one.
Don't fly away! You idiotic pigeon—Can't you see that I'm going to
    feed you?
You darling monkey! How do you swing on the trees so easily? Your
    body seems to be made of rubber bands.
You sweet puppy! Flopping ears and wet nose—so loyal and faithful
    you are!
Ooh! What a gory feline—this flesh-eating, prey-stalking panther—a
    regular threat to the human race!
And fish! How innocent and gentle you are! Swimming around lazily
    all day. . . .

   —*Nicole, age twelve, Usdan Center*

★   ★   ★

I saw some water on
a puppy   The puppy was
dead   The puppy
was in the dirty lot
You are a little
girl   I blow a kiss

—*Pauline, age eight, P.S. 29*

★   ★   ★

Guess What?

I looked
in my cousin's
secret book.
It was her
Diary.
She came
in her bedroom,
I closed the
diary fast.
She looked
at me real
strange
and asked
what
was I doing
with her Diary
I was scared.
Then I said,
Don't worry
I couldn't
read the
whole secret.

—*Michelle, age ten, P.S. 31*

★   ★   ★

My Cat

I got a cat
and my cat
died.

God took my
cat. I am going to
beat him up.

You dead.

God said to my
cat
What's up, baby?

I said, What's
up, God, you
want to fight me?

God said Yes.

  —*Albert, age nine, P.S. 31*

     ★   ★   ★

My mother
kissed
my father

My cat
is under
the bed

My teacher
is shouting

My dog
had puppies

My friend
is sleeping

The flower
pot is under
the sun

  —*Aitza, age nine, P.S. 29*

     ★   ★   ★

Annoying People

Annoying people comb their hair when it already looks good.
They drive their cars with jerks and short stops and purposely avoid
  bumps.
They go around singing off key.
They crack their gum during tests.
They always have ink marks on their faces.
Annoying people wear the wrong color lipstick.

They play louder than anyone else in the orchestra and play the
    wrong notes.
They complain all the time and their sneakers stay perfectly white for
    about two years.
Their clothes never match and their clothes always match.
Annoying people wear too much perfume and don't shave their legs.
They talk too much in class and suck up to teachers.
They always get high grades on tests and they say that it's not very
    good.
Annoying people's glasses always fall to the tip of their noses and they
    don't push them back up.
They waddle when they walk and they never mind their own
    business.
They wear too much blush.
Annoying people pretend they know how to smoke and don't inhale.
They button up their shirts to the top and then put up their collars.
They wear bell bottoms and high heels.
Annoying people swim badly and recite TV commercials.
They stretch out the elastic in their socks.
Annoying people leave a light on when they go to sleep and call
    during dinner all the time.
Annoying people don't really know their ass from their elbow about
    a certain subject and then try and tell you what to do.
They speak slowly and whine.
Annoying people tell really bad jokes and then laugh at them . . .
    alone.

   —*Samantha, age fifteen, Usdan Center*

★   ★   ★

A Stormy Night

It was a rainstorm. It was raining hard, and I mean hard.
In the sky I saw a hand and a face and another hand
and a leg and another leg
and the body looked like God's.

I asked my mother if I could go outside.
She said, no, it's raining. I said, but. . . .
But nothing. I ate my food
and went to bed.

   —*Kim, age ten, P.S. 31*

★   ★   ★

There's a fight and she don't get out of there.
She is in danger and she don't get out of there.
They're going to kill her and she don't move from there.
Poor her. She is in danger.
A car is coming, she don't move.
An airplane is landing on the floor.
She don't move from there.
Well, she don't move from there
because nothing that is happening
ain't where she is.

—*Magdalena, age nine, P.S. 31*

Nan Fry

Writing Riddle Poems
Secrets Meant to Be Shared

One of the first times I used riddles in teaching writing, I was working in a poets-in-the-schools program with a fourth grade teacher who had a strong interest in writing but who resented my intrusion into his class. The students, caught between two authority figures with different ideas about poetry, were rather tentative and subdued. The problem, I thought, was that the teacher had a formal, conventional view of poetry, while I had a looser, more free-verse approach.

Because I was writing riddles myself, I brought some in. I asked the students to describe an object, animal, or natural force—or to imagine how it would describe itself—mysteriously but accurately. We had already worked on comparisons, so I encouraged them to use metaphors or similes. Their response was dramatic. They wrote quickly and were bursting with eagerness to read their poems. They listened to each other carefully and tried valiantly to unravel even the most obscure riddles. The teacher and I were delighted. The focus was off us and where it belonged—on the students and their work. Perhaps it was the feeling of having a secret—and of knowing the answer—that energized the students, making them eager to share what they'd written. A riddle, I realized later, is a secret that's meant to be shared.

I also realized that the joke was on me. Though I had considered the teacher too traditional in his approach to writing, the most successful session I had with his class involved one of the oldest forms of poetry. Riddles first developed orally, so we don't know how far back they go in human history, but the earliest known examples were inscribed in cuneiform on Babylonian clay tablets around 2200 B.C. A riddle is featured in the Hebrew story of Samson's wedding celebration, and the ancient Athenians entertained each other with riddles at their feasts. According to tradition, Hesiod stumped Homer by asking:

> What I caught, I left behind,
> What I brought, I didn't find.
> What was the catch?

(Lice)

The riddle of the Sphinx (What walks on four legs in the morning, two in the afternoon, and three in the evening? Answer: a human, who crawls as a baby, walks on two legs as an adult, and uses a cane in old age) is integral to the story of Oedipus who, like all tragic heroes, had to learn what it means to be human. Riddles occur, often with regional variations, in folk literature, nursery rhymes (such as "Humpty Dumpty"), and fairy tales (such as Grimm's "A Riddling Tale"). Riddle poems flourished during the Middle Ages, and some of the finest were composed by the Anglo-Saxons between the seventh and the ninth centuries.

Certain contemporary poems that focus on familiar things—a green pepper, a door, a pair of shoes—have much in common with Anglo-Saxon riddles. In both cases, the poet uses metaphor and precise descriptive details to present the object in a fresh, surprising way. Depending on the amount of time I have and the class' interests, I sometimes use riddles as part of a sequence that includes object or persona poems, or both.

First I emphasize the use of sensory detail and metaphor. As I've said before, a riddle must be both mysterious and accurate. Mystery makes it challenging, and accuracy makes it fair. Without careful and detailed observation, the audience is apt to feel cheated or frustrated. For example, the fourth grader who wrote:

I am white. I fly. I sing and dance.
I feel so good. I fly over the sky.
Who am I?

knew she was describing a fairy, but the rest of us didn't have a clue. It's probably better to encourage students to write about real things or beings, but even these can result in vague riddles. Here, in contrast, is a poem, also by a fourth grader, that is accurate but not mysterious:

I'm grey and weigh two tons.
I always carry a trunk.
I have wrinkled legs. And I kill peanuts.

In spite of the lack of mystery, there is much here that is delightful: the internal rhyme, the wordplay, the distinctive voice. I especially like the precise detail of the "wrinkled legs." It shows how accurate observation can provide a fresh perspective.

In presenting riddles to a class, whether of fourth graders or college students, I often begin with one of two warm-up exercises. Both involve collaborative list-making. In some cases, I ask the students to come up with a list of comparisons, encouraging them to start with their immediate experience: What does the blackboard look like? What does the air conditioner sound like? This grounds them in the senses and also gets them thinking metaphorically. If we've already worked on comparisons in class, I talk to the students about how poetry derives much of its energy from strong action words, and ask the class to come up with a list of such verbs (*creep, slither, ooze,* etc.). This helps them to think concretely about movement and to imagine the sensations that accompany it.

In selecting examples to bring to class, I've found that students respond particularly well to riddles by their peers. I usually also bring in a contemporary poem or an Anglo-Saxon riddle. In discussion, I touch briefly on points made in the warm-up exercise, noting the use of sensory detail, metaphor, or strong verbs. I don't have any hard and fast rule about this sequence: sometimes we discuss examples first and then go to the prewriting exercise; at other times I start with the warm-up. Either way, most of the class period is spent with students writing and reading their own riddles. I haven't tried having a class do a collaborative poem, mainly because I feel that riddles result mainly from an intense contemplation of an object by an individual:

> I live in a clear, hard shell.
> With my sticky underside
>
> I curl round myself.
> A single foot extends
>
> to the toothed edge.
> If you pull me,
>
> I'll bite myself, peel off
>
> in strips for you.

When I wrote this riddle, I was staring at a roll of scotch tape on my desk. I tell students this in order to stress the importance of looking closely at ordinary objects and to show them how observation can release the imagination. To encourage the use of concrete details, I sometimes ask questions that focus on the senses: What would it feel like to be a blade of grass or a truck tire? What would it see? Hear? Smell? How would it move? What would its friends or enemies be? Would it have any secret knowledge?

Do they run with the wind?
Or do they flee from it?
They sprout up as yellow
blossoms of sun
Then they turn grey and
slip into the breeze
Why do these proud creatures run?
These lions of the sun

(Dandelions)

    —*Junior high student*

★   ★   ★

I look at the world
Through one large eye.
I have a long body,
I reach up toward the sky.
My children are your food,
My beauty is your pride.
I do not move,
I cannot hide.

(Sunflower)

    —*Junior high student*

★   ★   ★

Things go through me
The wind takes me over
I can be many different sizes
I can be soft or very brittle
I can be many different colors
But I am always there
You can never get rid of
me—I always come back.
I am hair.

    —*Junior high student*

Riddles disorient us. They focus on the ordinary and make it seem mysterious. Often they do this through metaphor. On the other hand, figurative comparisons can also make the remote or alien seem familiar, even cozy. The Anglo-Saxons had a particularly metaphoric turn of mind. The language they used in their poems was full of kennings, compounds that could be substituted for common words. For example, instead of saying "ocean," an Old English poet might say "whale-road," "gannet's bath," or "the wind's playground." The sun might be called "the world-candle," the body a "bone-house."

> A golden jewel on a sea of blue,
> A sea filled with white fish.
>
> (Sun and clouds)
>
> —*Junior high student*

★   ★   ★

> My house is not quiet, nor am I loud.
> Our lord set us within deep walls,
> shaped the road we travel together.
> I am swifter, sometimes stronger
> than my home; he will last longer.
> At times I may rest; he must run on.
> I dwell in him as long as I live;
> if we are parted, I will surely die.
>
> (Fish and river)
>
> —*Anglo-Saxon*

Both of these riddles seem like expanded kennings if we see the sun and clouds as sky-swimmers and the river as the fish's house. Kennings emphasize the similarities between the natural and the human, perhaps making the expanse of the ocean or the sky seem less threatening. At the same time, some Anglo-Saxon riddles recognize other species as equal partners sharing the world with humans. A similar view informs this riddle by a fourth grader:

> I can live for 1,000 years.
> I touch the clouds every day.
> I drink water without a cup.
> Who am I?

The answer is a tree, which emerges in the third line as a kind of giant straw. While the first two lines emphasize the great age and height of the tree, making it seem almost mythical, the third line brings us down to earth with a familiar yet unexpected detail.

To see a tree as touching the clouds suggests awe more effectively and sensuously than a direct statement could. Emily Dickinson said, "Tell all the Truth but tell it slant—" good advice for a riddle poet. Dickinson herself wrote riddles, including the anthologized "I like to see it lap the Miles," which uses extended metaphor, and the less familiar "Drab Habitation of Whom?," a series of comparisons for a cocoon. In "Metaphors," a riddling self-portrait, Sylvia Plath uses a series of comparisons to explore her contradictory feelings about being pregnant.

Other poems that use metaphor within the list structure include Wallace Stevens's "Someone Puts a Pineapple Together" and Craig Raine's "A Martian Sends a Postcard Home," which is a delightful series of metaphorical riddles. Here is the Martian's description of a common household object:

> In homes, a haunted apparatus sleeps,
> that snores when you pick it up.
>
> If the ghost cries, they carry it
> to their lips and soothe it to sleep
>
> with sounds. And yet, they wake it up
> deliberately, by tickling it with a finger.

It is, of course, a telephone.

Metaphor can be humorous in riddles. Charles Simic's "Watermelons" is—without the title—a delightfully playful poetic enigma. A similar sense of whimsy informs some of the Anglo-Saxon riddles. In one, a plow "sniffs along" like a dog with its nose to the ground. The Old English poets employed sly sexual innuendo as well. Older students often enjoy such double-entendres.

> Be careful with me—I'm rigid and frail, transparent and small. I'll be hard to find if you let me fall. Sometimes it's hard for me to get in but simple to get out. I can hurt you real bad if you don't know what I'm about. I suck and kiss Iris real tight, but break us up before you go to sleep tonight.
>
> (Contact lenses)
>
> —*Tony Howard, Corcoran art student*

★   ★   ★

> I live in a dark house.
> The white gate opens,
> but I never leave.
> Rooted to the floor,
> I flop and wag,
> poke into crevices
> slide into ridges,

bathe in juices.
Though I'm soft
and tender, I'm also
a weapon. A whip.

(Tongue)

 —*Nan Fry*

Riddles frequently use paradox, another source of their ability to mystify and disorient us. Such seeming contradictions that make a surprising kind of sense stretch our minds, enabling us to imagine other possibilities beyond the literal or logical. Perhaps because it pushes against the limits of language, paradox is often associated with wordplay.

I'm a circle.
My coat is glass.
I have two fingers
but I don't have hands.
I run every day
but never walk.
I tell you something
but I can't talk.

Built on a series of contradictions, this poem was written by a fourth grader who had recently come from China. Perhaps because English was still new to him, his metaphors are delightfully fresh—his clock has fingers rather than hands. The final paradox expresses a theme that occurs often in riddles, especially when they give voice to the voiceless.

Many "first-person" riddles are spoken by creatures or things that are usually silent. This aspect of the poems appeals to young children, who are bursting with things to say but are so often told to be quiet. Perhaps riddles help them to consider or explore other ways of communicating—including the written word. One fourth grader, writing about a book, said:

I talk a lot but don't have a mouth.
I show a lot but don't have hands.

She had not seen the clock riddle or this Anglo-Saxon poem:

I was by the shore, near the sea-wall
at the surging of waves,
settled firmly in my first state;
few saw my solitary home,

where at dawn the brown wave embraced me.
I never knew I was fated to speak
mouthless over the bench in the mead hall,
to exchange words. That is the wondrous part,
uncanny to a mind that cannot understand
how the knife point and the right hand,
the man's mind and the blade together,
pressed me purposefully, so that I should,
while we two are alone,
bring a message meant only for you,
speak it at once, so that no man may
spread far and wide our sayings.

(Runestaff or reed pen)

By allowing the silent to speak, riddles enable us to see the world from a non-human point of view. We are thrown off balance, not only because we don't know who or what is speaking, but also because we think of speech as uniquely human. As a result, we experience a sense of dislocation, seeing our familiar environment from a strange, new perspective.

I am soft and fibrous.
You wear me, although you don't like me.
I am beautiful in myself,
But when I like something,
I stick to it
Because it is my Maker.
I was born in a dry, windy place,
where no human lives.

    —Junior high student

★   ★   ★

Beaten by a hammer, my head was hurt
by sharp tools, scraped with a file.
Now I swallow all who stand up to me.
Surrounded by rings, I strike hard
at the hard thing, pierce the hole from behind.
In the dead of night, I drive out the guard
that keeps my master from his pleasure.
I pull back my nose, last barrier
to this hoard, when my lord desires
to take his treasure, left by those
slaughtered at his command.

    —Anglo-Saxon

I found the first of these riddles particularly disorienting. It takes an ordinary nuisance—a fuzz ball on a sweater—and presents it in surprising, even religious language. I didn't understand the last line, but when the poet explained that it was about a dryer, it made sense—and it also made that common appliance seem exotic and mysterious. In the Anglo-Saxon poem, the speaker is a key. It not only tells us how it was made and how it works, but it also seems to judge the lord who gained his wealth (and perhaps his woman) through slaughter.

> The sea fed me, water concealed me,
> and waves covered me as I rested close
> to earth, footless, my mouth open to the flood.
> Now some man wants to feed on my flesh.
> He doesn't bother with my bony rind
> but rips open my side with a sharp
> blade and eats me, ravenously, raw. . . .
>
> (Oyster)
>
> —*Anglo-Saxon*

By providing a persona, riddles give writers an opportunity to explore feelings difficult to express directly.

> I am hard.
> I beat up things.
> My hand is like stone.
> I hate things.
> You can hold me.
> My pants are black.
> What am I?
>
> (Hammer)
>
> —*Fourth grade student*

★   ★   ★

> I sparkle
> and endure the screams of
> the wind
> and the small, sharp
> pain of nuts hitting me.
> Beings stare at me,
> and look through
> me, as if I am
> nothing.

They see my
insides.
It's embarrassing,
really.

(Window)

   —*Junior high student*

In the midst of all that hard, stony anger, the speaker of the hammer
riddle says, "You can hold me." All riddles are ambivalent: they con-
ceal and reveal. They contain an invitation to "look through" them
and find the answer, the secret that is meant to be shared.

   Ultimately, the secret is connected to the writer's sense of self. I
am not suggesting, however, that teachers focus on the feelings or the
person revealed in the riddle. In *Sleeping on the Wing,* Kenneth Koch
and Kate Farrell give some good advice on this point when they emphasize the importance of "talking about the poem and not the
student."

   Though guessing the answer to a riddle has all the excitement of
discovering a secret, the result may be anticlimactic. According to
Emily Dickinson, "The Riddle we can guess / We speedily despise."
Post-riddle letdown is not inevitable, however. A riddle draws its audience in, involving them in actively imagining the scene the poem
creates. Once the answer is glimpsed, a shift in perception occurs and
everything falls into place. A good riddle doesn't lose all its energy or
excitement when this happens; rather, it stands up to being reread as
an object or persona poem. There should still be an element of mystery or surprise left, some new way of perceiving the subject of the
poem. If enough care has been taken to include accurate sensory detail and fresh, original metaphor, the riddle is strengthened rather than
deflated by its solution. When the small mystery is solved, we should
be left with an expanded sense of larger mysteries.

   Sly and slippery, I'm not
   what I seem.
   You look for me as you might

   for a fish in a river.
   All is moving light
   and shadow. Suddenly you see

   something hovering—there—by the bank,
   blending into the weeds,
   so close you could touch it.

Of course, you say. *I should
have known.* But you're wrong—
it's important not to know.

I come to you nameless,
wanting you to find me,
here in the weeds.

But when you name me,
remember all you don't know
and how it gleams.

(The answer)

    —Nan Fry

★   ★   ★

Riddles from Corcoran School of Art First-year Students

Three thin men in
a small round box, with a big picture window
and a floor that fights shocks,
each running a race with slowness and speed.
Spectators count laps
absentmindedly,
always starting over,
9, 10, 11, 12,
1, 2, 3, 4,
6, 7, 8, 9,
three predictable men
each thin as a line.
A pulse on a pulse,
almost always on time.

(Watch)

    —Nici Tietjen

★   ★   ★

With my mammal skin stretched to its fullest
I serenade the jungle. I am of wood and skin;
my voice bridges your subconscious and boards
your body. I am forever in the pocket.

(Drum)

    —Michael Brown

* * *

Endless microscopic organisms dwell in my belly,
swimming about and tickling.
A pair of webbed, slimy feet paddle across my chest
to the safe floating platform just out of my reach.
A cattail pokes and thrown stones skip, forever
disturbing my glassy outside.
And in the fall my life dries up, not to
be seen until the early spring melt.

(Swamp)

—*Ella Hurley*

* * *

I live on the smoothest sheets of glass
and watch everything, never closing my eyes.
Sometimes I lie on still water in the forest and
show the animals the sky.
And when I'm hurt, I scream
and break into thousands of pieces,
or I just float away.
And if I'm angry and you come
too close, I might just show you yourself.

(Reflection)

—*Colleen Hanlon*

Resources for Riddles

I often use examples from the work of student writers, but I also draw on other resources.

Life in Greece in Ancient Times by Paul Werner, translated by David Macrae (Friburg: Productions Liber, 1977) includes a selection of Athenian riddles.

Several translations of Anglo-Saxon riddles are available. Kevin Crossley-Holland's *Exeter Book Riddles* (London: Penguin, 1988) is perhaps the most comprehensive. I also recommend the handful of riddles included by Burton Raffel in his *Poems from the Old English* (Lincoln: University of Nebraska, 1971). My own translations are published in *Say What I Am Called: Selected Riddles from the Exeter Book* (Washington, D.C.: Sibyl-Child Press, 709 Dahlia St., N.W., 1988). Those interested in reading the riddles in the original Anglo-Saxon will find them, along with a glossary and extensive notes, in Craig Williamson's *The Old English Riddles of the Exeter Book* (Chapel Hill: University of North Carolina Press, 1977).

In *A Book of Puzzlements: Play and Invention with Language* (New York: Schocken Books, 1981), Herbert Kohl has a chapter on riddles that includes examples from British and African folklore and from student writing. *Crosbie's Dictionary of Riddles* by John S. Crosbie (New York: Harmony Books, 1980) contains a lot of the "Why did the chicken cross the road?" type of trick questions, but it also includes traditional riddle poems. *The Scott, Foresman Anthology of Children's Literature,* edited by Zena Sutherland (Glenview, Il.: Scott, Foresman, 1984), contains a section on Mother Goose and contemporary riddles.

For a discussion of the use of riddles by Emily Dickinson and Wallace Stevens, see Mervyn Nicholson, "Reading Stevens' Riddles," *College English,* Vol. 50, Number I, Jan. 1988, pp. 13–31. Brian Swann also considers Dickinson's use of poetic enigma in "Who Is the East? and Other Riddle-Matters," *Poet & Critic,* Vol. XI, Number 1, Autumn 1983, pp. 58–70. Swann analyzes riddles drawn from traditional sources, contemporary writers, and student work. Two contemporary poets whose work I often use in class are Sylvia Plath and W. S. Merwin. Plath's "Mushrooms" is a persona poem that—without its title—works well as a riddle, as do some of W. S. Merwin's shorter pieces, such as "Full Moonlight in Spring" and "Song of Man Chipping an Arrowhead." If I am doing a sequence that includes persona poems, I might also bring in Merwin's "A Contemporary."

The Whale's Scars (New York: New Rivers Press, 1974) by Brian Swann contains original riddles and translations. He has also published two books of riddles for children: *Tongue Dancing* (Boston: Rowan Tree Press, 1984) and *A Basket Full of White Eggs* (New York: Orchard Books, 1988).

Jane Avrich

Sonnet Writing
In the Fifth Grade

Last year I taught a fifth grader named Rachael whose confidence waxed and waned. Usually she'd slam her books down on a front row desk, ready to leap to the fore of class discussion. "Oh, oh! Please, me!" she'd pipe, waving her arm wildly, upper body lurching over her desk. But when Rachael was unsure of the material, she retreated. If I called on her, she shrank back in her seat, large-eyed and timid, her answer barely audible. That spring, Rachael wrote a sonnet about shyness:

> The waves build up and up until they're gone
> Gone up upon the shore hiding in the sand
> Retreating to the sea as other waves have done
> Then, gathering their courage, surge to land.
> The aspen tree so bold and bright stands tall
> It battles against all kinds of weather
> But when the wind blows its hardest it calls
> To mind the quivering of a lovely feather.
> The morning glory, the gold and the bold,
> Opens its petals to the morning like lions
> But when the afternoon does come it folds
> Into a timid little mouse who's crying.
>> As I retreat from my boldness I'm shy
>> But I know my courage will come by and by.

Rachael wrote this sonnet in my Language Structures class last year at Saint Ann's School. The sonnet writing project was highly successful; each student in the class of fifteen was able to produce a fresh, artful sonnet in his or her own voice. The success was partially due to the exceptional nature of Saint Ann's itself. A private school in Brooklyn, Saint Ann's is progressive in both curriculum and philosophy. By removing the pressure of grades, the school fosters a mood of curiosity and openness to new projects; the aim is to encourage individual growth and group interaction instead of competition. My fifth graders were a particularly supportive group, listening to and commenting warmly on each other's poems as I read the daily sheaf of homework aloud.

In addition, the school makes a point of introducing creative writing as early as the second or third grade and continuing its practice throughout the high school years. Lower school students are encouraged to write stories and poems without worrying too much about errors in grammar and spelling, so as to make writing as spontaneous and free of anxiety as possible. By the time I receive my students in the fifth grade, the students think of writing as fun. Language Structures, a course taught side by side with English, presents language as a versatile tool. As well as writing poetry, my fifth graders learn to trace etymological roots, read and write newspaper articles, use the resources of a library, and write research papers.

Finally, many of the children at Saint Ann's are gratifying to teach. Bright, curious, many of them very talented, they feed on intellectual stimulation. Small classes of thirteen to eighteen students allow lessons to take place on an intimate level, enabling the teacher to be constantly aware of each student's needs.

At the same time, it is important to note that many students at Saint Ann's, while motivated, do not possess exceptional abilities. The fifth grade humanities courses are divided into four levels; last year mine was third from the top. Many of the children were not strong readers and few were strong writers. Some had problems with spelling and retaining information, while others had learned English as their second language and were still shaky on usage and rules. Moreover, few students had formally studied poetry; although most of them had done plenty of free-form writing of stories and poems, a formal structure such as the sonnet was something new.

But the fact is that younger children in general, regardless of their education and background, have a strong instinct for poetry. Nine- and ten-year-olds are highly attuned to rhythm and sound. Words, not yet worn out and drained of life, are for them still imprinted with images. Much of what my own fifth graders were able to do, others of their age could do, too.

During the poetry unit that my class did that spring, I grew more and more impressed with their enthusiasm both for reading and for writing different kinds of poems. Children are remarkably clever imitators, able to read and appreciate a variety of forms and then to make those forms their own. The sonnet was a fitting final project because it wraps up many new skills, such as the uses of meter, rhyme, and imagery, into a neat and compact package. The sonnet is also an exercise in clarity: its tight, logical form disciplines students to focus on one idea, develop it in twelve lines, then bring it to a conclusion in the couplet.

I approached this writing assignment in cautious steps. The fifth graders started by looking at poetic images, so often the building blocks of a poem. The students read haikus and drew pictures of what the three-line poems let them see—a blossom, a loon, a reflection of the moon on water. Then, in seventeen syllables of their own, they tried to capture an image in a few swift strokes, leaving a lingering feeling of its "after-presence." Their haikus were simple, frank observations of insects, sunbeams, passing clouds, or snow freshly fallen on a meadow in Prospect Park.

They went on to read Imagist poems such as William Carlos Williams's "The Red Wheel Barrow" and Wallace Stevens's impressionistic "Thirteen Ways of Looking at a Blackbird." I introduced the terms *simile* and *metaphor*, which they tried thinking of as points of intersection between two images, like the joining place of two links on a chain. Ezra Pound's "In a Station of the Metro" served as a good example:

> The apparition of these faces in the crowd;
> Petals on a wet black bough.

After turning the poem over in their minds, the students began to nod in appreciation and murmur, "Oh, I get it," as they realized how the splotches of a hubbub of faces could look for a moment like wet blossoms clustered on a branch.

As we played with figurative language, we made the distinction between poems about abstract ideas—love, peace, or fear—and concrete ones—sensual impressions like the sound of glass breaking or the image of two plums in the icebox. We explored how abstract ideas could be represented by concrete images and thus rendered more familiar, more personal, as in Emily Dickinson's poem #254:

> "Hope" is the thing with feathers—
> That perches in the soul—
> And sings the tune without the words—
> And never stops—at all—
>
> And sweetest—in the Gale—is heard—
> And sore must be the storm—
> That could abash the little Bird
> That kept so many warm—

I've heard it in the chillest land—
And on the strangest Sea—
Yet never, in Extremity,
It asked a crumb—of Me.

The fifth graders warmed to this emotive poem, which is so simply written, and whose single image suggests so much about the woman who wrote it. Unlike the Imagist fragments that describe impressions coolly and deftly, Dickinson allows her feelings to show, extending her metaphor by drawing numerous parallels between the nature of hope and the behavior of a bird (the "thing with feathers" that she playfully declines to name). One girl flapped her hands and pointed out that "her words sound like this"; indeed the bird's frenetic fluttering is much like Dickinson's delicate bursts of verse. Like a bird, she is persistent yet fragile. At this point I asked the fifth graders to describe an abstract feeling by comparing it to something concrete and to sustain the comparison for at least eight lines. The resulting batch was mostly animal poems, many of them very lively. In one poem, loneliness took the form of a baying dog; in another, playfulness was a panda.

After experimenting with figurative language, we went on to rhyme and meter. Getting the children to rhyme didn't require much work. For exercises I gave them one-, two-, and three-syllable words and asked them to go home and find as many words as they could that rhymed with each. They brought back scores. (After all, most of them had been rhyming since *The Cat in the Hat*.) Some were already rhyming their poems voluntarily. Others were accomplished rappers; in the lunchroom they'd rap about subjects ranging from Nintendo to peanut butter cups.

Fifth grade ears were not as well tuned to meter, however. I tried bringing in examples—fluid iambs as opposed to plodding spondees, rapid anapests and waltzing dactyls—and showed them Coleridge's tour de force, "Metrical Feet":

Tro-chee | trips from | long to | short.

From long | to long | in so- | lemn sort

Slow Spon- | dee stalks; | strong foot! | yet ill | a-ble

Ev-er to | come up with | Dac-tyl tri- | syll-a-ble.

‿—　‿—　‿　—‿—
I-am | -bics march | from short | to long;

‿‿—　‿‿—　‿‿—　‿‿—
With a leap | and a bound | the swift An- | a-pests throng.

But when the students read a poem on their own, they had trouble distinguishing the stressed syllables from the unstressed. I encouraged them to read the poems out loud. In fact, the first poems were songs, I told them—that's where their rhythm comes from.

Then my own words gave me an idea. The next day, I came to class armed with a boom box and a Beatles tape. I pushed *play* and "Eight Days a Week" blasted out. The fifth graders mouthed the words and drummed the beat on their desks. Within moments they were keeping time in perfect trochees:

—‿　—‿　—‿
Ooh, I | need your | love, babe

—　‿　—‿　—
Guess you | know it's | true

Or iambic:

‿—‿—　‿—
I want | to hold | your hand . . . .

I wrote lines of the songs on the blackboard and asked for volunteers to scan them. Most of the students were eager to come up and mark the stressed and unstressed beats. For homework they were able to write two lines of iambs and two lines of dactyls for me to read aloud. They also began to like having the odd, consonant-cluttered metrical terms in their vocabulary; daily they announced discoveries of "trochees," "spondees," and "anapests" in limericks, TV jingles, and their own names.

Now it was time to put the pieces together and look at some sonnets; in order to construct such a strict form, the students first needed to see it in action. Shakespeare seemed a reasonable place to start. His sonnet #29 proved a good icebreaker:

> When, in disgrace with fortune and men's eyes,
> I all alone beweep my outcast state
> And trouble deaf heaven with my bootless cries
> And look upon myself and curse my fate,
> Wishing me like to one more rich in hope,

Featured like him, like him with friends possess'd,
Desiring this man's art and that man's scope,
With what I most enjoy contented least;
Yet in these thoughts myself almost despising,
Haply I think on thee, and then my state,
Like to the lark at break of day arising
From sullen earth, sings hymns at heaven's gate;
    For thy sweet love remember'd such wealth brings
    That then I scorn to change my state with kings.

I was surprised that the fifth graders did not seem intimidated by the antiquated language or syntax. They asked me the meaning of certain words (*scope* and *haply*) and they found it helpful to trace a few participial phrases back to their distant antecedents ("I" to "wishing," "desiring," and "despising," for example), but their basic response to the poem was immediate and strong. The students could relate to the bouts of insecurity and self-pity that Shakespeare talks about when he says, "I all alone beweep my outcast state." You feel that you're stupid and clumsy, that you look awful, while everybody else seems smart, popular, and cool. "Nobody likes me, everybody hates me, I think I'll go eat worms" was one student's chanted response. The students liked the bantering self-mockery of Shakespeare's tone and felt conversant with him rather than daunted by the old-fashioned language. Even their misunderstandings brought them closer to him. In the phrase "bootless cries," for example, they pictured someone kicking out tender bare feet in frustration, only to have them slam against a wall.

Perhaps most important, the students were able to trace the shape of the poem's argument. After the buildup of complaints in the first eight lines, they recognized the "turn" in the ninth, signalled by the pivotal word *yet*. The poet stops, remembers his love, and in the remaining six lines regains his confidence. The final couplet, chiming with the sound of "brings" and "kings," gives the poem a satisfying sense of closure.

Another poem that went over well was the anti-Petrarchan blazon #130 ("My mistress' eyes are nothing like the sun"). The students liked the fact that the poet's love is a real woman, palpable and earthy, who "treads on the ground." At the same time, a few of the girls admitted that they wouldn't be thrilled if some guy declared that their eyes *weren't* bright, their lips *weren't* red, and that "black wires" grew out of their heads. We tried to imagine how Shakespeare's mistress might respond in her own right, pointing out her love's spindly legs or his receding hairline.

The most helpful of the Shakespeare sonnets was #73:

That time of year thou mayst in me behold
When yellow leaves, or none, or few, do hang
Upon those boughs which shake against the cold,
Bare ruin'd choirs, where late the sweet birds sang.
In me thou see'st the twilight of such day
As after sunset fadeth in the west,
Which by and by black night doth take away,
Death's second self, that seals up all in rest.
In me thou seest the glowing of such fire
That on the ashes of his youth doth lie,
As the death-bed whereon it must expire
Consumed with that which it was nourish'd by.
    This thou perceivest, which makes thy love more strong,
    To love that well which thou must leave ere long.

This melancholy lyric about aging might seem beyond the experience of young students, but my fifth graders read the poem with understanding and compassion. They appreciated the sober beauty of its three images, each developed in a quatrain: the tree on the eve of winter, the vanishing twilight, and the nearly extinguished fire. Many of the children adopted this format when they came to write their own sonnets. In Rachael's poem (quoted earlier), the alternation of shyness and boldness is at first the ebb and flow of the waves, then the aspen tree in the wind, and finally the opening and closing of the morning glory.

Rachael chose to adhere to strict Shakespearian form: her poem is based on iambic pentameter and the lines follow a traditional *abab cdcd efef gg* rhyme scheme. But my students did not stick to established patterns of rhyme and meter if such formulas constrained them or didn't suit the themes they wanted to express. The modern sonnet is an adaptable form; the students saw how E. E. Cummings tossed out old rules of end-stop and capitalization so his sonnets speak in his own voice.

And so did the fifth graders' sonnets. I was delighted to see how each reflected the writer's own personality. There was a wide range of topics—musings on nature, statements about friendship, a description of a pet turtle, a tongue-in-cheek poem about the changing sports seasons:

As the season of spring comes in, behold,
A starting of baseball has come to spring.
The month of April it started, I'm told
It goes to fall and ends with a big ping.
In the season of fall, basketball comes.

Shoot a sphere through a hoop, try not to miss.
If you call a basketball player dumb,
He will be very mad and they will hiss.
In the season of winter football is there,
Big people play it and make people fall.
They tackle and block—what do people care?
The people are strong, big, fast, fat, and tall.
    The sports never stop, go through the season.
    More guys who watch it is the reason.

—*Mike Lee*

Also wry and humorous—and a bit naughty—is William Avedon's whimsical riddle poem:

What Is It?

Shooting over the ice and through the rain
The rain covers its tracks so they cannot be found.
Could this be a horse? Or a donkey in pain?
Not slipping and sliding, but merely gliding.
Maybe it's an animal of some special kind?
It could be a donkey whose nickname is a behind.
It could be real, it could be a fake,
It could be a child making mudcake.
Maybe it's Athena, maybe it's Zeus,
Maybe it's a runner with Nike A I R shoes,
Maybe it's God's messenger, maybe it's his mail.
But you know their motto, even through hail.
It looks like a Porsche, a real cool hot rod,
But if you ask my opinion, I think it's God!

William loved wordplay; his poem is full of witty tricks, like the derivations of Nike sneakers and the florists' logo of Hermes ("God's messenger") from Greek mythology, which we had studied earlier in the year. Aaron Neff's poem also mentions the Greeks, but is quite different in tone:

The dawn arises for a whole new day
The day is as beautiful as I thought it.
Dawn meets dusk and the daylight goes away
And the sky burns then is dabbled and lit.
Then it shows its ever-present beauty
The night is radiant with pure white light.
The stars and moon do their special duty
To summon all the gods up high and bright.
Andromeda, Perseus, Pegasus

All tell their story with their shining light.
Scorpio, Orion, and Artemis
Shine down from the heavens showing their might.
    The night is mystical and magical
    Gods conversing in light and madrigal.

Impelled by the structure of the sonnet, many of the children found themselves exploring new corners of their imaginations. Some created surreal fantasy lands:

Flowing water, purple, blue, green, and red.
More and more green goldfish first fly around.
Catfish, sea stars, sea slugs are at the head
Scurry around without making a sound.
Light dances around on the water's edge
Sun slowly goes into the horizon
Dances back and forth on a little ledge
Goes down like it has some sort of poison.
Blackness fills the sky as the sun goes down.
Darkness fills the sky and light from the moon.
Darkness makes people seem to have a frown
Good news is that dawn will be coming soon.
In the water melting into the twilight
I'm sure this is going to be my light.

    —*Rebecca Milburn*

Rebecca's clever rhyming of *twilight* and *my light* brings the poem to a gentle, glowing close. Other students experimented with the couplet in their own ways. One child, describing a tropical vacation resort, concludes with

In the pond there is an alligator
There are secret passages, so see you later.

I collected all fifteen poems in a book that I called *Fifth Grade Sonnet Sequence* and distributed among the authors. Seeing the poems in print, the children were amazed at how good they were. They complimented one another wonderingly.

I was no less impressed. The sonnet form provided the children with the guidance they needed to express their thoughts clearly and sequentially while allowing them leeway to improvise, to ride the crests and dips of language to realms of their own. One such realm is described by Nao Terai, whose knowledge of English as a language second to Japanese gives her verse its own special music. Nao's was the *Fifth Grade Sonnet Sequence*'s opening poem:

The Sky

In the sky, a great big white fluffy cloud,
There are angels with hulas and wings,
Playing a golden trumpet very loud,
The other angels in beautiful voices sing.
The other angels swim in the sky beach
While the others make cloud castles.
The angels walk their dogs on leashes
Cats jump on angels—what a hassle.
People down below cannot hear the noise
So most people do not believe in this.
But when you hear it they rejoice
But when you ignore it they hiss.
    Now you saw the secret of skyland.
    When teachers ask you about it raise your hand.

Dave Morice

Poetry Poker

Misfit Improvisations on Language

The turning upside-down in play—the misfit improvisations—are both self-congratulatory symbols of a child's achievement and means of reinforcing what he has learnt about actuality.

—*James Britton,* Language and Learning

Poker cards in the classroom? Poker with poetry? The very thought of it catches the attention of the class. It's easy to do, it's quick, and it's fun. For those (and other) reasons, I've used it with almost every group I've taught since 1975. More than 5,000 students from nine to ninety-six have played the game and won—a poem.

One objective of Poetry Poker is to explode any preconceived notions that students may have about poetry, such as "Poetry has to rhyme" or "Poetry is boring to read and hard to write" or even "Poetry has to make sense." By going to the outer limits of process, to an unfamiliar landscape where topic, sense, and form grow out of surrealistic wordplay, students are able to enjoy language in a different light.

The Beginning

In 1975, I began to teach the "Poetry Class for People over Sixty" at the Iowa City congregate meals site. For the first month or so, the students wrote poems on various topics in styles that they chose. One day when I walked into the room, two of the students were talking about playing bridge later that afternoon. "We ought to play cards here," one of them joked.

Next meeting, I brought in a deck of playing cards with phrases typed on each card, and announced in a W. C. Fields voice, "Today we'll play Poetry Poker!" They laughed, and I shuffled. The results were completely different from anything they'd written, and they wanted to do it again next time.

In the Schools

Soon after that, I tried Poetry Poker with children. As I'd hoped, they responded with mirthful enthusiasm, and their poems, like the older people's, were playful and imaginative.

During the next five years, I visited approximately forty schools throughout Iowa to conduct poetry classes with students in grades K–12. More recently, I've taught other workshops at local schools. Most of the time I've worked with around thirty students in grades 4–8.

Since I use nontraditional as well as traditional techniques, my sponsor, the Iowa Arts Council, came to think of me as "the avant-garde teacher" and told schools that I would present poetry in ways they might not be familiar with. That introduction (or warning, in some cases) usually helped to place me in schools that were open to alternative techniques. Many of the teachers prepared their students for my visit by announcing it as a special event, or by having them write poetry in advance, or both. Some, however, simply told the students that a poet would be coming to class for a week.

My main goal has always been to leave a positive memory that will stay with the students for a long time. Although I've usually been in each school for just a week, I've hoped that writing in strange new ways would provide students with a buffer against staid concepts of academic seriousness they might bump into later on. This desire grew out of my own first experiences in poetry, an alien topic in the early 1960s in the Midwest. One day my high school English teacher, Mr. Duggan, a square-jawed Irishman with a booming voice, read Gerard Manley Hopkins's "Margaret" so powerfully that I never forgot the experience. It turned on a poetic light for me that has never dimmed. Of my own school visits, I have the hope that one day in the future a student bored by literature class might look back on the week, introduced by Poetry Poker, and think, "Hey, wait a minute. Poetry doesn't *have* to be dull."

How to Play Poetry Poker

To introduce Poetry Poker, I ask students for their ideas on poetry, beginning with the basic question, "What is a poem?" After a few kids give their answers, I try broadening the scope by suggesting alternatives. For example, if a student says, "Poems have rhyme," I reply, "If you want them to. But many people would rather write poems that don't rhyme. The choice is up to the writer. I like to write both kinds." We also talk about sense and nonsense, fantasy and reality, lyric and narrative, or the differences between poetry, prose, and prose poetry. We sometimes discuss why people write poetry, and where, and how.

Here is a thumbnail sketch of the two steps involved in Poetry Poker:

1. *The Deal:* The teacher deals five cards to each student and explains how to play the "game."

2. *The Game:* The students write poems or prose poems using the phrases typed on the poker cards and as many of their own words as they want in order to connect those phrases. They can change the verb tenses, pluralize nouns, etc., but they should try to include all the words. They move the cards around their desks and put them in an order that seems to "click." Important: invariably a few will think that the goal of Poetry Poker is simply to rearrange the cards. The teacher should emphasize that they need to add many more of their own words to complete the poems. During the actual writing, the teacher should be available to answer questions, respond to ideas, and replace discards.

Making the Cards

Poker cards (as opposed to plain white cards) encourage a playful atmosphere. Each card in the Poetry Poker deck has a phrase typed (or taped) on it. (The phrase may be handwritten, but the typewriter gives the cards a more official look.) The selection of phrases is important, since those phrases suggest what to write.

The phrases I make up are of three general types, and each deck has roughly the same amount of each type:

1. *Complete phrases:* "to the store," "eating fish." These phrases are flexible, insofar as they can be dropped anywhere into a sentence—beginning, middle, or end.

2. *Incomplete phrases:* "without a new," "jumped off the." These phrases are a little more demanding. They need words at the beginning or the end to complete them.

3. *Unusual phrases:* "magic hamburgers," "with toenails flashing." These phrases nudge the poem into a fanciful, surrealistic context.

Here is a list of such phrases, divided into the three types:

Complete Phrases	Incomplete Phrases	Unusual Phrases
to the store	without the new	magic hamburgers
eating fish	jumped off the	with toenails flashing
stale piece of cake	gold as the dome of	a dinosaur or two
a pretty face	it was going	1,000 streets
I promise	smashed between	beautiful blue teeth
all the flags	in this tired	asking faces

red paint	knowing who	mouthful of cheese
the spaceships	the house as another	the evil factory
old train	oh, no, I	how to growl
a stereo	don't chase my	apples as gray as
I would like	cheese and	sloppy hippopotamuses
the roof leaked	up the puzzle	stop the table
banana split	the flags to	laugh slowly
going crazy	without her nice old	round eggs
the pickle jar	wherever the goat	phony ant
a balloon pops	spins the wheel	zoo monster
my stomach	almost got hit	colors of sleep
no sunlight	saw a hotdog	snoring a song

A Sample Session

To demonstrate how the game is played, here is a composite session based on my experiences. Twenty-five sixth grade students are about to play. The teacher (T) is giving directions, and the students (S) are asking questions. The dialogue begins after a brief warm-up discussion of poetry.

> T: And now you'll have a chance to write a poem.
>
> S: Right now? I can't write something off the top of my head.
>
> T: Oh, but this is a different kind of writing. It's called Poetry Poker. I'd like all of you to take out a sheet of paper and a pencil, and write your name at the top.
>
> *(Saying this, the teacher holds up one or more decks of prepared cards—three decks for a class of twenty-five students so that each student can receive five cards. On seeing the cards, the students' responses change dramatically.)*

S: Wow! Poker! We're going to play poker *in school*.

T: That's right, Poetry Poker. You'll use these cards to write your poems.

S: Do we write on the cards?

T: No, they're specially marked cards. Each has a phrase typed on it, and all the phrases are different. Some are pretty normal, like "to the store," and others are weird, like "magic hamburgers."

(The teacher removes the cards from one deck, holds up a few, and points to the phrases.)

T: I'll shuffle the deck and deal five cards to each of you. To play the game, you write a poem using all the words on the cards and as many of your own as you want. I would prefer that you not try to rhyme, and don't be surprised if what you come up with doesn't make sense. With Poetry Poker, it probably won't—at least not in the regular way. Your poem can be as weird and crazy as you want, but it still will probably make a different kind of sense.

S: But what do I write about? I don't have any ideas.

T: Whatever comes to your mind. Don't worry about that. When you get the cards, spread them face up in front of you, read the words on them, slide them around, and see what ideas you get. You don't have to concentrate on correct spelling, punctuation, or capitalization. You can change those things later, when you're rewriting. If you have any questions, just raise your hand, and I'll come over to your desk. See what you can do in ten minutes.

S: How long does it have to be?

T: Not that long. Say, somewhere between six lines and a page. If you want, you can write it like a story. Or a poem.

(The teacher deals the cards.)

S: I don't like this card. Could I have another one?

T: Sure.

(The student is satisfied with his new card, smiles, and comments that it works much better. But another student is not happy with her cards.)

S: Do I have to use them all? I can't fit this one in.

T: Here, pick another card and see how it works. If you can't fit it in, then write something using the other four cards.

After the students draft their poems (about ten minutes), the teacher asks who wants to read his or her poem aloud. In some cases, the class wants the teacher to read them. In others, the students read their own. Most of the poems are strange and humorous; some are lyrical, imagistic, and serious. During the reading, some students show surprise that what they wrote with the phrases actually sounds good.

Surrealism and the Students

To give the students a context for the writing, the teacher can introduce the concept of surrealism as it relates to fantasy and dreaming. One way is to describe a school desk from two different points of view: "A realistic way of describing this desk would be to say that the top part and the seat are made of wood, and the legs are made of metal. But surrealism is different. You can talk about the way things *don't* appear, except in your imagination. A surrealistic way of describing a desk might be to say the top is made of bats' wings, the seat is made of storm clouds, and the legs are giraffes' necks. But you could describe the desk in many other ways. Does anyone want to add to the description?"

Not being familiar with surrealism, students find this explanation intriguing. They carry the description farther out, chuckling at their additions. A fifth grade girl once said, "The bats' wings have eyes in them, and when they blink, the wings flap and carry the desk away."

Some educators feel that technical terms can turn students off, but I think such terms can intrigue them. Introduced in an entertaining way, "surrealism" becomes a word many can identify with. In fact, one fourth grade teacher told me recently that her class adopted the word *surreal* in their own slang to indicate when someone is behaving wildly: "Patty's acting surreal today."

The teacher should make certain points clear about this writing activity. First, it is not the usual way that people write. Second, it's okay if the results don't make complete sense. Third, the images from the resulting poem can lead to ideas for writing poems in more usual ways. Fourth, the poems needn't rhyme. And fifth, they can be written in lines and stanzas or in paragraphs.

Most importantly, the students are free to alter the rules to fit their own words.

Evaluation

To me, the best form of evaluation has been to watch students while they play Poetry Poker: clearly they enjoy it. Sometimes students finish early and ask for a new set of cards to make a new poem. Other students suggest playing it again the next day. Teachers also respond with gusto. Many have said they'd never seen the students so excited about poetry. Some have copied my phrases to make Poetry Poker decks, and I suggest they make up some with their own phrases too. School librarians have reported a big jump in the number of students checking out poetry books.

Student Examples

Below is a selection of poems written in Iowa City by three different groups—elementary school students, college students, and senior citizens. In most cases, the poems are not titled. None have been rewritten.

The first group includes fourth, fifth, and sixth graders who wrote their poems in 1976. The second group, graduate students in elementary education, wrote theirs in 1991 during the "Introduction to Literature" class that I teach at the University of Iowa. The third group, members of the "Poetry Class for People over Sixty," composed the first Poetry Poker poems in 1975, and their poems, reprinted below, come from the original session.

POEMS BY CHILDREN AGES 9–11

I ate a stale piece of cake.
My teeth have turned a beautiful blue.
You have a pretty face too.
I promise I won't tell.

    —Anonymous

★   ★   ★

I opened a door and this cat
comes and says, "Hi. Welcome
to the cat castle. We love
to have company. Come and I
will show you my talking house."
I said, "Oh, no house can talk."
But I was wrong. Even the stove
says, "What's cookin'?" The washer
says, "No wash today, no detergent
to spit around." It's kind of
spooky really. But I survived
that whole month without getting
roared half to death.

    —Debbie Svobodny

★   ★   ★

Once upon a time I saw it fly loudly
the zebras. I love the loudly of
the zebras. One day I heard my mom
say "Make it a good one." I love the
way it flies. It flies loudly

like the zebras. I love it when
you make a good one. One day me
and my friend went to the loudly
zebras. It flies and it makes
me feel like a good one. It
makes me feel good.

　　　—*Tammy Burr*

　　　　　★　　　★　　　★

Behind the Comet

Behind the comet
that was behind
the evil factory
there was a
sleek silver ship
Then out came
that woman, who
didn't know what
to do
All of a sudden
a balloon pops.

　　　—*Susie Pardoe*

　　　　　★　　　★　　　★

I certainly do want to say whose hair was on the side of the hill. If you
do not tell me I will make you swallow a pill 20 times and then barf it
up 365 times.

　　　—*Karen Budensiek*

　　　　　★　　　★　　　★

Have you ever dreamed of love zipped up
Yeah the roof just fell over somebody
Just laughed slowly

　　　—*Tammy Gjere*

　　　　　★　　　★　　　★

My Bike

You with your
Jumbled-up puzzle
Head toward
My bike.

　　　—*Anonymous*

*   *   *

My bike like a knife.
My kite like a knife.
That woman who I like.
Tomorrow like a butterfly.
Behind the comet I like.

    —Jeannie Starks

*   *   *

If I have a dinosaur or two,
   I hope they don't chase my rabbits
If they do my mouth yap yap yap.
Everybody needs a mouth,
    even a stereo.

    —Betty H.

GRADUATE STUDENTS AGES 20–22

You destroy asking faces
Comfort them with peaches now
Hear keys clicking from the dog's chain
Comfort them with peaches now
Peaches bright and juicy
Questions fade away
Peaches cool and sweet
Fears put in the shade

    —Kristine Weidel

*   *   *

I love the time I spend with you.
Yes, *you*, dark!
Riding your motorcycle.
The stupid stunts you try to entertain me with.
Sure, you almost killed me, but I grabbed on tighter.
And, yes, I loved every minute of it.

    —Anonymous

*   *   *

In the Land of Enchanted Animals, Where

The Wild horses are off snoring a song. Along comes the fairy floating over the Wild horses. She hears them snoring. Her mission: to stop the snoring so the other animals can sleep.

She wakes the Wild horses from the beautiful colors of sound sleep and grants them three wishes only if they stop snoring a song every time they drift asleep.

Three wishes are granted and the fairy floats on her merry way. The Wild horses return to their colors of sound and peaceful sleep. Suddenly a tune is heard, where is it coming from? The Wild horse that was sleeping behind the tree who was never woken from his colors of sleep and never granted his three wishes from the floating fairy.

—*Amy Rea*

★   ★   ★

When the sun sleeps she opened
the envelope & pulled out
a wolf who taught her how
to growl and said, "When the balloon
pops you tiptoe across my heart's
beat."

—*Heather Schmida*

STUDENTS IN THE "POETRY CLASS FOR PEOPLE OVER SIXTY" (AGES 60–82)

Ideas

What were you saying?
    Yes, they will buy it.
Your ideas are loose ends floating.
    Yes, you.
Your ideas are against the Silver Ship.

—*Louis Taber*

★   ★   ★

Car

Push the stalled car
For twelve long days.
It's like
Playing baseball

With ice for a ball.

With soap on the sponge
In the post office
Look through the boxes
And make them shine.

—*Alice Gratke*

★　　　★　　　★

Magic

Such magic in the house
Such magic in the telephone booth
Don't listen to the glasses & cups
Don't listen in the house
I've found it: such magic!

—*Pearl Minor*

★　　　★　　　★

Gold

I'm here
　　We're searching for gold
At the end of the rainbow
　　Mysterious clue
Planets aren't stars
　　I hear accordion music
Whatever you like
　　Is that my clue?

—*Julia Kondora*

Achille Chavée

Cadavre Exquis

Collaboration and Inspiration

A Vote of Confidence

Life
The one-way virtue
of a woman who gives herself for free
who loses her name for good
and who survives by defending
the memory of her murderers

A madman predicts at random
and a hundred artists suddenly lucid
with fits of brand-new anger
destroy their so-called masterpieces
a madman predicts at random
and a hundred patient revolutionaries
go back to their touching work
a madman predicts a man goes by
with his very last chance
to find love at last
A madman demands truth
he postulates an upside-down universe
and eating a colorless flower
he follows the river going back upstream

The redistribution of land is taking place
bombs are exploding nearby
railroad tracks are no longer parallel
the imagination takes off at top speed
here everywhere elsewhere and at last
there is a potential dawn
for one and two and so many fervent men

Time is ticking away
is it the end of the whirl
truth in a muslin veil
or hopeless despair
coming back one more time
pushing back the room of the horizon
for another hundred hours
A character incognito
in the ever-present gathering
keeps himself carefully hidden from everyone
he drinks at a table with no glass on it
and in the middle of so many obscure notions
he sees the eagle carrying the lamb away

Time simply stands still
the forces of nature are being reduced
to an old laboratory joke
the trees shed their fake leaves
and buy themselves golden wigs
at the very moment when a simple man
sees his chance nesting
in the ear of a poor and beautiful woman
in the ear of a woman identical
to the one he had been waiting for all his life

Adventure comes into our lives
as if virginity could still
catch our ancient hearts
or the bird fleeing its nest

What can we do with adventure
Tricks?
Pirouettes?
Puns?
Build houses of cards in the air?
ONE MUST BE DIGNIFIED
If you got angry
as I have in the past
if the sun did not rise
as was the case
love would still be possible
yes love love so sad
and we would have my certitude

The man very far away chases a woman
in one of those well-known landscapes
that we carry within us for life
and the snow is stained with a virgin's blood
and the snow is stained with our own blood
What is beauty after all this?
What is a patched-up solution now?
What is easy living now?
Believe me a little less than nothing
a tunnel under the Channel to blow up London
a waste of time

While the scientist pulverizes a secret
and the wings of doubt breathe an ancient sigh
a poet goes to jail or walks along a wall
or like the bear in my menagerie
makes them pay for his skin
before letting skinny hunters put it up
for sale

There is a surge of evil instincts
that want to take the floor
asceticism and its ascetic
with ears shaped like urinals
there is fortune
good and bad fortune
there is the revenge of destiny
so to speak
and all the perfect lies
and what under the system of exploitation
of man by man is pointlessly called freedom
But also there are
fortunately undeniable
reflexes all the reflexes
of the drunken coachman I love
of fear which is a terrible force
of the light silently turning on
of the bomb laughing at the scapulars

Amid a hundred questions being begged
what is your rich head of hair doing?
What does the tempest do as it wonders where to go?
It is forgiven

because it is the very tempest
we had planted in our hearts
it is dreaming
it is dreaming about the avalanche of eternal snow
like the mother cutting her child's throat
in the light of the complexes' burning torch
but that touch of the magic wand
those festive graves
those hypotheses realities
let us reject them with terror
or on second thought no
in the realm of absolute values
which do not exist
let us reject nothing
let us not be love minus man

If we fire our last cartridge
if our lost heart feeds on leaves
our heart which has no other food
to put between its famished teeth
the necessary crimes
all the sacrifices accepted
hatched first in our solitude
will not remain a dead letter
because sunning sickness
our sickness rich in epidemics
this hot beam of the hallucinatory triangle
of dialectics
is the eighth

the last wonder of the world
the Danube peasant
burning with communism
who transmits his burning to us

Yes
your chance
the one they have fooled us with for so long
can go tear its hair out
it's had it
don't worry
the mother of the son of man

will never be pregnant again
and corrupt once more
the women we have loved
don't worry
our arms
furbished by our destiny
our hands our hearts
will not sign a four-power pact
don't worry
the cannibals will play chess
with the bones of colonial empires
don't worry
our dreams will be filmed
the eel will coil around the knife
sexual freedom will be guaranteed
love protected
and all the martyrs from A to Z
will be avenged

June 24, 1938

★   ★   ★

Poetry Ought to Be Made by Everyone

The long poem above, called "A Vote of Confidence," was written around ten P.M. on June 24, 1938. I wrote it in a span of real time hardly greater than what it would take anyone simply to copy it, and under conditions worth relating to those interested in the problem of poetic inspiration and the automatic writing of poetry.

I was, at the time, in a blocked state, for reasons I do not wish to analyze here; it had been going on for more than three months, during which I had been unable to write one single good line, despite repeated attempts, and—still worse—I had been utterly unable to put myself into a state of poetic inspiration.

It is in these circumstances that, on June 24, 1938, at approximately ten P.M., as I was opening a file, I happened to fall—as if by chance—upon a long series of surrealist games I had practiced more than a month earlier on the evening of May 18 at a café called "The Wooden Leg"; it had been rather late at night and since the place was quite unusually empty, I had asked Raymond Dauphin, the owner, to play this game he had never heard of; he liked it immediately, and I thought it would be a good way to kill time while awaiting the arrival of a few friends.

Without any special kind of conscious goal in mind, I began to reread that long series of surrealist games which the reader will find in its entirety following this note.

I had read about ten questions and answers when I suddenly felt a compulsive urge to write and I started the above poem.

I wrote in this way, automatically, everything that came to my pen. When I finished writing, I resumed reading the games at the point I had left off. After another series of ten questions and answers, I took up my pen again under the conditions I have just described, and kept alternating between successive operations of quick reading and automatic writing, until I reached the end of my reading of the games, and until my pen stopped at last.

All this had lasted less than forty minutes.

At the time I paid no attention to this poem, which must be defined as an automatic text since the original draft has not been altered in the slightest.

Only later did I make up my mind to reveal, to the few friends to whom I had showed it, what mechanical device had triggered its birth. I did so because they agreed that the poem had poetic qualities which, in their opinion, were undeniable—poetic qualities I myself would hardly dare to be so positive about.

On my friends' advice (since the poetic value of this text is not irrelevant to the conclusions I want to draw from it) I'm going to take the liberty of talking freely about all this, which I hope no one will hold against me.

But first, it is important to explain to those people who still don't know anything about it—and wrongly so—exactly what the surrealist game called Dialogue is. Let me say what the simplest of these games consists of: theoretically, one of the players writes down on a piece of paper any question that pops into his head, but keeps it hidden from the other player, who then gives an answer to the question he knows nothing about, in a similarly spontaneous fashion.

In the case that concerns us, one of the partners would, in order to avoid any possibility of cheating, write down, in record time, a series of five questions, and the other partner would answer in the same way. After each series of five questions and answers, we would check their content and immediately begin a new series.

An in-depth analysis of these games would no doubt provide much valuable information about the dialectical, unconscious movements that come to light in them.

At certain times, the parallelism, even the concordance of the questions and answers could lead us to believe that each partner sees into the psychic reality of the other, as if it were an open book.

But it is important to emphasize that surrealist games are authentic sources of irrefutable images. To quote André Breton's definition, the most powerful image of this kind is the image that reaches "the highest point of arbitrariness, the image that takes the longest to translate into practical language, either because it conceals an enormous dose of apparent contradiction, or because one of its terms is strangely missing, or because it first appears sensational but then seems to develop weakly (it abruptly closes the angle of its compass), or because it draws from itself a formal, uninteresting justification, or because it is of an hallucinatory order, or because it quite naturally gives a concrete mask to what is in fact abstraction, or because it implies the denial of some elementary physical property, or because it provokes laughter."

In this case, my unconscious took over a set of games that included surrealist images.

You can see how my unconscious simply rejected a certain number of questions and answers it could not or would not use; how some questions and answers got integrated into the poem without even the slightest change in their interrogative structure; how my unconscious appropriated, transformed, and developed certain passages for its own particular purposes.

You can also see that it showed no tendency to reject my partner's questions and answers in order to use only mine; on the contrary, what came out of my partner's rough thoughts became quite naturally its own.

I wish Raymond Dauphin had agreed to my request to at least attempt to write a poem under conditions he could have tried to render identical to those which happened to be there for me.

Since he would have composed it at my request, the poem he would have written would obviously have lacked an undeniable air of necessity. On the other hand, I think that it, too, would not have failed to illustrate the preceding observations.

What I want to show here is how poetic material—and this is true for any secret device responsible for the birth of any other kind of production—has been gathered through games that, when you look closely, are like an abridged version of what is commonly called a human experience; these games let filter through all of my recent preoccupations and locate them in the time contained in the harsh contact of other realities: my partner's preoccupations. And I want to show how this material has been subjected to a long unconscious gestation in order to suddenly appear completely transformed, developed, and mixed inside the automatic poem.

The surrealist method and discipline always seemed shallow to me, but I owe to them the ability to express myself often, regardless of any conscious aesthetic or moral preoccupations. Because of that method and discipline, we have all of the poem's original elements, the exact circumstances in which they were assembled, the exact length of their gestation, the particular conditions of the poetic surge, and finally the result, which is the poem itself.

We have everything we need to undertake a good, serious analysis of a text's preconscious life—everything we normally lack.

And when you take a close look at the operations I went through, from the moment I began the games to the moment I wrote the last word of the poem, you can see that schematically they are the exact reproduction of the psychic process invariably involved in every kind of creation.

Isn't this an excellent illustration of how skilled the mind is in drawing—from the external reality it has induced—all the elements that will be likely to combine with its former internal reality so that the elaboration of our personal myth can continue?

"I is another—*Je est un autre*," said Rimbaud. To anyone whose individualistic deformation would cause him to want to separate out from the concrete entity of this poem that which he considers to be mine and that which he considers to be my partner's, we would have to say that his ambition is illegitimate and even impossible to realize; because at this moment, nothing yet in that poem can be considered my own for the simple reason that nothing belongs to anybody.

We are dealing here with one of the tangible manifestations in our minds of the law of universal interaction and interdependence, a law which some people do acknowledge but which a far greater number choose to reject because their acknowledgment would undermine and blow away their idealism, their mysticism, their subjectivism, and, consequently, what they take to be their nice little genius, their silly flirtation with the gods, the pointless vanity of their effort to pass down in history a name that history will not allow to be rescued from oblivion.

But it is not my concern here to indulge in invective of a kind that would make all noble hearts rejoice.

Let me repeat that everyone is in possession of poetic reality. How could it be otherwise, since every man retains enough imagination for us never to despair of his destiny—despite the attempts of so many enemies who plot his ruin and have an interest in keeping him enslaved.

The exteriorization of his poetic reality will depend on the power he uses to "stage" his imagination.

Surrealism wants to deal the last blow to the hundred-headed hydra of poetic slavery and intellectual betrayal by working for a takeover: everyone will take poetic power over himself; surrealism gives us the means to achieve that goal; it gives us the absolute reassurance that such an endeavor is not foolhardy by providing multiple devices that have been widely and successfully tested.

It is from the liberation of the poetic potential each man carries within himself—once revolution has similarly freed him from all exterior constraints—that the day can come when, according to Paul Eluard's prophecy, "Every man will show what the poet has seen."

★   ★   ★

Surrealist Games Called Dialogues

Night of 18–19 May 1938 at the Wooden Leg Café.
Partners: Raymond Dauphin and Achille Chavée.

D: When virtue is one-way only
C: Women give themselves for free.

D: When the horse comes before the cart
C: The waves of the sea go crazy.

D: When the notes jump out of their staff
C: Axioms drink a glass of beer.

D: When the madman predicts
C: Artists finally destroy their so-called masterpieces.

D: When blood rushes up to the brain
C: Revolutionaries put an end to capitalism.

★   ★   ★

D: What does man seek?
C: His last chance to find love.

D: What is truth?
C: It is the return to primal truths.

D: What is the universe turned upside down?
C: It is bad luck all the way.

D: What is a river flowing upstream?
C: It is a fly playing the accordion.

D: What is a colorless flower?
C: It is an ultraviolet ray getting engaged.

★   ★   ★

C: When phenomena are moved
D: The planet wanders through a dark universe.

C: When the redistribution of land triggers the revolution
D: Nymphs join the whorehouse.

C: When a bomb explodes nearby
D: Music soothes the savage breast.

C: When railroad tracks are no longer parallel
D: The imagination takes off at top speed.

C: When it is 5:00 A.M. in Singapore
D: Birds sing classical music.

★   ★   ★

C: What is a mirage that turns into reality?
D: Time ticking away.

C: What is the end of the world?
D: The hidden truth.

C: What is hopeless despair?
D: Retreating horizons.

C: What is the character we carefully hide within us?
D: A table with no glass on it.

C: What is the triumph of the law?
D: The eagle carrying the lamb away.

★   ★   ★

D: When time stands still
C: The forces of nature turn into laboratory jokes.

D: When a concept becomes obscure
C: Trees shed their leaves and buy themselves a wig.

D: When the individual is drowned in collectivism
C: Chance finds its nest in the ear of a poor and beautiful woman.

D: When a dictator dictates
C: The anachronistic law of gravity is peopled by silence.

D: When a star dies out
C: The eyelashes of anger flip coins.

★   ★   ★

C: When Gypsies swear at each other
D: Kings desert and deserts fill with people.

C: When there is nothing left to do
D: The forces push and shove.

C: When the day reaches its end
D: A cataclysm restores order.

C: When poetry says screw you to the bourgeois world
D: Flowers wither away.

C: When the woman says farewell to her child
D: The students at the high school don't swap their pens for
   lollypops any more.

★   ★   ★

D: If art remained the only reality
C: There would be something new at the other end of the planet.

D: If the atmosphere couldn't hold on to anything
C: Nothing could be done to avoid war any more.

D: If the victor kissed the loser's feet
C: We would all have one last chance.

D: If love was only for sale
C: Love and science would be reconciled at last.

D: If everything got settled my way
C: There would be trouble at The Wooden Leg.

★   ★   ★

C: If adventure suddenly erupted in our lives
D: I would enforce the law on everybody.

C: If virginity could still be of interest
D: Birds would leave their nests.

C: If I didn't ask a question to play a trick on the Dauphin
D: Houses of cards would challenge buildings.

C: If I got angry, as I have in the past
D: Love would be possible.

C: If the sun did not rise
D: I would have my certitude.

★   ★   ★

D: What is the man who follows a woman?
C: It is the snow stained with a virgin's blood.

D: What is an unfinished symphony?
C: It is something that gives me the shivers.

D: What is beauty?
C: It is less than nothing.

D: What is a solution?
C: It is the digging of a tunnel under the Channel.

D: What is life?
C: It's a waste of time.

★   ★   ★

D: When the scientist pulverizes a secret
C: The wings of doubt breathe a sigh of relief.

D: When a poet meets a poet
C: Jails turn into country homes.

D: When the man walks along a wall
C: The people in the neighborhood are at one of prettyboy Leon's rallies.

D: When the bear leaves its skin behind
C: The good old ways are lost.

D: When the ascetic believes
C: Ears turn into urinals.

★   ★   ★

C: What is fortune?
D: It is the light turning on.

C: What is destiny's revenge?
D: It is fear.

C: What is a miracle?
D: It is the reflex of a drunken coachman.

C: What is a perfect lie?
D: It is a bomb exploding in the middle of prejudice.

C: What is freedom?
D: It is a huge joke.

★   ★   ★

D: What is a rich head of hair?
C: It is begging the question.

D: What is a tempest?
C: It is a serious mistake that must be forgiven.

D: What is a dream?
C: It is an avalanche of eternal snow.

D: What is a mother who cuts her child's throat?
C: It is the magician's wand.

D: What is a festive grave?
C: It is the hypothesis that must be rejected in terror.

★   ★   ★

D: What is an absolute value in universal relations?
C: It is a bad joke that must not be repeated.

D: What is a poet without a lyre?
C: It is the shortest distance between two points.

D: What is an ace?
C: It is life which will have no end.

D: What is love minus man?
C: It is the last cartridge to be fired.

D: What is a crowded urinal?
C: It is a lost heart that feeds on leaves.

★   ★   ★

C: What is pot luck?
D: It is the destruction of concrete data.

C: What is an attempted crime?
D: Truth as bland as an English tune.

C: What is sleeping sickness?
D: It is the hot beam of the hallucinatory triangle.

C: What is the eighth wonder of the world?
D: It is the Danube peasant.

C: What is communism?
D: It is a fever.

★   ★   ★

C: If chance tore its hair out
D: The cheese would remain the strongest.

C: If the Virgin Mary were pregnant again
D: Velocipedists would use steam power.

C: If firearms signed a non-aggression pact
D: The ideal would become nebulous.

C: If cannibals played chess
D: Internationalism would be particularly appropriate.

C: If our dreams were filmed
D: The eel would coil around the knife.

—*Translated from the French by Nicole Ball*

Daniel Judah Sklar

Playmaking

Setting a Tone

In this piece, Daniel Judah Sklar describes his first two classes with elementary school children, the beginning of a series of playwriting workshops that are fully described in his book Playmaking.—Editor

Why write a play?" That's the first question I asked the kids at P.S. 34, the Bronx. "Why not a letter or a clear paragraph describing your best qualities?"

"So we can get rich?" answered Hector, a chunky boy of eleven in a turquoise sweatsuit. Hector belonged to Ms. Finney's fifth grade class, but like many younger kids, he seemed to assume that writing a play is the same as acting in a soap opera and that plays are the same—or poor cousins of—TV shows and movies.

I had to explain that very few people, alas, actually get rich from writing plays.

Maria Margarita, a tall girl who spoke with great precision, said that plays have a "moral." Her tone was dutiful and correct. She sounded like the many students who tell teachers what they want to hear.

I agreed with her, but again asked why she and the others should have to write a play. If they learned to write proper letters and essays, those skills might help them get jobs. But a play?

To my delight, Luz, a pretty girl with long black hair in the second row, said, "It's fun."

"Yes, yes, but why?" I asked. And we began discussing how much fun it is to get up in front of other people and how cool it is to put on a costume and make-up and be someone else.

"What happens when we're being somebody else?" I asked. "What part of ourselves are we using?"

Monique, an intense black girl who sat next to Maria Margarita and whose proper skirt and sweater mirrored the tall girl's, said, "Brain."

"What part of your brain are you using when you make up a story?" I asked.

"Mind," said Hector. He sat just in front of Ms. Finney's extra desk at the back of the room and looked around to see if she had heard his contribution.

"There's a special kind of thinking when we let our minds go, when we make things up. Does anyone know?" I said and waited.

Finally Kim, a light-skinned black girl, said, "Imagination."

"Yes. Writing a play helps develop the imagination," I said, "and a healthy imagination will help you sooner or later in life, regardless of whether you become an explorer discovering a new island, a parent breaking up a fight between kids, or a carpenter bracing a building that almost collapsed in an earthquake. It's how we solve problems when there are no instructions or rules."

The kids, like most other kids—especially teenagers—found that explanation satisfying, so I pressed on. "But why write a play to develop the imagination? Why not a poem? Or a story? Or science fiction? They all use the imagination, don't they?"

The kids agreed guardedly. "So," I persisted, "what's different about a play?"

"The actors," Luz called out. It took a bit more probing for the kids to acknowledge the set designer, lighting person, make-up artist, backstage crew, etc. But once they did, they realized that doing a play means working together. And that it's a way to learn cooperation and discipline.

At that point I recapitulated: "Fun. Imagination. Cooperation. Discipline. Those are all fine goals. If we accomplish any one of them, we will have used our time well. But if we put them together we can do something really special: we can make magic."

This assertion, greeted by smiles at P.S. 34, has elicited cheers, doubtful glances, and even cynical stares at other schools.

My reaction to the smiles was the same as it has been to the stares, glances, and cheers: I showed a video of *The Twins in the Lobby*, written by Erica Hore, an eleven-year-old from Harlem.

In *The Twins in the Lobby*, Sissie and Sally, eleven-year-old twin girls, wait in the hospital lobby while their mother gives birth. Frightened and lonely, the two girls bicker—until Annbellemay, a bag lady, slips into the lobby and teaches them a song and gives them some fruit. Annbellemay not only gets them through the wait, she also helps them to understand and appreciate the Annbellemays of this world.

The P.S. 34 kids loved the video, but when I asked them why, only Kim raised her hand. She said, "It seemed real."

I agreed and asked the other kids if they thought so too. They nodded tentatively, so I asked if they could name a specific part that seemed phony. Monique raised her hand and asked what I meant by "phony," and as I explained, I realized that she and a number of others believed the video was real, a kind of *cinéma vérité*. (It had actually been shot and edited by my friend Theresa Mack and directed by me.) Still others refused to believe a child had actually written the words.

To reinforce the point, I said, "Yes, a child just like you wrote every word. She lives less than twenty blocks from here—five minutes on the subway." As I spoke, my eyes scanned the classroom, finally resting on Jaime, a small boy with a devilish look in his eye.

He cried, "Not me!" as if I had just accused him of running the local crack house.

"Oh yes, you and you and you. Everybody. As I said, you're not only going to write a play, it's going to be magical."

"But how?" asked Kim. The intensity of her expression made me feel that she planned to write her play as soon as I revealed my secret formula.

"That," I said, "is the question I've been waiting for. Can anybody guess the answer?" I paused. Nobody responded.

"The answer is 'honesty,'" I said. "You are all going to explore yourselves—your private worlds.

"That may mean writing about the time you let down your best friend. Or the time you felt so silly that you rolled over and over in the mud or sang the same song fifty times in a row. Or the time you really hated your mother. Or the time you went up on the roof and stayed half the morning, doing nothing . . . without knowing why. But whatever you choose, it will be yours and yours alone."

"But you said the video wasn't real," said Maria Margarita. Her body seemed to rise in righteous indignation, and I looked down at her feet to see if she had stood. She hadn't, but I noticed how close together the desks were—and how scuffed the floor was.

"The story was made up, but the *feelings* were real. The writer's imagination transformed—does everybody know that word? It means to *change*, like the way you change a Transformer toy. So in this case, Erica, the girl who wrote this video, transformed what she felt into a play.

"And that's my job," I continued, "to teach you how to do the transforming. Sometimes the transforming will lead to a serious drama, sometimes to a crazy, wonderful comedy, sometimes to a mystery or a piece of science fiction. But always it will start with you: what you really want, what your bodies, senses, and emotions tell you—what you really feel. What you care about."

"I don't care about writing," said Hector.

"Then maybe you'll write about that—some stupid drama teacher coming in and making you do the most horrible, monstrous task—write about your feelings. You can start with that and maybe it will end with you tricking him and him catching you or not catching you and. . . ."

Hector looked at me carefully.

"Yes, I'm kidding, but I'm also serious. If you write what you really feel, you can't lose. And more than that—we're going to have fun."

"He's crazy," said Jaime quite audibly.

"Maybe. But I'm going to be honest with you—and I'm glad you're already being honest with me. You will have to be honest when you act, too," I continued, looking right at Jaime and then at Saul, a big, husky boy in a dark blue sweatshirt with a hood. Saul's eyes darted to the coat closet, which extended from the front door to the back door along the hall-side wall. I imagined him trying to hide among the winter gear when it came time for acting.

"And when you direct. Or design the set or costumes. And if you are honest, you will be saying 'This is who I am. This is what I believe.' So when your parents and friends and neighbors see and hear your play on the stage, they will enter your world. Not Walt Disney's world or even Hans Christian Andersen's. It will be yours, the world of you people in Ms. Finney's class at P.S. 34.

"And that's where the magic comes from—all those people, your parents, friends, and neighbors, learning from you, appreciating you, and discovering what you believe, really embracing who you are. All of them at once."

The kids paid attention, but clearly had difficulty digesting what I said. I was about to try again when Luz raised her hand and said, "Could we see the video again?"

Somehow that made more sense than another explanation. They would be learning this point in action soon enough. So the kids watched the video and I looked out the window of that fourth-floor classroom at a large housing project a few blocks away. In between, all of the buildings had been burned or demolished. I meditated on that scene and my "explanation" until the bell rang.

*   *   *

"I'm a little confused by this 'magic' business," said Ms. Finney. We were depositing fifty cents each in the kitty and getting coffee from the pot in the teachers' lounge. "Is it a good idea to use such words with kids? Especially if I have to do the explaining when you're not here," she added with a wry smile as we sat down. (These weekly sessions, part of an artist-in-residence program sponsored by Teachers & Writers Collaborative, included work with the classroom teacher.)

Looking at Ms. Finney, a handsome woman in her early forties dressed in a grey skirt and a baby blue cardigan sweater, I thought, "You could do this with your eyes closed," but diplomatically replied, "It's all based on a technique with clear exercises."

"Honesty exercises?"

"Oh yes. Most of them are."

"Well," said Ms. Finney, also trying to be diplomatic, not wanting to burst my bubble too abruptly, "where I live in Westchester County, we have a children's theater and it does Creative Dramatics—as well as stunning productions of classics—but it is hardly magic, as nice as it is. I don't think it's wise to set kids up to. . . ."

"Creative Dramatics is only one part of a play written and produced by children," I asserted.

"Don't the kids make things up in Creative Dramatics? Isn't that the point?"

"Yes, but that's just the beginning for a playwright. The playwright starts with the kind of spontaneity that goes into Creative Dramatics games and goes on to writing exercises, which lead to deeper exploration, which leads, in turn, to the writing of the play, which leads, finally, to the production," I said a bit pompously.

Ms. Finney seemed dubious.

"Creative Dramatics nurtures creativity," she said. "Formal plays and elaborate costumes and sets squelch it."

"Think of Creative Dramatics as step number one in a three-step process," I said. "Exploring feelings through games and exercises, writing, and a production." Then I described how one Creative Dramatics exercise had grown into a play.

It was an improvisation done by twelve-year-old boys in an upper middle-class neighborhood in Atlanta, Georgia. Each child had developed a character through Creative Dramatics techniques. As a next step, we agreed to assemble those seven characters, whose ages ranged from six months to seventy-three years, in a rumpus room. We also agreed on a situation: the seven characters would be the male members of a family and they would be setting up a bachelor party for the twenty-three-year-old character. As the improvisation progressed, a conflict between the boy playing the fourteen-year-old and the boy playing his forty-year-old father grew progressively more intense and finally overshadowed everything else.

At that point, we agreed that it should be the central conflict for a "real play." The play was then written and rehearsed and finally performed with an extraordinary ending that emerged during the writing: the fourteen-year-old would go to live with his mother.

The mother had not existed in the earlier improvisations, but with time to think and write, the boys decided the fourteen-year-old rebelled because his parents had divorced. His confusion about the situation surfaced as rage at his father.

When the kids performed the play, the audience of parents and friends, many of whom were divorced, watched transfixed. And afterwards almost every adult told me they were "shocked" or "chastened" or the like. The kids had started with Creative Dramatics but had taken it much further.

Ms. Finney found that example interesting, but said she had questions, which she didn't have time to ask. She had to return to class. We agreed to meet after every session. I felt as if I had survived the first cut.

★ ★ ★

After my talk with Ms. Finney I began thinking about the word *magic*. Was it pretentious, as her tone implied? I was certain that children writing and performing their own plays was different from Creative Dramatics. I also firmly believed in the magic of a truly realized theatrical production. But how could I claim that the kids at P.S. 34 would make magic?

I forgot about that question as I headed home, making my way past a burned-out building in front of which stood young men with their hands in their pockets. They had been there at 8 A.M. when I passed by on my way to school.

Not breaking stride, I continued on 138th Street, the bustling main drag of P.S. 34's neighborhood. If I had taken a few more steps I could have entered the subway and headed downtown, but I looked up and saw an espresso machine through the window of La Taza de Azul, a Puerto Rican restaurant. The thought of *café con leche* (hot milk and espresso coffee) seemed much more attractive than the subway.

Over the steaming cup, I looked out the window at the shoppers and the tacky Christmas decorations on the store façades, and contemplated the drug supermarket half way between the school and 138th Street.

Unable to make sense of it, I decided to return my attention to "magic," and began reviewing the other places I had taught kids to write plays. It was a long list, including many places in New York City, various towns and cities in Georgia, and a few on the West Coast. But as I thought about the work in each of those places, my eyes kept returning to the street and suddenly I realized why teaching children to explore an impulse and then helping them to develop it into a fully written, fully produced play makes magic: it brings back the first function of the theater, evoking a community.

Today we associate theater with Broadway and its road companies or comfortably established regional theaters—professionals dispensing entertainment to us. Or we imitate what they do with our own amateur companies. Sometimes these plays relate to our lives and we identify with the characters—but always from a distance.

It was different in ancient Greece, in twelfth-century English cathedral towns, and in villages throughout the Third World. Plays emerged from the local community. The writer and his compatriots, who produced and acted in the play, spoke directly to family, friends, rivals, elders, and outcasts. And when all those people came to see the play, they experienced a new understanding of their world. The magic came from the community's embracing and reevaluating itself.

Which is exactly what happens with plays written by children, I thought, and *The Mansion* came to mind.

The Mansion, a mystery drama written by preteens, told a story of reclaiming a large abandoned house.

That action, it turned out, mirrored what had happened in Stilson, a farming community of 600 people in south Georgia: as the farm crisis grew and farm after farm failed, the community shrank significantly—until a major highway connected Stilson with Savannah, a city of 200,000. At that point, ex-farmers began commuting to factory jobs and city people moved to Stilson. The play's action illuminates the changes the people of Stilson faced as they redefined their farming community.

Looking out the window again, I found myself excited by the memory of that powerful play. Or was it anticipation of the plays that would come out of this neighborhood in the South Bronx? Probably both.

Setting the Tone

At the beginning of the next session, I announced that we would create a work space by pushing the desks and chairs against the walls. Some of the kids groaned, others waited, but a third group jumped up and began banging chairs and dragging desks as loudly as possible.

"Freeze," I shouted, and everybody did—except Felix.

Felix, a lithe, dark-skinned boy, had gotten up and was sauntering in the direction of the front door. "Is that freezing?" I asked, but Felix kept walking. "You in the green T-shirt. What's your name?"

"Me?" he answered innocently.

"Yes."

"Felix," he said, tossing a crumpled piece of paper into the wastebasket by the front door.

This was clearly going to be a test, so I told the other kids to unfreeze and sit.

"Now, Felix, let me explain something about the theater: when a director tells an actor to freeze, the actor freezes. And if he tells a lighting person to bring up the house lights, the lighting person brings up the house lights. . . . Does everybody know what I mean by 'house lights'?" I said, interrupting myself. Nobody knew, so I, ever anxious to teach, explained that "house lights" are lights that shine upon the audience, not the stage.

"And that's true of everybody else who's part of the theater," I continued. "Do you know why?"

Felix's answer was "I had to throw out some paper."

"Because we count on each other in the theater. For example, let's say Luz is acting"—Luz's smile at this suggestion was love itself—"and she's counting on you to pull the curtain after she says 'And I never want to see you again,' and at that moment you decide you want to throw out some paper or go to the bathroom or joke with your friend. What happens? She's stuck on the stage saying 'And I never want to see you again . . . I never want to see you again . . . I never want to see you again,' till you get back to pull the curtain."

"That's her tough luck," answered Felix. And the kids laughed.

"No, it's yours—because you'd be fired. And do you know why?"

"Because you got it in for me."

"Because you've let her down. You'd have also let down the kids working the lights, the rest of the crew, the director, the playwright, the other actors, and the audience."

Addressing the class as a whole, I said, "We don't let each other down in the theater. We need each other. We count on each other. And if we can't count on you, you go down to the principal's office. We don't waste our time with you."

At that point, Ms. Finney looked up from her desk, where she had been working on her roll book, and said, "Oh, we don't need the principal. We can take care of him right here," and the kids murmured.

"Actually, I wasn't talking about Felix specifically," I said quickly. "Because now that he understands, he won't be doing it again. I meant anybody," and scanned the room.

After that significant pause, I said, "Now we're going to move the desks row by row. When it's your turn, pick up your desk and chair, move them against the nearest wall as quietly as possible, find a spot in the center of the room and stand on it—without talking."

The kids executed these instructions remarkably well, and a twenty-by-fifteen-foot scuffed wooden work space emerged.

I moved to the center of that space and said, "Now, why do you think I had you move?"

"To waste time," yelled Jaime. "So you don't got to teach nuthin'." He stood near the back of the room. On the wall behind him I noticed the words HARD WORK PAYS OFF in multicolored construction paper.

"Yeah, you just keep us runnin' around," seconded Felix, who stood right in front of me.

"Well, Jaime—and Felix—you may have had teachers like that, but I'm not one and I have a strong hunch Ms. Finney isn't either." The kids giggled nervously. They clearly agreed with my assessment of Ms. Finney.

"So why?" I asked again.

"Man, you ask why a lot," said Felix.

"It's my favorite word," I said. "So . . . why?"

Finally Luz raised her hand. "To get more space to act," she said.

"Right, that's definitely part of it. And what else?"

When nobody responded, I said, "To shake you up. Now why would I want to shake you up?"

"I don't know!" Maria Margarita blurted. Her tone revealed her irritation with such foolishness.

"When you're in your regular seats, you can rely on habits. But when you're out here, you don't know what's next, so you feel more, think quicker, and really use your imagination. All of which makes your writing and acting better."

"It's hard to just stand here," said Deana, a pale, sad-looking girl in jeans and a yellow sweater with a gaudy, green flower design. She stood near Ms. Finney's desk at the back of the room and stole a glance at her teacher as soon as the words were out of her mouth.

"Good point. Ordinarily I would have had you sit on the floor Indian style, but so many of the girls are in dresses and. . . ."

"I wouldn't sit on that floor if you paid me," said Tyrone, a short black boy. He was wearing neatly pressed brown slacks.

"Not today, but let's do it next week. Wednesday, a week from today, everybody wear jeans or clothes they can sit on the floor in."

"What does all this have to do with writing a play?" asked Monique, who stood next to Maria Margarita just as she sat next to her in their seats. They, I surmised, worked well in their seats.

I answered Monique by asking her if she remembered what I said last week. Monique dutifully said we would learn to use our imaginations, and we would learn cooperation and discipline.

After complimenting Monique on her memory, I asked, "Does anybody remember anything else?" Nobody did—until Felix said, "Yeah, you said something about magic."

"'Magic,'" mimicked Hector, who stood behind me. I was between him and Felix. Felix said, "What you lookin' at?"

"Nuthin' much," said Hector.

"Hector, what do I mean by 'magic'?" I asked quickly. Hector didn't answer.

"Do you know, Felix?" I asked, switching gears when I saw Felix smirk. He didn't answer either.

"Does anybody remember? What makes the 'magic'?" Nobody responded.

"Okay," I said, "the magic comes from honesty about yourself. What you really feel in your heart, what your body tells you, and what you sense with your eyes, ears, nose, mouth, and skin. And sharing all that with an audience. So the question is 'How do we do that? What's the first step?' And the answer, Monique, is that we have to switch the setting—to shake ourselves up. So we'll be alert and open, and so our imaginations will work as well as they can. We will do that every time we work."

"And that's it?" asked Maria Margarita. "Just standing up in the middle of the room will do that?"

"No, once we change the setting, we begin working with our bodies, senses, and feelings. We begin the transforming I told you about last week."

"How do you work with feelings?" asked Kim. She wore the same jeans and pullover as the week before.

"Actually, we're not going to get to feelings today, but that's because feelings are often built upon the body and senses; they help us get to feelings. So we do body and senses first. And of the two, it's best to start with the body. Does anybody know why? No? Then let's think about football. What do you do before you play?"

"Warm up," said Clarence, a tall, rangy black boy, who apparently considered himself the class authority on sports.

"Right. So you get loose. And what happens when you get loose?"

"You move better," said Clarence. He stood still, evenly balanced on his feet, arms dangling. I felt he could have moved effortlessly in any direction.

"And what else? You move better. You're looser, you're focused on what you're doing, you're not worried about anything else. You're what?" I looked at a girl with bright eyes. She wore tan pants and a pretty, beaded blue sweater. Her name was Venus. "What do you think, Venus?" I asked, feeling she had followed the lesson as intently as she had the first day's.

"Relaxed," she said firmly, and then gave me a shy smile.

I smiled back and was about to say "Yes, and when you're relaxed, you can express who you really are," but the bell began ringing and the kids lined up in front of the green chalkboard in the front of the room for a fire drill. I made a mental note to emphasize that link between relaxation and self-discovery, as I followed the kids down the stairs to the street.

★　　　★　　　★

"I couldn't help agreeing with Felix on one point," said Ms. Finney when we were sitting in the teachers' lounge later that day.

"Actually, I thought I headed him off quite well."

"Oh, you did. Your instinct was absolutely correct there. In fact, it bolsters my point. I was referring to the 'why' business. You do ask that quite a lot."

"It may seem like a contradiction, but when they're loosening up. . . ."

"Yes, I understand all that. But there was a lot of standing around."

"I felt they should understand what they are doing," I said defensively. "I want them to be responsible and you can't do that if you're just following orders."

"We're dealing with a forty-five-minute session," said Ms. Finney, ignoring my whine.

"Less," I thought, remembering the fire drill, but I decided to tell Ms. Finney why moving the desks and finding spots in the center was a pallid compromise.

"If I had my druthers, I would do what I did in a private school in Atlanta. I would have the kids take off their shoes and lie flat on their backs. I'd also turn off the lights. It would be so much easier for their unconscious impulses to emerge."

Ms. Finney nodded politely and said, "And another practical consideration—Deana, who said she was tired. She is. She lives with her grandmother. They are extremely poor. But more important, when her father died of AIDS, her mother threw herself out the window." Ms. Finney paused and said, "She died too. Deana is exhausted."

The enormity of what Ms. Finney said brought me out of my defensiveness. Teaching in the South Bronx was different from the more affluent neighborhood surrounding Emory University in Atlanta. Worrying about unconscious impulses "emerging" seemed terribly precious. What these kids needed were basic skills to deal with grim realities. I needed to work more directly and let go of the frills. That was what Ms. Finney had been gently telling me.

*   *   *

After Ms. Finney left, I went back to pondering my technique. Was "setting a tone" an indulgence for the upper middle class? Kids with time and space to slow down and "get in touch" with themselves could benefit enormously from this "professional" approach. But what did it do for kids in the South Bronx? Wasn't their time better spent on fundamentals, as Ms. Finney had hinted? Wasn't I just wasting valuable class time moving furniture? Especially if there wasn't space and a nice soft rug like the one in Atlanta?

On my way home past the burned-out building and its denizens, those questions seemed even more pertinent. I decided to stop for a *café con leche* and re-examine the notion of "setting a tone." Taking the same booth by the window, I thought about how I had set the tone in other inner-city schools. What about the Harlem school where I had taught the previous year?

In that school, we had changed the tone without a rug or proper space, and without moving our chairs to the side of the room (the teacher had preferred that we did not). The kids had stood behind their chairs. But even that small change had distanced the children from the security of their seats. And they had gone on to write wonderful plays like *The Twins in the Lobby*. Their teacher, who clearly distrusted me as yet another "specialist," agreed the plays worked and even said that after the playwriting section the kids seemed to like writing—some for the first time.

Taken by itself, this example proved little, but it reminded me why I had developed the technique. I had designed it to appeal to non-readers and non-writers as well as to the speedy, the plodding, and the average. "Shaking the kids up" puts everybody on an equal plane. Non-readers and plodding readers can perform as well as anybody else. Equally important, the non-readers feel motivated to learn: after they are shaken up, they go on to create scenes through improvisation and other theater games. That, in turn, leads to an interest in grammar and spelling, because they realize those skills will help them build their improvisations into plays.

So an interest in writing skills often depends upon the success of the improvisations. And good improvisations often happen after a break from traditional classroom thinking. That's why I try to shake the kids up, why I set a special tone.

Herbert Kohl

Making Theater

Developing Plays with Young People

Theater does not take place in real time and consists of creating convincing illusions of possible realities. The world of illusion is a very familiar and comfortable one for young people. Imagination—the free play of the mind with possible worlds, beings, and events—is easily engaged wherever children come together. For many children one of the saddest aspects of getting older is the closing down of the imagination as the price of fitting into adult-controlled worlds such as school and the so-called workplace. Too often, growing up means closing down.

This need not be the case. The imagination can and should be nurtured throughout life and the sense of play natural to childhood can be a continuing source of pleasure. We do not have to "grow up."

Theater is one source sustaining the life of the imagination. For many young people I have worked with, as well as for me, participating in the creation of theater is a source of joy and an escape from the dull routines that school too often represents. Improvisation, acting in classical or modern scenes and plays, and performing plays of one's own all engage the imagination.

Over the last twenty years, I have been playing around with theater in my classes. I have had no training, I am not a good actor, and I can't memorize lines. Yet I love the stage, and decided when I was teaching in Berkeley in 1968 to try to teach drama. Seeing and reading plays and discovering Viola Spolin's *Improvisations for the Theater* were my only qualifications to teach drama. I taught in order to learn how to teach, and my students were wonderful about my fumbling attempts to teach what I was afraid I couldn't do.

One of the students in my first improvisation class, Phil Krauter (who was sixteen at the time), understood how tentative and insecure I was about teaching theater. When acting, he had an intensity and focus that sometimes scared me. There were times when I wasn't sure he was in control of himself, yet he always knew what he was doing with his face, voice, and body. Once we did an improvisation on going mad. Phil went mad, or at least I thought he had. He frothed and foamed and rolled on the floor, and then, like a paranoiac, started threatening people. I insisted that all the other students leave the room, resolved to give up teaching improvisation, and set out to bring Phil back to reality. He was taller and stronger than I. I was afraid of him, but somehow my fear has always been tempered by my stubborn refusal to allow myself to be intimidated. I grabbed him and tried to shake him back to sanity. Phil just looked at me and laughed. He was in control all along. He had been acting, and told me that if I wanted to do serious theater I had to deal with serious actors.

Phil is involved in the theater professionally now, but most of the young actors, playwrights, set designers, and technicians I have worked with are not. Yet I hope that their experience with being a part of theater has given them a love for the stage, a continuing sense of playfulness, and an intelligence about performance that will provide lasting pleasure for them and create an audience for Phil's work and for the work of people who are seriously engaged in entertainment and education through performance.

The goals of doing theater with young people are:
• to provide group experiences that break out of the competitiveness (and its tendency to isolate people) that dominates school life
   • to learn to be part of an intelligent audience
   • to learn how to speak well and control gesture and movement
   • to introduce young people to classic and modern drama
   • to learn how to create environments for performance
   • to have fun being part of the illusory world of theater.

The fun of doing theater with young people is that, playing off the traditions of classic and contemporary theater, myth, fairy tale, and other literature, one can spin out new worlds and share them with others. First approaches to plays are magical. You start with young people who will not be who they are, with some characters, an empty stage, perhaps some props or costumes, and a story outline or theme, and then bring them together to the point where you are ready to share this created world with an audience. When you start out, you can't tell what the final play will be like and that uncertainty, coupled with the experience of living through the development of a performance, is an invaluable educational experience. Performance is not like filling out a workbook sheet or doing what an adult tells you. It emerges from within and from learning to become part of an ensemble. Consequently it provides a great opportunity for personal growth and for the development of group solidarity. And since the stage is illusion, it provides the rare opportunity for a shy child to take center stage, a timid one to be brash, and a bully gentle. A number of students I've worked with have had severe stuttering problems, but on stage they speak and sing beautifully. In some cases, they were even able to transfer the confidence they developed through theater to their everyday speech. You never know what power and energy may emerge from young people as soon as they step into character.

The Four Alices and Their Sister Susie in Wonderland

Last year I did a production of *Alice in Wonderland* with five- to ten-year-old students at the Acorn School in Point Arena, California, where I was teaching. Actually it was a production of *The Four Alices and Their Sister Susie in Wonderland,* a country-western and blues version of *Alice* that owed its spirit and some of its story to Lewis Carroll.

Initially what I had in mind was a simple puppet show version of *Alice in Wonderland,* which had been read to the children during lunchtime over the course of several weeks. I made a very crude posterboard puppet of the Mock Turtle, modelled on Thai stick puppets. There was a movable hand and head and I played with it in class. The idea was to provide an accessible, easily constructed model of a character you could talk through. I thought the whole *Alice* puppet construction and show would take no more than an hour a day for a few weeks.

During free time and art class the kids made puppets—Alice after Alice after Alice, with one March Hare, a few White Rabbits, and an occasional Mock Turtle, Carpenter, Mad Hatter, Duchess, or Queen. As one of the girls explained to me, "After all, there are so many Alices in the story that you can't make just one." She gave me three puppets: a tiny, tiny Alice; an Alice stretched large and out of proportion; and a regular-sized everyday Alice.

I didn't know what to do with all the puppets, and initially thought that we might end up with three or four troupes performing their own versions of *Alice* for each other and possibly for their parents.

We did improvisations with the puppets. The idea was to become familiar with the puppet characters in different situations before reading Lewis Carroll's story again and adapting scenes from it. It was a lot of fun to have many Alices talking to each other and to all of the other characters in ways that freed them from the structure of *Alice* and yet kept them within the spirit of Carroll's work.

During one of the improvisational sessions, a girl in the class said that the puppets were boring. She wanted to *be* Alice, not just play with an Alice puppet. Everyone in the class agreed and I realized that the play would have to move in this new direction.

I abandon my plans if students come up with more interesting and challenging ideas. There was no harm in trying to do a live *Alice in Wonderland* with the group. So, naïvely, I asked the children who would like to be Alice. There were five volunteers, one of whom dropped out and opted to be Alice's older sister. So it was up to me and Deborah, my co-teacher, as well as Susan, our aide and the music teacher, to decide who would be Alice. I begged off doing it on the spot and decided to think through the criteria for selection that night.

The more I thought about who should be Alice, the less I could choose and the less I wanted to. I had adapted classical plays for student performance before. In *A Midsummer Night's Dream,* I had twelve Pucks, and since most six- and seven-year-olds want to be Puck, dividing up the role gave each of them an opportunity to speak a few lines of Shakespeare. Besides, Puck is everywhere, and in the spirit of Puck there was no reason why he couldn't have twelve faces. In *Macbeth* we had six or seven witches. After all, what was one witch more or less to the spirit world? So why not four Alices? Any book that has magic mushrooms, talking rabbits, and an entire monarchy consisting of a deck of playing cards is perfect for fantasy and elaboration.

The next day in class I made the suggestion that we have four Alices. The kids were disappointed. They wanted to experience the competition between the four girls who wanted the role. However, I believe that education works best in the context of cooperation and joy, and I had no intention of yielding to their will. Children often pick up bad habits from the culture they are born into; besides, I have never felt obliged to perpetuate things that tear some children down and limit their aspirations.

So it was going to be four Alices and their older sister, but how could we do it in a way that would be convincing and exciting for the children? I discussed that problem with the whole group. We agreed that Alice, like any other person, has many aspects to her character, so there was no reason why four of the parts of Alice couldn't be on the stage at the same time. In other words, the children didn't want to take turns being Alice. They all wanted to be fully Alice, and Susie wanted to have a part that was just as prominent as the Alices'. I remember turning to the Alices and saying, "But which one of you is the real Alice?" They all raised their hands and shouted, "Me!"

At this point Susan Spurlock, the class aide and music teacher, started strumming on her guitar and someone in the room sang "Will the real Alice please stand up" and the girls responded, in song, "That's me." I suggested that Susan and the Alices compose a song called "Will the Real Alice Please Stand Up." Here's what they came up with:

Will the Real Alice Please Stand Up

(Note: During this song the whole cast, with the exception of the Alices, sings everything but the words in quotation marks in the chorus parts—these are sung by the Alices.)

I'm so pretty
It's a pity
My neck's so long
From dusk to dawn

Chorus:
Will the real, real Alice
Please stand up.
"That's me." That's who?
"That's me." Uh huh.

Blond hair
Blue eyes
Can you tell me why
I grow so high

(Chorus)

My friend is mad
And he's so glad
The tea's not hot
And the mouse is in the pot

(Chorus)

What's the matter
With the Mad Hatter
Haven't you heard
He's crazy as a bird

(Chorus)

Why me
Can't you see
I'm so glad I'm Alice
In my palace

(Chorus)

When, a few days later, the children and Susan performed the song, I realized we had moved from a simple puppet show to musical theater. I had to struggle with how far to take the play, how much time to spend on it, and where to fit it into what was already a very full educational program at the school. These problems are common when you are about to get carried away with doing theater and have other educational demands at the same time.

After talking with my colleagues, the first thing I decided was that the play could not completely take over the work at the school, even though I was tempted to drop everything else and do *Alice* exclusively. So to do the whole thing, I compromised and spent a half-hour to an hour a day for about three weeks, and then an hour or two a day for a week, and finally two full days before the performance. Fortunately Susan and Deborah were willing to be part of the creative process. And we had parents who, as the production developed, contributed generously to costumes, make-up, sets, and props.

Most teachers are not lucky enough to collaborate with other teachers. However, there are many ways in which similar situations can be created. Two classes, working together with parent volunteers and high school and junior high school students, can provide the backup needed to mount a major production, and one teacher and his students, with a few parent volunteers, can also do very fine children's theater. And plays performed in the classroom or for another class can be just as much fun as big productions. Theater can happen anywhere and on any scale and still be wonderful.

For me the central aspect of doing children's theater is to enjoy the fact that it is children's theater and not professional theater. It has to be fun, and need not lead to performance, though if it does, it should play for a friendly audience of children, parents, and other friends, as well as take advantage of the freedom of not having to aim for a move to Broadway. It exists for the sake of the children.

The Four Alices developed gradually and by sections. The White Rabbits worked up a comedy routine during recess; the Mad Hatter's tea party gained and then lost "guests." The Mad Hatter's version of "Twinkle, Twinkle, Little Star" was rewritten by Susan and the students and turned into a jazzy tune that the four Alices danced to in chorus-line style:

Twinkle twinkle little bat
How I wonder where you're at
Up above the world so high
Like a tea tray in the sky

Chorus:
Twinkle twinkle little bat
How I wonder where you're at

Twinkle twinkle little rabbit
Why is being late your habit
You're always rushing here and there
But never getting anywhere

(Chorus)

Twinkle twinkle big fat queen
I wonder why you are so mean
You always scream, "Off with her head"
But if you do it, she'll be dead

(Chorus)

Twinkle twinkle Mister Hatter and Hare
Teacups spilling everywhere
Every time you drink you switch your cup
And then the dormouse fills it up

(Chorus)

Twinkle twinkle little Alice
We never see you in a palace
Wonderland, it is so strange
When you're there you always change

(Chorus)

Of course, there was simply too much in the book for us to use on stage. Time constraints and the size of the class dictated that some things be eliminated and some be overemphasized. The overall outline was simple, too simple for some people, who wanted a finished script to work with from the start. Here is my working outline:

1. A narrator introduces the play and keeps it moving.
2. The Alices and their sister Susie are on stage.
3. White rabbits appear and do something.
4. The Alices and Susie follow the rabbits into Wonderland.
5. Bizarre things happen in Wonderland involving characters from the book and others the students might invent (one invented character at the Mad Hatter's tea party was called Dungeons and Dragons, a warrior who didn't know how to stop fighting and sat at the table stabbing and stabbing away at a tea biscuit, while shouting "Stagger, jabber, dagger, stagger, jagger. . . .").

6. The Alices and the whole cast end up at the Court and the Court scene ends with the Alices shouting, "You're nothing but a deck of cards."

7. The Alices return to the bank of the river and the un-Wonderland (the play almost ended this way but Susie didn't want to stay in the "real" world and so she provided the ending by saying, "It's boring here. I'm going back," and plunging down the rabbit hole a second time).

The body of the play developed in sections, with the students picking their favorite parts. In this way everyone had great latitude of choice. In addition, all the sections of the play could be rehearsed independently (though the Alices and Susie had to rush around from group to group). That way parents and high school students could help fine-tune different sections of the work. I talked to our parent group and asked for help and patience.

For some of the adults and children, this piecemeal and improvisational approach to adaptation was frustrating. They wanted to know how the final product would look, but I didn't have the slightest idea. Part of helping people improvise plays is to encourage them to accept uncertainty and to realize that the whole endeavor is imaginative and fun. Improvisational adaptation is a form of theme and variation on a classical play or story, or the development of an idea; it doesn't need to be predictable. Most of the children had little problem with that openness, but I had to work hard to convince the adults that a performance would emerge from our improvisations on *Alice in Wonderland*. However, I did provide structural diagrams of how the play looked as we progressed. Here is the final structure:

1. Overture and introduction by narrator.
2. Reality with the Alices and Susie.
3. The rabbits come on and do comic routine.
4. The Alices follow the rabbits.
5. Susie sings her song and then runs off after them to Wonderland.
6. They encounter the Caterpillar on a mushroom.
7. Then they encounter the Cheshire Cat and do Jabberwocky.
8. Then comes the Mad Hatter's tea party.
9. Then comes the Court at which the Mock Turtle leads "Won't you join the dance."
10. Then comes the confrontation between Alice and the Queen; Alice says, "You're nothing but a deck of cards"; and everyone throws cards into the air.

11. The Alices and Susie go back to reality.
12. Susie returns to Wonderland.

We created a script as we went along, improvising each scene over and over, exploring character, voice, and movement. At this point, I wanted the children to act rather than to memorize lines and recite them. Improvisation also provided alternatives if students forgot the lines that they eventually were given. As it turned out, many lines were forgotten during the performances, but there was no panic and some of the best dialogue in the play emerged spontaneously when the actors were on the spot before an audience.

A week before the play, there were some children who still were not involved. By that time, the high school combo was rehearsing the songs with the kids and there was a need for sets and a tech crew. Some of the shyer children were willing to do the tech work, and others had watched the rehearsals enough to decide how they would like to jump into the production. I've learned to add characters at the last minute and console children who find they can't deal with the pressures of performance, while redefining their roles to keep them in the process. There's always room on the tech and lighting crew, posters and programs must be made, and ushers might be needed. My goal was to involve everyone. If one of the children had not been engaged, the performance would have been empty for me.

We had one dress rehearsal, and spent two full school days dealing with the logistics of costumes, makeup, sets, props, etc. We did two performances, one for the school and one for the community. Then we had a cast party. The essential educational and emotional success of *The Four Alices* was not the quality of the performance—which I think was pretty good—but the fact that everyone played a part and knew that they made a contribution to the whole.

On Cast Parties and Performances

When you do drama with young people, the first thing to plan is the cast party. The party has to be fun for the actors and technical crew as well as for parents and friends. Before beginning work on a play, I like to imagine the party, and think back from there to the steps necessary to get to that celebration. Thinking backwards in time allows me to anticipate what might go wrong and plan ways to avoid obvious mistakes.

First I imagine ways the cast party can fail. For example, someone might be sulking in the corner because he didn't get the part he or she wanted; or some might be tense and angry because they wanted to participate but were afraid. Some parents might feel their children had been treated unfairly. Some students might feel that others had looked down on them for the minor roles they played, lines they forgot, or entrances they missed. The joy of being part of the theater can easily be lost in an atmosphere of jealousy and competition, and that's what I try to prevent. When doing theater with young people, you should pay as much attention to the pleasure of the participants as to the success of the performance. Successful cast parties become the criterion for the success of the whole theater program.

Moving backwards in time from the cast party to the performance, rehearsals, development of the script, and improvisations, try to imagine all of the mistakes that could prevent students from being part of an enjoyable experience that has contributed to their growth.

Some of the problems I've imagined emerging at the cast party are:

• A child who has refused to participate in the production stands in the corner sulking, or sneaks around the room spilling soda and insulting the actors. My fear of this makes me remember, even at the last possible moment, to push recalcitrant children into the production no matter how much they resist. Have them hold the script while you prompt, or have them knock on the stage three times to signal the beginning of the action, or have them put posters up in the community, take tickets, seat the audience, or be in charge of the costumes and props. It doesn't make any difference how small the role is. What is essential is that every child have a sense of belonging, of being useful. Teachers have to learn how to create useful work for reluctant and scared children and to encourage them to take larger roles the next time around. Over the years, I've found that having a few unfilled jobs just before the performance provides the opportunity for even the most reluctant of students to help out and feel that the production could not happen without them.

• Jealousy is something to avoid at the cast party at all costs, even if it means four Alices, two Hamlets, twelve witches, or forty-eight dwarfs. Jealousy can spread throughout a cast party and throughout the class over the rest of the year, becoming a major impediment to learning. So I try to devise strategies to avoid the star syndrome and all of the disappointments that can emerge if students don't get the parts they want. Again, one of the guiding principles of young people's theater is that it is not a route to TV or Broadway. One way to get around the problem of jealousy is to provide every student who wants a part with one he or she feels is appropriate, and not to care how much revision or adaptation this may involve. Some people have told me my attitude is foolish, that I should pay more attention to teaching students how competitive and harsh the world is. My response is that I don't have to teach that—the kids already know it. I prefer to provide them with the love, success, and communal feelings that are all too lacking in that hard world everybody wants to prepare them for.

• Moving from the cast party back to the dress rehearsal, I try to figure out what specifically might go wrong: lines might be forgotten; props can disappear at the last minute; the set could be only half finished by curtain time. Students have to be told this, and how to fake it when something goes wrong. I like to show the performers how to recover from disaster. Some recovery methods are:

To keep on talking no matter what you're saying; to use a prop, examine something on the set, and in general mutter about waiting for something important to happen; to step out and talk to the audience out of character; to begin a conversation with another actor on stage; to tell the audience to be patient, and show your composure— all of these depend upon having one person in each wing who is prompting and can be turned to for help, and another person whose specific job is to follow the script and hunt down missing actors. It's better to anticipate disaster than encounter it unprepared.

If someone misses an entrance, it's always possible to produce an instant monologue or dialogue while the director runs around looking for the absent or absconded actor. With five-, six-, and seven-year-olds this is a particular problem, as urinary and bowel control tends to decrease as performance time approaches. When you and the actors on stage anticipate this, the scared and incontinent ones can recover, perform, and have a good time at the cast party.

• The details of a dramatic performance are as important to young people as they are to members of the Royal Court Theatre or the New York Shakespeare Festival. Children who don't like their costumes or makeup, or who feel that their props are cheap and unconvincing, spend time apologizing for them and can be bores at cast parties. Therefore, it is of particular importance to ask actors to participate in the designing of make-up, costumes, and props.

• Performing is difficult for children who don't understand the play, and that means not just their roles, but the whole of the drama. To be able to feel good about what they have been a part of, they have to know what it is all about. Improvisation, discussion, and diagrams help give everyone a sense of the whole. All of the actors should know what is happening on stage when they are in the wings. This is especially true if you have adapted a play to the needs and personalities of your actors. One technique I've used during rehearsals is to have members of the cast who are not on stage sit in the audience and watch the action. I also encourage them to help me with blocking (deciding on the positions and movements of actors) and to make any suggestions for improving the performance. In addition, I act as a stand-in for the lead characters several times and have the actors watch from the audience so they can get a feel for what they might look like on stage. Then I suggest that the actors take turns directing scenes or parts of scenes. I encourage the fullest possible participation of the students in the whole process.

• Thinking of the cast party, you have to imagine the proud parents. Therefore you should think carefully about how to prepare an audience for student performance. A young person, who feels she or he has done very well and worked very hard, can be devastated by an offhand comment at a cast party. If your mother or father doesn't praise you, or if someone else's parents put you down, it can ruin the whole evening. For that reason, it is important to make it clear to parents that performance is part of the process of the development of imagination and, if necessary, make them realize that thinking that the school auditorium is just a step away from Broadway is not good for their children. Of course, the more you involve parents in small aspects of the performance and have them see and participate in improvisation, rehearsals, costumes, and sets, the more they will feel that they are part of what their children are doing. It is also good to involve them by having them prepare a potluck dinner for the cast party; after performing, children are hungry.

• A cast party can become a bore if only a few children get the credit for the performance. It takes a lot of effort to negate, at least in its most invidious forms, the gloating that children often indulge in when they think they're stars. Improvisations help because everyone gets to play all the roles in informal exercises. If there are multiple performances of a play, I like to have different children play all the major roles in each performance. If the actors put down the tech crew, I'll turn off the lights and suggest that the play be rehearsed in the dark. If they make fun of the prop master or the kids in charge of sound effects, they might find themselves fighting with invisible swords or waiting on stage, in the middle of a scene, for the sound of a phone call that never comes.

The goal is to create a sense of community through theater, one that just might spill over to the rest of the time the class spends together and even to life beyond the school.

• No matter how hard you try, there will be some kids who hate the cast party and won't be part of the play. It is important to learn that there are times when it will be impossible to get everyone involved. Expect trouble, and don't let it destroy the whole process. Keep on trying to get the most reluctant ones involved in the next performance or in the cast party itself. They can plan it, serve food, call parents, set tables. If none of this works, offer them a piece of cake and suggest that there is a good part for them in the next play. Or back off and see if poetry, mathematics, science, computers, music, or dance might be their modes of expression. And plan the next group activity so that you might have a better chance of getting them involved.

★　　　★　　　★

Recently I've been playing chess with five- to eight-year-olds. We have a chess club that meets once a week and I set up games so students can learn some of the sophistication of the game. A few weeks ago one of my students, Galen, who's six, beat me and, as proud as he was, tried to console me for losing. I laughed and told him that the goal of teaching is to have your students be decent people who are better and smarter than you are. It was a pleasure to see him acquire chess skills and use his mind in such sophisticated ways. That feeling was the same feeling I have when I see my students on stage, playing with ideas and taking control of their voices and bodies in ways I could never do. There is perhaps no greater pleasure one can get as a teacher that that of stepping back and grinning like a proud parent at the cast party of a play that has worked for everybody.

Margot Fortunato Galt

The Story in History
Writing Your Way into the American Experience

Margot Fortunato Galt's piece is an excerpt from her book The Story in History, *which integrates imaginative writing and the study of American history.*—Editor

Circle Poems of Praise in the Native American Spirit
(For elementary school level to adult)

This exercise introduces students to the differing attitudes and customs of Native Americans and Europeans, in what I call "A Circle Poem of Praise in the Native American Spirit."

Step One: Reading Model Poems

First I read a poem by Darrel Daniel St. Clair, of the Tlingit tribe. Born in Alaska, St. Clair was a teenager when he wrote this poem, which suggests another kind of school, one without walls:

My school the earth.
My teachers,
The sky, the clouds, the sun, the moon,
The trees, the bushes, the grass,
The birds, the bears, the wolves,
The rivers, whom I claim to be
My mad genius.
Once I missed a day
Because they tried to make
Me learn it from the books
In a little room
That was really too stuffy.
I hope my teachers don't
Put me on the absent list.
I enjoy going to that school
Where the air is fresh.

Where nothing is said and I learn
From the sounds.
From the things I touch,
From all that I see.
Joy to the world and
I've fallen in love with my teachers.

Step Two: Using Stickers and Circles

After the students and I discuss how St. Clair's school is different from theirs, I hand out a wildlife sticker to each student. (I collect these stickers showing trees, birds, or other animals from organizations such as the Sierra Club, the National Wildlife Federation, and Greenpeace.) I then hand out big sheets of newsprint and have the students fold them in half and draw a moderate-sized circle on one half, leaving enough room to write on either half. "Stick the sticker somewhere on the circle," I tell them.

It's possible to do this exercise without the stickers, but I find that the activity of licking and sticking appeals to young students, and gives them an illustrated example of some growing, living thing—a spruce tree, arctic fox, leopard, chipmunk, or chickadee. This gets them started thinking about what they know of the outdoors.

Step Three: Two World Views

Next I outline two ways of looking at the world: the Native American way and the way of people of European ancestry. To schematize these differences, I draw a pyramid and a circle on the chalkboard.

I tell them that the Native American way sees the world as a circle: humans occupy a place in the circle, but so does everything else in the natural world—rivers and hail and beavers and cardinals and jackrabbits and canyons and meadows and roses and thistles and creeks and oceans and whales and on and on. As I say these names I write them around the circle, as in:

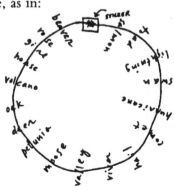

Then I tell students that although humans may kill animals and plants for food, humans belong to the circle, too, and must also learn from everything else in it. In other words, we are neither better than, nor separate from, the other life forms in the circle.

The European way tends to see the world as a pyramid, with a supreme divinity at the top. Further down the pyramid are angels and then humans, after which come other living things, ranked according to their smartness or complexity or similarity to us. Students quickly grasp this concept, and can soon say that apes and monkeys should come under humans, then dogs and cats and hoofed animals, then other mammals, then birds and fish, then insects, then trees, then plants, then maybe water, maybe fire, maybe air, maybe dirt. The reasoning goes this way: as we descend lower on the pyramid, the things we add have "less life" and "less importance"—it is all right for humans to use them because these things can't feel anything and don't have a spiritual life.

Step Four: Writing Nature into the Circle

In the next step, the class adds any forms of natural life they want to their circles. I help by listing categories on the board: Animals, Plants, Fish, Birds, Weather, Sky (and What's in It), Water, Landscape, Dirt, Fire, Air. I urge students to be as specific as possible in their lists, to put *salmon* rather than *fish*; to put *eagle* rather than *bird*.

Step Five: Looking at Another Model

Next I read N. Scott Momaday's "The Delight Song of Tsoai-Talee." Momaday, one of the best-known contemporary Native American writers, comes from the Kiowa tribe that originated in Montana but migrated to Oklahoma.

> I am a feather on the bright sky
> I am the blue horse that runs in the plain
> I am the fish that rolls, shining, in the water
> I am the shadow that follows a child
> I am the evening light, the luster of meadows
> I am an eagle playing with the wind
> I am a cluster of bright beads
> I am the farthest star
> I am the cold of the dawn
> I am the roaring of the rain
> I am the glitter on the crust of the snow
> I am the long track of the moon in a lake

I am a flame of four colors
I am a deer standing away in the dusk
I am a field of sumac and the pomme blanche
I am an angle of geese in the winter sky
I am the hunger of a young wolf
I am the whole dream of these things

You see, I am alive, I am alive
I stand in good relation to the earth
I stand in good relation to the gods
I stand in good relation to all that is beautiful
I stand in good relation to the daughter of *Tsen-tainte*
You see, I am alive, I am alive.

The "Delight Song" beautifully expresses the connection of humans to all the wealth and variety of nature. I ask the class to notice how precisely each description brings to life what Momaday has noticed. We also talk about what it means to "stand in good relation." Students often suggest that relation means relatives and good relation means treating relatives kindly and respectfully. I tell them that this poem is a love song, of course, not just to the daughter of Tsen-tainte, but to the whole world.

Step Six: Writing Poems about Nature's Teaching

I tell the class that we are now going to write our own songs of good relation. In our poems, one part of the circle will teach something to another part. Students should begin by connecting with a straight line two names in their circles, such as beaver and moon. To get them started, I take beaver and moon and write the first line of my poem on the board: "The wet brown beaver leaps in the stream and shows the sad sliver of moon how to fill with rain."

Next we brainstorm some words related to *teach*, such as *preach, demonstrate, educate, show, display, learn, understand, prove*, etc.

Then on the other half of the paper, beside their circles, I have students start drafting their poems, making each stanza take off from a connection they've drawn between two parts of the circle. Here is such a poem, by Heidi Bakken, a fourth grader:

The goat teaches
    the mountain how to sing.
The moon told
    the people how to be quiet.
The old woman made

        the elm tree come alive
        and he liked that.
    The hail was in the sky, so
        he told the star to come too.
    The deer told
        the old man, I like you.
    The goat got shaped
        like a cloud because
        he looked at it.

To cap off this exercise, you can also have students create a collaborative poem using some of the best lines from each student's circle poem. Here is an example from a fifth grade class:

    The parrot can show the moon how to talk.
    The ladybug teaches lava to fly.
    The snake shows the hurricane how to eat a mouse.
    The Appalachians teach the moon how to make rocks.
    The stars demonstrate to the garter snake how to shine brightly.
    The rattlesnake teaches the ground to rumble.

Like the circle diagram itself, these poems circle around and around in an endless chain of influence.

★   ★   ★

Writing a Tall Tale
(For junior high level to adult)

From the very beginning of European settlement, travelers and settlers fell into the habit of exaggeration. Since the game, crops, rivers, forests, storms, and distances in Europe were dwarfed by those of America, exaggeration was a natural device for conveying the newcomers' astonishment. Loneliness and solitude no doubt contributed to the tale-telling. Settlers yearned for someone to tell about their adventures. When the occasional traveler—particularly one fresh from Europe—knocked at their door, they were more than ready to let out long pent-up tales. The wilderness settler could embroider as much as he liked. Who would correct him? He could make out his difficulties three times worse than they'd been, or even go as far as to create an entirely new persona for himself. His fancy could range free, and the long trips by stagecoach or on horseback gave him plenty of time to refine his exaggerations.

Think of Paul Bunyan, with his blue ox Babe, the hero of lumber camps. With his superhuman strength Paul could uproot huge trees with a twist of his wrist, reroute a raging torrent, or stop a tornado, and then sit down in the lumberjack dining hall and consume mountains of pancakes and cascades of syrup. Paul Bunyan was more than a match for the immense new land, and the tales about him heartened lesser mortals who quailed before the endless forests and flash floods.

Step One: Reading an Excerpt from a Tall Tale

True-life accounts of American fecundity suggest some possible origins of these hyperboles. Francis Higginson's 1630 account, *New England's Plantation*, had this to say about corn: "Thirty, forty, fifty, sixty [fold increases] are abundant here." The numbers of animals almost made Higginson stutter with amazement: he knew of fishermen who filled two boats at one time with nets so heavy they could scarcely draw them in. New England, Higginson told his English readers, is more healthful than anywhere else in the world.

Two centuries later (1845) an advertisement for Arkansas talked up the place with even more enthusiasm and exaggeration:

> Strangers, if you'd asked me how we got our meat in Arkansas . . . I never did shoot at but one, and I'd never forgive myself for that, had it weighed less than forty pounds. . . . You see, the thing was so fat that it couldn't fly far; and when he fell out of the tree, after I shot him, on striking the ground he bust open behind, and the way the pound gobs of tallow rolled out of the opening was perfectly beautiful.

Not all the reports of America boasted of its vast benefits; some bemoaned the immensity of American catastrophe. In the 1840s, traveling by stagecoach in West Virginia, J. S. Buckingham recounted hearing men talk about the unhealthy condition of the Illinois river: "One asserted he had known a man to be so dreadfully affected with ague from sleeping in the fall on its banks, that he shook . . . all the teeth out of his head." The next two storytellers topped that tale by describing a man so sick with ague he shook off all his clothes and the fourth had the poor man shake a house down around his ears.

It took men and women larger than life to control and combat the immensity of America. Davy Crockett (1786–1836) was a shrewd politician, hunter, fighter, drinker, and raconteur, and eventually was elected to Congress. An English captain traveling through Kentucky heard about Davy Crockett everywhere:

He took hailstones for "Life Pills" when he was unwell—he picked his teeth with a pitchfork . . . fanned himself with a hurricane. He could . . . drink the Mississippi dry—shoot six cord of bear in one day.

The anonymous tale, "Mike Fink Beats Davy Crockett at a Shooting Match," demonstrates how such exaggeration built on itself. At one point in the exchange of boasts, Crockett bends back Mike's ear with the following tirade:

Mike, I don't exactly like to tell you you lie about what you say about your rifle, but I'm d—d if you speak the truth, and I'll prove it. Do you see that 'are cat sitting on the top rail of your potato patch, about a hundred and fifty yards off? If she ever hears agin, I'll be shot if it shan't be without ears.' So I blazed away, and I'll bet you a horse, the ball cut off both the old tom cat's ears close to his head, and shaved the hair off clean across the skull, as slick as if I'd done it with a razor, and the critter never stirred, nor knew he'd lost his ears till he tried to scratch 'em.

Step Two: Creating an American Frontier Character

Some standard types on the frontier from which students can choose are: farmer, blacksmith, tanner, teacher, politician, boatman, trapper, hunter, peddler, housewife, merchant (both male and female), cook (women cooked in logging camps), lumberjack, and fisherman. Unlike their urban counterparts, women on the frontier often worked alongside the men.

Part of the fun of developing these types into distinctive characters comes in creating humorous names for them, such as combining a familiar first name with a compound last one (joining an item from the person's life with a common suffix): a boatman might be named Jim Sternfoot; a teacher might be named Nancy Rulerman; a farmer's daughter might be named Karen Shootfast.

Using word mapping, students place the name of the character in the center of a piece of paper. Then they brainstorm the tools the character would use at work, making sure that these are accurate to the frontier: hoe, harrow, plow, oxen and horse, churn, iron kettle, anvil. Next I have students add features of the landscape: a waterfall, meadow, canyon, high bluff, road, or path. Finally, I have them add weather (tornado, hailstorm, drought) and clothing (buckskin breeches, gingham apron, sunbonnet, clogs, sheepskin coat, coonskin cap).

Step Three: Creating Drama through Exaggeration

Many of the tall tales begin with small boasts and end with earth-wrenching occurrences. So rule number one for writing a tall tale is to start small and gradually build larger and larger. This gradual approach makes the tale more credible.

Next I have students imagine a situation that plays with the standard elements of the American tall tale: fecundity, extreme weather, loneliness, isolation, competition, and reversals of expectations. I ask students to recall the advertisement for Arkansas where the bird falls out of the tree and disgorges gobs of tallow, and to imagine pumpkins the size of wagon wheels, partridges so plump that . . . , corn so tall that . . . , rivers so unhealthy that . . . , hail so big that . . . , snow so deep that . . . , trees so tall that. . . .

A variation on this is a tall tale about school. Older students can write such tales, using the strategies suggested in this exercise, but transferring them to such topics as lunch, teachers, lockers and the amount of stuff in them, grades, books, the library or media center, water fountains, stairways clogged with students rushing from class to class, gym, teams, the principal, and so on. Then they can read the tales to younger students from the same school, who will probably make a very appreciative audience.

Back to pioneers. Another thing I remind students is that just as the pioneers competed with the wilderness, they also competed with each other. When the frontiersman who has bested the biggest bear in the mountains meets up with another hunter, he's going to want to boast and outdo him with the same stamina that brought down the bear.

Surprise is a staple of good stories; in tall tales it often means that what first seems a blessing turns out to be a curse in disguise: the ten pumpkins the size of wheels rot and spread their stench over the barnyard, the chickens flee, the pigs stampede, and the horses break through the barn walls in their eagerness to get away.

Step Four: Reading Some Models

Here are some tall tales by students. Listen for the distinctive voice of the narrator in each example. This is not the normal speaking manner of the author; instead, the narrator is a fictitious persona, a garrulous talker who won't let the listener get in a word edgewise. In a sense, the narrator is a fast-talking con artist, aiming not so much to capture the listener's belief as to keep the listener so interested and so quiet that the question of whether the incidents really happened will never come up.

Karen Shootfast, Farmer's Daughter

Karen Shootfast was a weird child, she did not grow like a regular farmer's daughter. "No way," she must have said at birth, because this child grew strong and beautiful, she had the looks of an angel princess and the shape of a picture that would never be drawn more perfectly. Well, let me tell you about this Karen Shootfast. Her daddy was sickly and her mother died at her birth. She was such a different child. They were so poor they did not even live in a barn. They lived in a cave near town. Karen Shootfast thought from the age of five months that she had better start talkin', walkin' and shootin', and believe it or not, she did. Ol' Karen Shootfast learned to talk an alligator into giving her his skin; she learned to walk better than Lady Isabel herself and shoot, this girl could shoot an ant a mile away. That's where she got her name, Karen Shootfast.

At the age of thirty-two, she came to town with her sickly father and there was a bank robbery. She grabbed her daddy's fifty-year-old pocket pistol and before the sheriff could move to shoot, she shot the socks off both of the robbers as they ran out of the bank, without touching a hair on their legs. Then she showed the town just how good a shot she was. She had a showdown with both robbers and these were the fastest gunmen in the west. She shot them both with one shot. Three women and the sheriff fainted and the preacher dropped dead with such a shock in their bones. Old Karen grew up to be the best and the prettiest gal in the west.

—*Markeela Thomas, tenth grade*

★   ★   ★

Fisherman

How do you do! I'm Mike Salmon, fisherman. I'm gonna tell you 'bout a day that I went fishing. Boy, that day I needed more than one man to catch the fish as I brought them in with my pole. I could actually walk on the water there were so many fish. I had to walk (on the water of course) to the shore to get another boat because the one I had was starting to sink from all the fish. I tried to pull up the anchor, but the fish were so thick that it was like trying to pull through ice. By the end of the day, I caught so many fish they filled five boats. I caught all of the fish in the sea with a bare hook. It is now called the Dead Sea.

—*David Bixler, tenth grade*

★   ★   ★

Henry Joes, the Trapperkeeper

Once there was a trapper named The Trapperkeeper, alias Henry Joes. His arms were the size of redwood trees. He could lift a log cabin at the blink of an eye. When he walked around, he made trenches wherever he walked. His skills at trapping were excellent. He didn't even use traps. With his monstrous voice, he screamed at the top of his lungs and scared all the animals in the forest to death. To shave his face he had to use a saw blade, and he took baths in the Pacific Ocean and showered at Niagara Falls, and then dried off in a tornado. His knife Charlie was so sharp that he could cut the earth in half. For dinner he ate nails and drank lava from a volcano. Him and Paul Bunyan had a fight and made huge crevices in the ground, which is now called the Grand Canyon.

—*Vinny Corbo, tenth grade*

★   ★   ★

Lena Lutefisk

One day Lena Lutefisk decided to go fishing with her husband Ole Lutefisk and some Germans. They left at 6 A.M. and were to arrive home at 5 P.M. When noon came they still hadn't caught anything and wanted Lena to make a dinner for them. Lena wanted to stay fishing, unlike the others who were playing cards. Lena decided to go fishing and serve dinner at the same time. She put the pole between her long toes and mixed up some soapy water. She then waited for a fish to bite. She felt a tug and pulled up the fish with her feet. Then while she cleaned off the scales with a knife, she baited the hook with her feet. She cast the bait into the water with her long toes and threw the fish in the soapy water, which produced lutefisk! She repeated the process over and over again and soon the others noticed what she was doing and thought it would be a good idea, only they were still playing cards. Each of them tried it, but Ole was the only one to succeed, for the Germans' toes were too short and the pole kept slipping. Soon the news was all over Delaware about the Norwegian's great feet.

—*Joya Bromeland, eighth grade*

Step Five: Shaping the Tale

A good way to start the story is to set the scene and introduce the main character. It's a good idea to emphasize one or two characteristics of the person, using lots of details.

Then the exaggeration can start. It's important to begin with something fairly commonplace—pumpkins, a bear, some logs, pancakes, horseshoes, etc.—then gradually increase the exaggeration until the whole world in the tale seems out of control.

★   ★   ★

Creating a Writing Assignment with an Historical Slant

Many of my writing ideas come from collaborating with classroom teachers. Usually I arrive for a one-week writing residency and find, after discussion, that the teacher and I agree where writing will fit into the curriculum. Maybe the teacher already uses an "American Studies" approach, teaching about a particular historical period not only from the political and military perspective but also a cultural one, playing records of seventeenth-century English folk songs and showing slides of Williamsburg houses, candle-making molds, cross-stitched samplers, and curtained beds.

Imaginative writing fits almost anyplace in the history or social studies curriculum. Some courses offer this opportunity more readily than others, of course. Learning about the houses of Congress and the doctrine of separation of powers is fairly abstract and hard to respond to personally, but following a tax bill all the way from its proposal to its application can show how families with different incomes are affected by such a bill. In such a case, creative writing can draw out an empathetic response.

But how to structure an exercise? What models to use? Let's start with the last question first. Over the years I've developed a sense for what kind of literature makes teachable models for elementary or high school students. I can't trace how this sense developed, but I can indicate some hallmarks of a good model.

First, it has to be structured clearly. Structural techniques include ones you probably learned in freshman English: comparison and contrast; sequence (in other words, an organized list of some kind); a gradual accretion of detail that reaches a climax; a story (or image) within a story (for instance, an essay might begin with a contemporary experience, recall an historic one, then return to conclude in the present). If by its structure a piece of writing can't help students order and focus their ideas, it won't work well in the classroom.

I've also learned that the historically apt model isn't necessarily the one most likely to elicit interesting writing from students. Writing a ballad about a Williamsburg tailor, in the mode of ballads popular in the 1700s, might give students practice using details of daily life from the period, but chances are it wouldn't spring them across the distance between their own lives and the past. A contemporary model, however, might lead students to see the relationship between "hip" styles of dressing and the tools and fabrics of the 1990s, and so begin to give them an understanding of the history of the dandy. Such an approach links an historical period and a contemporary writing model, and brings a sense of empathy to the students' writing, one fundamental reason for introducing creative writing into the study of history in the first place. When students empathize with people from the past, they dig a tunnel through the years and the accumulated ideas about the past, and let voices echo back and forth between past and present.

But a contemporary model has to be rooted in the same cultural background as an historical one. Having a Williamsburg tailor sketch out his life in Japanese haiku might be funny, but the value would end there. Haiku is too divergent from the Western tradition to capture the swagger and panache of the comic-heroic Western dandy, circa 1750 or 1990. A rap song, on the other hand, blends rhythms and oral exaggeration that have come into the U.S. from the complicated cultural mixture of the Caribbean: distinctive but not totally divorced from the mixture that formed the ballads sung in a Williamsburg tavern a few hundred years ago.

The point is to help student writers take a fresh look at the past. If you're dressed in knee pants, with your hair in a queue, and wearing a flared frock coat, you may be almost as well suited to riding a motorcycle as a horse, but fighting a battle in the French and Indian War from a motorcycle would be nearly impossible: no roads through the woods, no gas stations. When students bring contemporary models to bear on historical experience, they begin to appreciate significant differences in the way life was lived, felt, and valued.

Contrasting past and present is not the only hallmark of an evocative literary model or writing exercise. Sometimes introducing an unusual point of view into the past can also activate the imagination. Take the poem "Dog" by Lawrence Ferlinghetti. A modern work—free verse, urban details, 1950s politics—this teachable poem is easy to analyze, with its repeating refrain, jaunty rhythm, and humorous take on the urban scene from a dog's perspective. All these elements are easy to adopt, but the crucial one is the dog's attitude toward human affairs: he sees through human pretense, and measures it against his own reality.

When I first brought "Dog" into a classroom, I hadn't begun to plumb the psychological possibilities in the dog as an historical witness. I simply used the poem to help students of all ages become keener observers of their surroundings. The poems that students wrote were all contemporary. Then a social studies teacher asked me to create an exercise on racial prejudice. I wanted to show his ninth grade class that racial prejudice existed even in Minnesota, with its small percentage of people of color and its history of racial tolerance. A trip to the state historical society's audio-visual room netted a surprise: engravings and photographs of lynchings that had taken place in the state between the 1880s and 1920s. Since I had already used photographs to inspire other writing, I sensed that I could devise an exercise around the photos. I made photocopies and wrote down what little information existed about them.

I still needed a point of entry, some slant to help the class address the admittedly horrible scenes. For some reason I can't explain, I thought of "Dog." Using it, I could show the students how to create an animal witness to the lynchings, and the relief from the heavy human atmosphere would, I hoped, help the writers leaven the horror and see past the rationale for the lynchings to their sad reality.

The results were mixed: the students did a good job of trotting out animal characters, but their take on the lynchings was too pat. The animals either simply reported what happened without interpreting at all, or they mouthed the standard liberal assessment of racism.

Back to the drawing board. An eighth grade teacher gave me another hint: using *To Kill a Mockingbird* in conjunction with "Dog" gives students a full-fledged reading experience about the racism that led to lynching in the early decades of the century. You can't read Harper Lee's novel without experiencing from the inside the complicated social and psychological realities of living in a racist town. Students today may experience their own versions of prejudice, but they probably need this novel, or other readings like it, to understand the particular mixture of ignorant suspicion, hair-trigger mob psychology, and the codified division between the races that spawned lynchings. The children in Harper Lee's novel not only grow up learning the racial code, but they are also innocent enough to see around it: similar to the animal character that initially attracted me.

It was, then, an easy step from reading the novel to writing about the trial in it or an historical lynching from an animal's point of view. I had fleshed out the exercise with enough background information to help students understand the complications of historical experience, and in "Dog" I had also given them a fresh, provocative model for framing their insights.

Where can you find wonderful models like "Dog," and how can you bring students through a writing process that will prepare them to draft their work? As a writer myself, I am always on the lookout for poems and stories and essays that inspire me. I happen across lots of writing simply by dipping into anthologies, attending readings of new writing, and taking tips from friends about good books. None of these activities demands any special expertise—anybody with a reasonably open mind and some teaching experience can encounter pieces of writing that bring out an "ah-ha" of certainty: this poem (or essay or story) will work with students.

Mainly, you have to be on the lookout, and not only for the standard fare. Try established writers and newcomers, writers from various ethnic, racial, and geographical backgrounds. Pablo Neruda's odes appeal to many contemporary poets in the United States, yet few classroom teachers seem to know of them. The odes exist in various editions and anthologies in good bookstores and libraries, but they haven't really made it into standard textbooks. The moral here is: branch out. Go into a bookstore or library occasionally on Saturday morning, wander around, leaf through books, let yourself read a little here and there. If you find something that you like, pause and ask yourself if you can make it relevant for your students. If the answer is yes, buy the book or borrow it from the library. You're on your way to devising an exercise.

Then, as you create the exercise, remember some of these general steps for leading students into and through their own writing:

• Use conversation to explore students' personal responses to the historical and literary material. Conversation in a classroom can do more than a mere question-and-answer approach. Conversation can begin to give students language about their own experiences and reactions to history that can then be set down in writing.

• The next step is to create a classroom collection of words and images. I usually do this on the board, with some sort of word mapping to which the whole class contributes; or, with older students, I make a map of my own on the board, and let the students make their own. Often what students put on their maps is a flushing out of received or hackneyed ideas (sometimes along with fresh, personal observations), but when the time comes to draft, the students will go beyond what they've put on their maps and write with new inspiration.

• Talking about ways to organize a piece of writing with a class can next point students toward selecting, shaping, and intensifying what resources they have gathered. The exercises in my book *The Story in History* offer examples of how this has worked with various models and historical resources.

• I try to remain attuned to the mood and understanding of a class as I am presenting an exercise. Each group of students differs—some need a lot more talking to, a lot more breaking up of directions into little steps, than do others. Sometimes I have to improvise on the spot when I discover that students don't know what to do with a set of instructions that I thought were clear and helpful. Often, first doing some of the work collectively will then allow students to proceed individually.

• Once students are writing, I move from desk to desk to identify strong phrases, answer private questions, read aloud good drafts, and help students who are stuck. As I work with individual students in this public setting, I am beginning to develop the class as an audience for writing and to prepare the students for reading their work aloud.

• Reading aloud satisfies students' curiosity about each other's work and helps them learn other strategies for writing. For the readers, the experience helps gauge what is communicated—the class laughs or responds soberly at appropriate places. Reading aloud also lets the writer hear clunky or marvelous phrases and begin to assess the total impact of the piece.

• Revision is an important step, but is not necessary for every piece of writing. I often pair students to work on revision and ask them to give each other several questions or comments to identify strengths and weaknesses that the authors can then address.

• As a final step, a class can consider what their creative responses to the past have helped them understand. This response may be as simple as a second grader's, who created a new name for herself "in the Indian spirit," and said, "I like my new old Dakota name." Or, it may be as complex as a high school student's reflecting on his new understanding of war after writing a Civil War ballad. This analytical coda to the writing exercise is important, because it allows students a wider sense of the various purposes of writing and the many ways we gain new knowledge of an historical period.

So you see, there isn't a simple method that will result in an instant assignment. What matters most is that the historical material really interests you, that you think it can interest your students, and that you remain willing to enter into the adventure of trying it with them.

Elizabeth Radin Simons

The Folklore of Naming

On this earth everybody has to have a name or they are no one," wrote Veronica, a seventh grade Mexican-American student. A classmate made the same point in different words: "If I wasn't named, I'd be called 'no name.'" Not only are we literally no one without our names, our names are powerful: they identify and define us, they contain our personal histories, and when we study the folklore or traditions that go into our names, they provide clues to the values our families and our country hold.

For the last eight years I have been experimenting with modern folklore (contemporary oral tradition) in the classroom. I've taught the folklore of names to students in urban and suburban schools, often as part of a larger unit on family folklore. I've found that whatever the setting or the grade level, students like to study names, especially their own.

There is a story behind everyone's name, and each one is important and interesting—although many students do not realize this at first. Consider the story behind the name of Pamela Denise Wells, a high school student.

> My mother and father have always told me and my sisters how we got our names. My father named all of us. All of our names start with P, all our middle names with a D, and our last names with a W.
>
> There was one mistake with my sister under me. Her name is Thelma. My father said my mother's mother (my grandmother) beat him to the hospital and named my sister after herself. My father was mad.
>
> When my baby sister was born my father's mother tried to get to the hospital before my father to name my baby sister after herself. But my father said, "No! What would the name Geraldine sound like for a baby girl these days?"

Pam's classmates, predominantly African-American in an inner-city high school, appreciated her story very much. The students liked the tradition of having initials in common and talked about why parents would want their children to have the same initials. It makes the family closer, they thought, and Pam agreed. They noticed that Pam's parents felt the stories about their naming were important, because they had made a point of telling the stories to their daughters over and over again. Pam's classmates also enjoyed the image of her grandmothers rushing to the hospital after each birth in an attempt to sabotage the parents' plans and get those babies named after themselves. Since many students in the class were in fact named after their grandmothers, they wondered if Pam's parents, by creating their own tradition, were violating another tradition, an older African-American tradition of naming girls after their grandmothers.

Students like the folklore of names, not only because it is about themselves, but also because they appreciate having their lives brought into the classroom and honored as important historical material. The topic is also useful in teaching writing because students have strong feelings about their names and nicknames and a lot of first-hand experience with names. Once they have gathered their data—the folklore surrounding their names—students can look for clues to their parents' values. To do this requires some training in analytical thinking, specifically in being able to identify the functions of folklore and oral tradition.

Understanding the value of naming traditions requires a bit of background in modern (or contemporary) folklore. Modern folklore is definitionally the same as traditional lore. It is the stories, jokes, traditions, customs, and the like that we have put into oral tradition and kept alive by passing them from person to person. Traditional folklore is that of ancient peoples, epics (such as *The Iliad*), folktales ("Cinderella"), legends (the headless horseman), proverbs, riddles, and folk music. All this folklore is not "ours" in the sense that we no longer keep it alive through oral tradition; we know it from books. However, we still do have a rich oral tradition, and it is to this that I am referring when I say "modern folklore" or "modern oral tradition."

Modern folklore includes children's games and play (tag and playing house); it is slang and school desk graffiti; it is ways to pass notes in class, dating rituals, and teenage folklore; it is heroes and heroines and modern urban legends such as "The Babysitter" or stories of albino alligators in city sewers; it is jokes. It is family folklore, rituals, and traditions, from family whistles to what we eat at Thanksgiving dinner and whom we invite. Be it Hispanic, African-American, or white Anglo-Saxon Protestant, we all have our family and ethnic lore. Most recently I taught the folklore of names in a high school of mostly white middle-class suburban students. In my ninth grade class, I started by writing my full name (Elizabeth Jane Radin Simons) on the chalk-board and saying, "Ask me questions about how I got my name."

Eric, the first student to speak, was confused by my having so many names and asked, "What's your real name?" I laughed; it was a good question. They are all my names but when I married I dropped the Jane. Tait, whose mother has been married three times, said laughing, "It's a good thing my mom didn't keep all her names from the past."

Next came a good question from Brian, "What other names did your parents think of?" "If I had been a boy," I told him, "my name would have been Edward."

Susan, one of the more playful members of the class, asked, "Didn't anyone ever call you 'Peaches' or something like that?" "Alas," I told them, "no one ever called me Peaches, but I do have a nickname, Liz, and when I was a child I was 'Lizzie.'" Susan wasn't satisfied with this, she wanted something "crazy." And at that moment I remembered a family nickname I had totally forgotten, "dear, dear Elizabeth." My father had coined it—the first dear because he loved me and the second because I was so expensive! My father delighted in this nickname and still likes to tell stories about why it was so appropriate. "Dear, dear Elizabeth" wasn't quite "Peaches," but Susan seemed satisfied.

"Why did you drop the Jane instead of the Radin?" Brian wanted to know. Alison had an answer, "No one ever does that." A hot discussion ensued about keeping last names after marriage and divorce. And Michelle brought some closure to the discussion with this observation: "Just because she got married she didn't want to forget where she came from." A beautiful point. Michelle understood that my name, a symbol of my past, was something I might want to keep after marriage as a way of maintaining my ties to my family—"where I came from."

I mentioned that I thought a really important change in this country was that now more women, when they married, were keeping their maiden names, something that was not done when I got married, twenty years ago. There were murmurs around the classroom, girls telling one another, "I'm going to keep mine." Then Alison asked, indignation rising in her tone as she was beginning to realize the significance and power of names, "Why do they [girls] take guys' names instead of the girls' names?" She had asked an important question, one which went directly to the heart of a Western European value. Alison eventually answered herself. "It shows," she said, "that men are more important than women." What decisions couples make about their last names at marriage tell a great deal about them and the culture in which they live.

At this point, Sissie announced proudly that her real name was Heleena Dawn Marti Donaire Watson Belcher. Since we all knew her just as Sissie Marti, we were impressed. Sissie explained that she had been named according to a Spanish tradition. In school she used only one last name, her father's, but she had three other last names, which came from both maternal and paternal grandparents. Sissie told us that she liked her name because it showed her heritage, which was both French and Cuban.

Finally Eric asked the question that is usually the first in these classes, "Why were you named Elizabeth?"

"I'm Jewish," I explained, "and the Jewish naming tradition is to name after someone who has died." At this point we had a discussion of the reason for such a tradition, focusing on the question, "What does it tell you about the values of Jews?"

Then I told them the rest of the story behind my first name. "I was named for my grandfather who had died seven years before my birth and whose name was Elijah. My parents are first-generation Americans and when they named me they had two concerns: they wanted to carry on Jewish traditions but they didn't want my name to sound too Jewish. So they took my grandfather's name, translated it into Hebrew and back again into English and came up with Elizabeth. They felt then they had preserved our heritage but had not burdened me with a Jewish name."

Whenever I taught the folklore of naming, I told this story. Recently I saw my parents and told them my little speech about how I got my name. They looked at each other and started laughing. When my father got control of himself, he looked me in the eye and said, "Liz, your grandfather's name was Jacob!"

Now I tell both stories to my students because both versions—my parents' and mine—are equally important; both are family folklore.

"Do you have any brothers and sisters?" Danny asked. He wanted to know their names and if they too had been named after people who had died. This, too, was a good question because Danny was branching his inquiry, looking now for family naming patterns.

Alison changed the subject a bit and introduced another aspect of naming. "When my grandpa died, my mother almost had my brother named after him, but since our last name was Henry and his name was John, that really couldn't go." The rest of the class didn't understand, and Alison explained who John Henry was. We had a brief discussion about what it would be like to have the name of a famous person.

Ralph told us his father's name is Paul Neuman, spelled differently but pronounced the same way as the famous actor's.

"What about your middle name?" someone asked. I told them that "Jane" was simply a popular name when I was born, a name fad. Many women my age are named Jane. "What are the faddish names today?" I asked. Tait, who jokingly offered his as a popular name, said, "David is the second most popular name, I got that from the *Book of Lists*."

"My last name is from my great-grandfather who was from France," offered Christine Olivette. This led Tapeeka to observe, "Some families have a coat of arms." Christine and Tapeeka had opened up the world of last names, a subject that interested some of the students, especially those who knew the histories of their surnames.

In twenty minutes of class discussion, the students had raised most of the questions I wanted them to pursue when studying their own names. They had asked about nicknames; they had wondered about other names considered by parents; they had talked about changing names and naming decisions at marriage; they had touched on name fads; they had discussed the situation of having the same name as a famous person; they had thought about their last names and how their first names were chosen.

To further dramatize the significance of our naming traditions I usually read to my students about other traditions and we talk about how they are similar to or different from our own. For example, chapter 1 of Alex Haley's *Roots* is the story of the naming of the hero, Kunte Kinte. The traditions of the Mandinka tribe speak powerfully of the Mandinka's knowledge of the history of their tribe, of their desire to perpetuate it, and of their belief in the great importance of this new child.

Writing about Names

Usually I have the students repeat with each other the activity that they did first with me. Each writes his or her name on a piece of paper while two or three other students do the interview. Then they do a piece of free first-draft writing about their names. I encourage all the students to write about the history of their names, but not all students know the full history. So I offer them several options. They can write about their nicknames, how they got them and who can use them. They can describe how they feel about their names, whether they like them or dislike them, and why. If they ever wanted to change their names, they can write about it and tell the other names they considered. If they choose, they can make up a story of how they got their names.

The students then take their drafts home and read them to their parents. Often this provokes a discussion, the parents remembering the thinking that went into the names. In case it doesn't, the students are armed with questions to ask, so they come back to class with more information to use in revising their original pieces. For many parents this is a lovely moment, a first chance to talk with their child about the choice of name. Conversely, it is wise to plan for the students who cannot interview parents. They can do the first draft, but when it comes to interviewing they may want to switch to someone else's name, that of a friend or a teacher in the school.

The study of naming can stop here with the revision of the original piece of writing. If it does, the writing, which is invariably interesting, should be presented either in a class read-around or by printing a booklet of the naming stories on ditto sheets.

The folklore of naming, however, can also be just a beginning. Listening to one another read, students can start thinking about or recording the naming traditions in their class and looking at them as history. The following examples from the first drafts of a junior English class give an idea of the richness of this activity, both as a subject for writing and as ideas for follow-up expository writing. In the first excerpt, Ron writes of "the best thing" his father could have given him at birth:

> My father chose my name Ronald Lain Nordyke, Jr., because it was his and at the time it was the best thing he could give me. Also he wanted it to last and go on in the family. . . .

Trish (Patricia) writes of her parents' and grandparents' desire that her name be an expression of her heritage.

> My parents and grandparents named me this (Patricia Kathleen Day) because my parents are first generation from Ireland! So they wanted the first-born to have a full Irish name! . . .

Writing of her name, Lisa brings up a religious tradition:

> Before I was born my parents decided what my name was going to be if I was a girl. Like most Catholic families, they chose my name after a saint. Saint Isabella and Mother Mary were the saints my parents chose. They changed Isabella to Lisa and Mary to Marie. I now have the name Lisa Marie Richnavsky. I feel happy with my name because it also belonged to two other beautiful women. . . .

When George learned the origin of his name, he changed his opinion of it:

> My father named me after my great-grandfather. My great-grandfather
> died in the Crimean War against the Russians and the Turks. He died in
> the famous battle of the Charge of the Light Brigade. Before I found
> that out I didn't like my name. . . . Now I am very proud to have George
> William Mitchell as my name. . . .

The following Chinese student asked to remain anonymous. Traditions such as his are invaluable when studying names: they make the
point that one can learn about the values of a culture through its naming traditions:

> In my language _____ is a name of a tree which lives the longest of all
> among other trees in the forest. Because of its meaning, my uncle got
> this wild idea about naming his nephew a name which describes the
> lifespan of his nephew. Of course as you already know, younger people
> can't disobey whatever their elders tell them to do; so therefore, my dad
> agreed with his older brother, my uncle, in naming me _____ since
> it means that I shall live a long life. . . .

In every piece in the class, there were traditions worthy of explanation. Why did Ron consider his father's name "the best thing he
could give" him? Did Trish feel connected to Ireland? How had her
name affected her? Why should knowing the history of his name
change George's attitude? Why is it a Chinese tradition that younger
people cannot disobey their elders?

The students also discovered patterns. While sons were often
named after fathers, daughters were seldom named after mothers. They
speculated on the meaning of this tradition—more evidence that males
are more valued? Some students were named after movie stars, a common American tradition and evidence that movie stars are heroes and
heroines in our culture. It is not by chance but an expression of American values that Ronald Reagan was president.

This first writing activity on the folklore of naming also can be
the basis of another writing assignment, an expository piece. Using
their first writings as their folkloric data, for instance, students can write
an essay on what the oral naming traditions in their families can tell an
historian or anthropologist about their families. Or after hearing all
the stories from the class, students could write about the naming traditions in their class and what these traditions reveal about the values
of one American community.

Another expository piece that leads naturally from this activity is
one on nicknames. Students write about the nicknames they get both
from family and from friends. "Pretty Panties," who wished to remain
anonymous, got this nickname from friends. She explained that she is

called "Pretty Panties because all my underwear are like five or six dollars a pair because they are all lace and I like lacy pretty underwear." Steve also wrote of his nicknames ("Beake" and "Beave") and explained their origins. "Beake because I'm skinny and have spiked hair like Beaker on the 'Muppet Show.' I get called Beave because it rhymes with Steve and there's a 'Leave It to Beaver' fad going on." Students can study and write about the origins and functions of nicknames. Nicknames make an interesting comparison to birth names because often they are acquired later in life and, unlike birth names, are descriptive. Like birth names, however, they define and mold us. Children's nicknames especially can affect their lives.

A unit on the folklore of naming has other uses as well. I use it to introduce the study of Family Folklore. When students write autobiographies in English classes they can include something on their names. And in history classes working on oral history, interviewees can be asked for the history of their names.

"On this earth everybody has to have a name or they are no one." Veronica might have continued, "But once a name is bestowed they become someone." The names we are given define us and stay with us for our lifetimes. At first glance the oral traditions behind the giving of these names seem unimportant, but they are not. A good look at these traditions not only produces interesting writing but also connects the lives of the students to history and can show them the relevance and connectedness of their lives to the larger culture.

Bibliography

On nicknames:

Harre, Rom. "What's in a Nickname?" *Psychology Today*, January, 1980.

Morgan, Jane; O'Neill, Christopher; and Harre, Rom. *Nicknames: Their Origins and Social Consequences*. London: Routledge & Kegan Paul, 1979.

On names:

The journal *Names* publishes articles on all aspects of naming, including the naming of persons. All books in public libraries on first names and surnames are good resources for students studying their own names.

On family folklore in general:

Zeitlin, Steven S.; Kotkin, Amy J.; and Cutting-Baker, Holly. *A Celebration of American Family Folklore.* New York: Pantheon, 1982.

On American folklore in general:

Brunvand, Jan. *The Study of American Folklore: An Introduction.* New York: Norton, 1978.

Elizabeth Radin Simons

The Folklore of Childhood

When I start this topic, the students have already had an introduction to folklore and know what it is, so I plunge right in by asking, "Tell me some of the games you played as a child, ones you learned from other children." Some classes answer in a big competitive rush, others take their time as they warm to the subject. In one class the list developed this way.

"Jacks?" Rocio asks tentatively; she is not quite sure what I am after. "Good," I say, and then because this is a prewriting as well as a brainstorming session and I want to encourage details to use later in writing, I ask, "What do you remember about playing jacks?"

Lorenzo interrupts and starts laughing, "You start from 'onesies' and 'twosies?'" Everyone joins him laughing at the memory of "onesies" and "twosies." Maria suddenly remembers "Cherry in the basket!" and laughs. "What else do you remember?" I prod.

No hands are raised yet, but from somewhere in the back of the room I hear another tentative suggestion: "Jump rope?" "Good," I say, "Do you remember any jump rope rhymes?"

"Teddy bear, teddy bear," Olga chants, imitating a young child, and everyone laughs again. Gradually the girls begin to remember their jump rope rhymes: "Windy, windy, weather . . . ," "I was born in a frying pan . . . ," "Ice cream soda, with a cherry on top . . . ," "Apple on a stick, makes me sick. . . ." Rocio is getting impatient with the jump rope rhymes; she wants to talk about something else. "I don't remember what it was called with the hands?" Lorenzo helps her out: "Patty clap." Suddenly the class remembers the elaborate handclapping games the girls used to play. In some classes, the more extroverted students try to demonstrate the handclapping. Often they cannot remember the words and have lost their touch, but they enjoy trying to regain their childhood skills. In this class, the girls are shy about demonstrating. The reminiscing continues. Lorenzo suddenly remembers a popular playground game and shouts out, "The boys against the girls!" The class is laughing again when someone quips, "We still do that!"

The opening discussions about children's folklore are a pleasure. High school students are nostalgic about childhood. Perhaps one reason is that childhood, so strong and sweet and poignant, seems so far away that it makes adolescents feel adult. Left to their own devices, students would happily reminisce for days about their childhoods; one strong appeal of this folklore unit is that it allows students, for a few weeks, to relive their childhoods.

This folklore study may start with nostalgia, but as it unfolds, students begin to understand that their early play was more than entertainment. In their childhood games, they tried out future adult roles, in playing with Barbies or "dressing up" or playing war. They learned sex roles playing house. They acted out being "bad" when they played Chicken or Doctor. In their play they were getting an education, learning the values, attitudes, beliefs, and behavior that would continue into their adult lives.

After the entire class does some preliminary brainstorming, I have the students break up into groups of four. Usually at this time I segregate the sexes because many of the games of childhood are gender-specific and they seem to brainstorm better in such groups. I give directions first: "Try to remember as many kinds of games and play as you can that you did as children. Each time you mention a game, give as many details as you can." Each group has a scribe, who writes down the games as they are mentioned.

Most groups do fine, but to spot groups that are floundering, I circulate and listen in. If the memories aren't flowing, I drop a few hints. For a group of girls I might ask, "Did you play with Barbies?" or "Did you have slumber parties?" or "Did you play with dolls?" Mentioning Door Bell Ditch and prank telephone calls works with both boys and girls.

Day Two: The Master List

The next day each group reports, and together we make a master list on the chalkboard. These usually have 100–150 items, which surprises the students—they have remembered a lot of folklore from their childhoods.

Speculative talk accompanies the making of the list. Students discuss, for example, which games they think their parents and their grandparents played.

I often ask the students about gender-specific games. Which are girls' games, which are boys' games, and why? We talk about age too. At what age was a game played? And as we add items to the list, we speculate a little about function; why do children play these games? The discussion that accompanies the making of the list is relaxed and exploratory talk about issues that we will address in more depth later.

Day Three: Choosing a Topic and Writing the First Draft

"Take a look at the master list," I tell the class, "and choose a game that you liked to play when you were young." Many students know immediately what they are going to write about. Their faces light up as they remember. For the students who look blank at this point, I suggest that they think back to a game they loved as a child, perhaps a game they played often and remember in some detail.

After the students choose their topics, I have them do some prewriting and additional brainstorming with a partner.

After the prewriting, it is time for first drafts. "Write down everything you can remember," I tell them. "If you are writing about 'levitating' at a slumber party, try to remember the details, such as what you chanted. Was it 'Light as a feather, stiff as a board?' If you levitated, describe how it felt." I remind the students that this is a first draft, a place to get ideas and to focus on their memories, and that they shouldn't worry about producing polished writing. I also suggest they try to include enough description that a reader could learn to play the game just by reading their account.

In one suburban classroom studying children's folklore, Jane Juska and I team-taught. For this assignment Jane stipulated that the memory be written in first person and in the present tense to create a sense of immediacy. One student, Lynn, wrote about playing Red Light, Green Light:

> Coming home from grade school, I can't wait to change out of my school clothes and into a pair of jeans, grubby, old and faded. It seems the whole neighborhood is in the same state of excitement, for every day at approximately 2:30 P.M. we kids meet in the park by the drinking fountain, dressed in play clothes and ready to play "Red Light, Green Light." Standing in a circle, our fists thrust into the center, we wait as a boy, his brown hair messy from running, counts out, "Eenie—Meenie—Miny—Mo." This is one game when everyone wants to be It. Calling "green light" and watching the pack of kids scrambling forward to tag you before you yell "red light" is always fun. We play until the sun sets in the west and we are weary and rosy-cheeked from running in the cool autumn air.

In an inner-city classroom, a boy named Lue wrote:

> Shooting craps is a game of luck and cheating. If you cheat good enough you don't need luck. First you need players, dice, and money. You need to be alert because some people use loaded dice. The first man makes a certain number and in order to win you must match your number. When people win they become happy but when they lose (crap) they get mad and sometimes fight. . . . But there are dangers if someone sees you playing they might tell your parents. Once your parents find out your dice throwing hand will be broken. Oh yeah, if you roll a one or a seven you crap.

Lue's classmates laughed at his humor, especially his opening lines. Lue was a senior, and although he was a skilled talker, he had not done well in writing. At first he was incredulous that his off-the-cuff draft was a success, but when he realized that he could entertain on paper as well as orally, he began to enjoy writing. The students who hadn't shot craps, however, did have a suggestion. From his description they could not play craps; they requested more details and information.

These early drafts are valuable. From them I learn about the early years of my students and I learn more folklore. I also learn about regional and ethnic variations on traditional folklore. In her draft on hopscotch, Olga, a Mexican-American student, wrote: "In the middle of the street I would start drawing the game while Rose got a bowl of water and thread." "Why a bowl of water and thread?" I asked. "We played with the water and thread because it was easier for wet thread to land on the number, not like other little objects that you throw and which bounce and roll away." In turn I told Olga about the small, flat stones I used as a child, called "potsies."

These drafts are usually a good read. The content is compelling because the students like the subject and are in control of the material, which comes from their lives.

Day Four: Responding and Revising

If students revise their writing and complete the unit at this stage, I have them simply write a memory piece. For a longer unit, this can be the catalyst for a longer paper on childhood folklore. To begin, students read their drafts in small groups, get responses, and do a first revision.

A fuller study of children's folklore, however, requires at least another week of research (in the form of interviews) and analysis of the folklore.

Day Five: Starting the Research—Interviewing

A deeper study of children's folklore requires information beyond the students' own memories. Like professional folklorists, the students can gather information through interviews. I ask them to interview three people: an older person who remembers playing the game as a child; a peer who also remembers the game; and a child who is still playing it.

Together we devise the interview questionnaire, discussing what type of information we want to gather. Each student makes up several questions. From these questions we select the best ones and create a questionnaire. (If the class does not suggest numbers one through five on the questionnaire below, I add them myself—these are essential. Questions that can be answered "yes" or "no" are best avoided.)

Children's Folklore Interview Questionnaire

1. Interviewer's name _____
2. Interviewee's name and age _____
3. Date and place of the interview _____
4. The topic (Hide and Seek, for example) _____
5. How did you learn to play? _____

Here is a list of questions one class used:

- Do you remember the first time you played "Hide and Seek"?
- What is the best part of the game?
- What do you need to play?
- Did you get into any fights or arguments?
- How many people play?
- Where do you play?
- How does it feel to win? Lose?
- Do both girls and boys play? Why?
- What is the purpose of playing?
- What kind of people did you play with?
- How often did you play?

Beforehand, students practice on one another. Two volunteers conduct an interview in the front of the room while the class watches and takes notes. Afterwards we discuss what worked and what needed adjustment.

Lorenzo, who was studying a game called Smear the Queer, agreed to do an interview, and Miguel, who remembered playing it, agreed to be the interviewee. Before starting, I asked them which interviewers they liked on TV. "Barbara Walters," Lorenzo answered. "Good," I told him, "pretend you're Barbara Walters." Lorenzo was rather ill at ease, which was not surprising; he had never done this before, and the whole class was watching. To mask his embarrassment, he spoke in stilted tones, imitating the style of a formal interview. "Umm, umm, umm, umm, what is your name?" he began. The class laughed. Miguel played it straight, however.

M: Miguel.

L: How old are you, Miguel? (*Laughter*)

M: Seventeen right now.

L: What nationality are you? (*Laughter: everyone in this class was Hispanic*)

M: Mexican-American.

L: Okay, do you remember the first time you played?

M: Played what?

L: Smear the Queer.

M: Yeah, in junior high.

L: Why?

M: 'Cause everybody else did it.

L: How did you learn?

M: I was—I watched my friends do it.

L: What was the best part of it, of playing Smear the Queer with your friends?

M: Hitting somebody, hitting somebody, hitting somebody you didn't like.

L: Do you still play this game since you are older now?

M: No.

L: What do, oh damn, did you get in fights or arguments?

M: Yeah.

L: Why?

M: (*Laughs*) 'Cause somebody thought they'd hit 'em on—you know, somebody'd get hit and they didn't have the ball or something.

L: Go on. Is that it?

M: That's it.

L: What did you gain by playing this?

M: Bruises, bruises, brother. (*Laughter*)

L: Did your mother approve of this game?

M: No, (*Laughs*) she didn't know about it actually.

L: How many people played?

M: I think it was about ten guys.

L: Did you guys play with a football, softball, can, or pillow?

M: No, we played with a football.

L: How does it feel to hit somebody, I mean just really hit 'em? (*Laughter*)

M: If it's somebody you don't like, it doesn't matter, it doesn't make a difference.

L: How did it feel when you got hit?

M: When I got hit, man, I felt like hitting somebody else.

L: Was it fun?

M: Yeah, sometimes when there wasn't any fights.

L: Is it for boys and girls? And why?

M: One girl played, she got stuck [hit] though. (*Laughter*)

L: So you're saying this is only for boys.

M: I'm not saying that, I'm referring to the fact that (*Laughter*) that ladies can play but they have to take it like everybody else, not just like a man but like everybody else does.

L: I agree with you. What kind of people did you play with? You know, were they older than you?

M: No, they were my age but they were like, they were big.

L: How often did you play this game?

M: Oh, I think every day—at lunch.

L: Did you ever get in trouble playing this game with the principal or you know—

M: No, the security guards stopped us from playing like that.

L: Did you guys go to jail?

M: Ne–ver.

L: Have you ever been convicted of a crime?

M: No, (*Laughter*) you're getting off the subject, man.

When the interview was over, the class critiqued it, starting with what they liked about it. "The fun!" Martin said. Good point. I told the class that if they made the interviewing fun for themselves, it would help the interviewee to relax. We complimented Lorenzo. I noted that several times he had departed from the list of questions, which is good; ad-libbed questions can turn out to be the heart of an interview. Lorenzo added some questions: "Did your mother approve of this game? How does it feel to hit someone, really hit them? Did you ever get in trouble [playing Smear the Queer]?" These questions elicited valuable information. Lorenzo was genuinely curious about the answers. By comparison, his last question was not appropriate. He had a dilemma: he didn't know how to end the interview gracefully. Also, while Lorenzo had asked a few spontaneous follow-up questions, he had overlooked other good opportunities. For instance, Miguel mentioned that he remembered the first time he had played the game, but Lorenzo didn't follow it up. During the class discussion of the interview, Miguel described the first time:

> Well, my friend—one of my friends—told me to come in and play 'cause he used to just watch me sit there, watching them play, so he told me to go out there and play, and I was scared at first because most of them guys were pretty big. But then, so I went there and after you hit somebody, you know, you get used to being hit. So I was cool but when I got hit, I got mad—

Maria interrupted Miguel. "I have a question: did you guys hit each other hard?"

"Friends we didn't hit them that hard, we just kind of bumped them and that's it, but people we didn't like, we stuck 'em," Miguel explained.

Since I wanted the students to be constantly thinking about following up promising leads, I pointed out things that I would have followed with more questions. I was curious about the girl who played; I wanted to know more about her. Also I noticed that during the interview Miguel often mentioned fighting, often joking about it. It seemed an important part of the game, but when asked what made a good game, he said a good game didn't have any fights. I would have asked Miguel to explain this contradiction.

In the discussion that followed the interview, no one brought up the title of the game. The game, a common one, is widely known as Smear the Queer but has other names, such as Kill the Pig and Get the Man with the Ball. It is a folk game that is a kind of preparation for football and is best played with a group. One player throws the ball, another catches it and then tries to break away from the pack and avoid being tackled. The player who catches the ball is the "queer," and if he fails to get away, he gets "smeared."

Part of the appeal of folklore in the classroom is that it is real—folklore tells it like it is. This game's name, with its prejudicial message about homosexuality, reflects societal values. When teaching folklore, it is imperative not to gloss over such inherent complexity and contradictions. In this case, the students should discuss the title. Was this a bad game? Were the kids learning prejudices playing it? Miguel's memory of the game was complex—sometimes it was fun, sometimes it was too violent. (I felt it important that Miguel not be made to feel guilty about the title; he didn't name it.) It's interesting to see the subtle ways in which prejudices permeate society, how they are learned unconsciously by children playing games, but also the interesting contradictions: for instance, the queer, the boy who catches the ball, when he gets away from the pack, is the hero. All the boys want to catch the ball and successfully pull away from the crowd. Furthermore, not all children playing the game know the word *queer* as a pejorative word for *homosexual*.

Two more issues in interviewing are note-taking and serendipity. For a project this size, it is relatively easy to keep a running written record of answers while seeking questions. (However, tape recorders are ideal.) Often the most informative part of an interview occurs accidentally or incidentally in asides, or before and after the interview. While asking the questions on their list, students should be aware of these serendipitous moments.

Homework for the next two nights is to conduct at least three interviews. The interviews can be eye-openers. Rhonda, for instance, discovered that her friend Mary's recollection of Simon Says differed with hers. Rhonda's memory of the game was dominated by the competitive pressure she felt while playing:

> When playing the game, I tend to get a little tense, tight, stiff, also a bit of a headache from carrying out commands, from the sunshine beaming down on the top of my head, from the fear that I might lose and from the excitement that I might win.

Mary, Rhonda's interviewee, remembered the game's violence. She explained, "Simon would say, 'Simon Says slap Jane Doe,' and you would have to slap her or be out of the game."

Day Six: Scholarly Analysis of Children's Folklore

In preparation for analyzing their own folklore, I have the students look through works by professional folklorists. Looking at books and articles serves two purposes. The writings not only provide models for what the students will do, they also legitimize the study of folklore.

A fine book to start with is *The Lore and Language of Schoolchildren* by British folklorists Iona and Peter Opie. The Opies's work is unusual—scholarly work that is also successful and popular. (It does have one major oversight: it glosses over scatological and erotic lore.) The Opies's presentation of British children's lore includes many examples of the closely related American lore. It's a well-written book that gives the reader a good feel for the variety and volume of children's lore. The Opies also do a commendable job tracing the historical roots of children's lore. Another useful collection that offers some analysis is Herbert and Mary Knapp's *One Potato, Two Potato . . . The Folklore of American Children.*

These two books are good sources for variations on the folklore the students are studying. Raymond, an African-American student, was concentrating on the children's legend "Johnny I want my eyes back," a "scary" tale that had delighted him as a child. In Raymond's version, Johnny's mother sends him to the store to buy some black-eyed peas. Johnny, a bad boy, spends the money on candy. On the way home he cuts through a cemetery, pokes out the eyes of several corpses, and presents these to his mother instead of the peas. That evening the corpses rise up from their graves in search of their eyes. Ever so slowly they walk down the road, turn up the path to Johnny's house, mount the stairs, and enter Johnny's bedroom, chanting, "Johnny I want my eyes back, Johnny I want my eyes back." In *One Potato, Two Potato . . .*, Raymond found a version where the liver is stolen from the corpse. (See also "Gotcha" by Sylvia Grider in the "Children's Folklore" issue of *Center for Southern Folklore*, 1980, Vol. 3, p. 12.) Raymond and his classmates were amused by the African-American twist to the legend— the black-eyed peas (they didn't mention the pun). Having assumed that the legend was known only to them, they were further surprised to find that it is a modern variant of a traditional folktale, "The Man from the Gallows." In the traditional tale a man steals the heart or liver or stomach from a person who has been hanged and takes it to his wife to eat. Later the ghost arrives to claim his stolen part and carries the man off. There is little doubt that these are related stories.

The books by the Opies and the Knapps are essentially collections; students need to see analytical studies as well. Sometimes I have them read articles, sometimes I give a lecture on several articles so students can see how different folklorists approach the same subject. The telephone prank, a widespread and continuously popular folklore, is a good subject for this.

In my lecture, I begin with Norine Dresser's article "Telephone Pranks" from the *New York Folklore Quarterly*, a good model study for students. Dresser shows that the most popular telephone pranks serve the social needs of "making positive social contacts [and] . . . releasing hostility and frustration with a minimum risk of retaliation." First she discusses nonhostile pranks, the pranks that allow for positive social contacts. Some are played on peers. Boys and girls, for example, call someone they know, usually someone of the opposite sex, giggle, and then hang up. Some are played on adults, for example the prank of calling a number at random, asking for Grandfather and singing "Happy Birthday" to him.

Most of the calls Dresser discusses, however, are hostile and directed against adults. She discusses two-victim calls, telephone company calls, obscene calls, phony contest winner calls, the formulaic call, and survey calls. Of the two-victim calls, the best known is the Pizza Call— calling and ordering several pizzas, often for a neighbor. In one version of the telephone company call, the callers identify themselves as telephone repairmen working on the line. They ask the person not to answer the phone for the next half hour because, they explain, it would be dangerous for the repairman. Then they ring the number over and over until out of desperation the victim answers. At this point the callers let out bloodcurdling screams, pretending they are being executed. Phony contest winner and survey calls are parodies of the real thing. The formulaic calls are the best known, such as the classic:

"Do you have Prince Albert in the can?"
"Yes."
"Well, let him out."

As for the hostility behind telephone pranks, Dresser writes:

The best possible explanation would appear to be linked with the age of these callers (eleven-fifteen). They are at the onset of adolescence, when the first stirrings of rebellion against adult rules are beginning.

The anonymity of the phone call, Dresser observes, is essential. The victim is unknown. "The protection of anonymity," Dresser explains, "provides a very safe method for releasing hostility or frustration and with little fear of retaliation."

Dresser concludes:

It would appear then that the telephone pranks serve a very important social need for the adolescent, and are a valuable means for expressing and communicating his ideas and his conflicts.

At first the students are incredulous that a folklorist has studied telephone pranks, their clandestine activity, and is condoning, even praising them. This is a good moment for students to write a learning log entry on their opinions of telephone pranks. Are they a valuable means for expressing ideas and conflicts? Or what are they?

Students agree with much of Dresser's work, but they have some questions. In a footnote, Dresser suggests that telephone pranking does not begin in earnest until eighth grade. Dresser's article was published in 1973. Students now report starting earlier, as early as fourth grade. She also suggests that students with better language skills tend to make up their own pranks and vary the traditional pranks. The students liked this idea and began to vie with one another for the best invented prank. Maria told us that when she was very little, she and her friends called the operator and pretended they were being robbed. Within minutes they heard police sirens. Before the police arrived at the door, Maria and her friends escaped over the back fence.

To demonstrate that there are different approaches, I also tell the students about Marilyn Jorgensen's article, "A Social-Interactional Analysis of Phone Pranks," in *Western Folklore*. It focuses on the types of dialogue used and the formal features of that dialogue, such as rhymes, alliteration, polysemy (words with multiple meanings), and puns. Jorgensen contends that one reason for the continued popularity of telephone pranks is their verbal play.

There are, for instance, the formulaic parodies of the way businesses answer the telephone. She mentions:

Morgan's Morgue—
You stab 'em, we slab 'em.

and points out the alliteration and rhyme. Pranks that depend on double meanings of words are also continually popular, such as calling a market and asking:

"Do you have chicken legs?"
"Yes."
"Well, wear long pants and they won't show."

For yet another perspective, I bring up Trudier Harris's "Telephone Pranks: A Thriving Pastime" in the *Journal of Popular Culture*. Harris notes that the pranks are as old as the telephone. Her focus is different; she categorizes the pranks according to commercial and residential calls. She disagrees with Dresser, maintaining that the purpose "is always the same—make an idiot of the person on the receiving end of the prank . . ." and makes another point of interpretation: the power the callers have over the anonymous adult on the other end.

All three—Dresser, Harris and Jorgensen—identify the genre, collect versions, and then analyze their data. Dresser focuses on the functions of the jokes, Jorgensen more on verbal play, and Harris the longevity of the pranks. They are all trying to figure out why children play telephone pranks.

I finish by telling the students that they will all have something not found in the works of the scholars—their own first-person narrative accounts of the folklore. Furthermore, I point out that no analysis is ever final. They can always ask new questions, bring in new information, and make new analyses. Already they can see some gaps in these studies. For instance, there is no mention of the ethnicity of the players, and no attempt to see if there are any gender differences in the types of pranks played. Each writer seems to assume all American children play the same pranks the same way.

I want my students to come away from reading the articles and hearing the lecture knowing these three steps: identifying the folklore, collecting data, and analyzing it; knowing that there is more than one way to look at the material; and trusting their own experience.

Day Seven: Student Analysis of Children's Folklore

Once the students have chosen their topics, written their memories of the topic, done several interviews, and had some exposure to the work of professional folklorists, they are ready to do their own analyses. As a prewriting activity, I sometimes have students exchange their memory papers. At the end of the papers, the readers write down their impressions of the functions of the folklore. For example, Trisha had written about playing Hide and Seek. Jennifer read her paper and wrote this note:

> Hide and Seek has the functions of entertaining the people who are playing it and it could be that it teaches you to hide from something bad or scary, because if you are hidden it can't find you, and if it can't find you, it can't hurt you. It also teaches kids to cooperate because they have to decide on certain rules. It's a game of strategy because you have to figure out where to hide and if there's a base, how to get back.

Jeff wrote about Capture the Flag, which he and his friend had called War. (Twenty boys were divided into two groups. Each team had a flag. The object was to capture the opposing team's flag without getting "killed.") Jon read his paper and wrote back:

> War was played to teach you to be patriotic and proud. It helped bring out the male dominance role that is programmed in society.

Sissie wrote of playing a neighborhood game of softball and got this note:

> Sometimes when friends get together, just sitting around talking can be uncomfortable. Finding a favorite game that everyone likes can bring you closer together so you really have a great time.

Another prewriting activity is to have the students discuss their topics with partners or in small groups. After hearing a paper, students can ask, "What did you learn playing the game which is still important?" or "What was important about the game just at the time you were playing?"

Next, the students write drafts, giving their ideas on why the folklore they are studying stays alive in oral tradition. Some use the ideas of their classmates, others do not. This draft can be started in class or done as homework, and then read to others for a response.

Last Days: Writing the Final Paper

The final papers vary. Students without much writing experience can successfully complete the unit with three separate pieces of writing: the childhood memory, the interviews, and the analysis. More skilled writers can write a single paper that includes their memory, describes the folklore, and analyzes it.

At the end of the school year in the class I describe here, we published a booklet of the students' writings. Most of the students had never seen their written words in print before. Within a given class, especially a heterogeneously grouped class, there is a wide spectrum of final products. William, one of the least skilled students, chose to include his essay on playing Doctor. He rewrote it five times before it was ready. William opened with the sentence, "The game Doctor reveals all closed doors." He went on to describe how he remembered playing:

> First I pretended to examine her reflexes. I hit her knee. I grabbed her hand and touched her breast and looked in her eyes and said, "They're okay," and checked her lips and kissed them, and said, "They're okay," and giggled a little.

William was proud of his writing, and the class loved it. They joked about their own memories of playing Doctor.

The next piece was written by Pam, a senior and a very capable young woman who often was a truant with little interest in school. In folklore class, however, she turned out to be a fluent writer. Her paper was on jump rope:

> Jump rope has been around forever. I played it, my mother played it, her mother and her mother played it. When I was little about twelve girls played jump rope with us. The more we had, the more fun it was. The only thing I hated was when my socks fell down. The way we played was two people held the ends. Whoever got out had to hold the rope and the previous rope holder got in line. You could jump with one or more persons if you wanted, but whoever got out held the rope. We didn't have steady-enders, because everyone wanted to play.
>
> What I loved the most was when it was time out for Kool Aid. We always had plenty and even today I still drink it every day.
>
> I didn't know that the game was originally a boy's game (this information was in one of the readings). When we played, boys always teased, or grabbed the rope and made us miss. They would jump in and jump out and laugh and tease us about our songs.
>
> You can learn from jump rope too. We learned how to get along and take turns. We learned rhythm. We jumped to music, singing, and sometimes to our own humming.

Pam's classmates especially liked the details of her socks falling down, the memory of "steady-enders," and the description of the boys disrupting the game. They liked her interpretation that in playing jump rope the girls were learning to cooperate. They also liked the mention of rhythm in the game. African-American musical patterns were an important part of their childhood play, a part they delighted in recalling and reenacting.

Ava, who had been playing telephone pranks for years, wrote a fine paper about her own pranks and about new pranks she learned while interviewing friends and family. Studying her data, she noticed something not mentioned in the literature: at different ages children play different pranks. In her paper, Ava traced the developmental stages of herself as telephone prankster. Of the beginning, Ava wrote:

> First came the sort of "starter" pranks—ordering flowers and food (Chinese and pizza). . . . Another early prank was calling to say "hello" or just to bother somebody. . . . My version of this was to call and try to chat at two o'clock in the morning.

These were followed by more complicated pranks, such as those that require a series, usually four calls:

1) "Is Lisa there?" "No."
2) "Is Lisa there?" "No."
3) "Is Lisa there?" "No."
4) "Hello, this is Lisa, have there been any calls for me?"

Ava went on to describe the scatological and sexual pranks she and her interviewees graduated to when they got older. This survey call is typical:

> "Hello, I'm calling from a local market whose name cannot be revealed to you, but we would appreciate it if you took part in our survey. How often do you shop?"
> "Three times a week."
> "What is the average total of your bill?"
> "Thirty dollars."
> "What brand of peanut butter do you buy?"
> "Jiffy. . . ."
> "How long does it take you to reach orgasm??!!"

Norine Dresser mentions that the primary audience is the friends watching the caller, not the person being called. Ava agreed, but she made some interesting additional observations. As she got older, she got more interested in the reaction of the person called. When she was younger (she played from age seven to fourteen), she hung up immediately. But as she got older, she waited and engaged people in longer conversations.

Like Trudier Harris, Ava felt the power the telephone gives kids over the adults at the other end of the line is key to understanding the appeal of telephone pranks. Ava wrote about the historical changes in the playing of telephone pranks that she had noticed in her research:

> To my parents' (or perhaps grandparents') generation, the form of the prank was much different. Instead of calling to say something, they listened in on the party line, only occasionally saying something to bewilder the other people.

She concluded with the observation that the emphasis placed on sex by today's popular culture is reflected in the game nowadays. Telephone pranks by students her age (fifteen) are mostly about sex. Finally, she predicts that telephone pranks are here to stay unless "video phones" come in.

Bibliography

Sources for student (and teacher) readings

Knapp, Herbert and Mary. *One Potato, Two Potato . . . The Folklore of American Children*. New York: Norton, 1976.

Opie, Iona and Peter. *The Lore and Language of Schoolchildren*. New York: Oxford University Press, 1967.

Sutton-Smith, Brian. "The Folk Games of Children," in *Our Living Traditions*. Edited by Tristram Coffin. New York: Basic Books, 1968.

Further readings for teachers

Dresser, Norine. "Telephone Pranks," *New York Folklore Quarterly*, Vol. 29: 121–130, 1973.

Harris, Trudier. "Telephone Pranks," *Journal of Popular Culture*, Vol. 12: 138–145, 1978.

Jorgensen, Marilyn. "A Social-Interactional Analysis of Phone Pranks," *Western Folklore*, Vol. 43: 104–106, 1984.

Juska, Jane. "Levitation, Jokes, and Spin the Bottle: Contemporary Folklore in the Classroom—A Teacher's View," *English Journal*, Vol. 74: 37–38, 1985.

Mechling, Jay. "Children's Folklore," in *Folk Groups and Folk Genres: An Introduction*. Edited by Elliott Oring. Logan, Utah: Utah State University Press.

Newell, William Wells. *Games and Songs of American Children*. New York: Dover Publications, 1963. First published in 1883.

Opie, Iona and Peter. *Children's Games in Street and Playground*. Oxford: Clarendon Press, 1969.

Samuelson, Sue. "The Cooties Complex," *Western Folklore*, Vol. 39: 198–210, 1980.

Simons, Elizabeth Radin. "Levitation, Jokes and Spin the Bottle: Contemporary Folklore in the Classroom—A Folklorist's View," *English Journal*, Vol. 74: 32–36, 1985.

Sutton-Smith, Brian. *The Folk Games of Children*. Austin: University of Texas Press, 1972.

Ron Padgett

Phrases in Grammar and Dance

I've always liked prepositional phrases. In school it was relatively easy for me to learn what they were and to diagram them. *In the house. Under the bed. Over the rainbow.* There were no horrible complications of voice, mood, or agreement. And the diagrammatic structure for prepositional phrases was so crisp and neat: a line slanting down to the right, then turning to run horizontally.

I think that when I was first taught diagramming, in the seventh or eighth grade, this graphic depiction caused me to associate prepositional phrases and human arms: the preposition was the upper arm, the noun object the forearm. In fact it was as if an entire sentence, its structure laid bare in diagramming, mirrored the human body. The subject corresponded to the head, the predicate to the trunk, the arms and legs to prepositional phrases. (I can't remember if I went so far as to relate conjunctions to genitals, though given my willingness at thirteen to see sexual connotations in everything, it's possible that I did. I'm sure I dimly felt the main clause to be male, the dependent clause female.) Such associations have a visual as well as psychological basis: relating sentence diagramming to the human body came naturally—after learning to draw the traditional stick figure.

Prepositional phrases still not only remind me of arms, they also give me a visceral sensation of motion, at least when they're concrete. *Under the ground* drives me lower, *across the river* whizzes me forward, *in the sky* elevates me—and not only because of content. *Under* has a Germanic sound that seems to attract other such sounds, guttural and heavy. The two syllables of *across* are like the two steps for shooting a projectile: the first syllable cocks the mechanism, the second is the sound of the projectile whizzing through the air. *In* is so small a word as to be lighter than air, calling forth other airy sounds, along with images of helium balloons.

The physiology of uttering these three prepositions reinforces their respective impressions. Say them aloud: *under, across, in. Under* begins low in the throat and ends by being pressed down by the tongue and lips. *Across* begins in the back of the mouth and then is hissed outward into the air. The short *i* of *in* rises to the long (and "high") *i* sound in *sky:* it rises. (Perhaps this is why the image of balloons came to mind a few sentences back.)

In any case, such concrete prepositional phrases make me feel— perhaps where mind and body meet—the actual motion suggested by the phrases. Combined with appropriate rhythms, these phrases become powerful vehicles: by the time we get to "we go" in "Over the river and through the woods to grandmother's house we go," I've already gone!

"Behind the Door"

The movement inherent in concrete prepositional phrases can be seen by contrasting them with abstract ones. "In this case," "of the agreement," "in my opinion" have rhythm (as any words do), but they are static. They are plunked right down where they are. Perhaps this is why people who wish to appear dignified, firm, and stately overuse such phrases. Built into their usage is the prejudice that to move one's body quickly is usually to appear juvenile. Children run and jump. Heads of state move with studied slowness. Middle-aged people seek youthfulness by jumping about in aerobics classes. I jump around on a tennis court. No wonder we get drowsy and doze when hearing a talk bogged down in phrases such as "under consideration," "in deliberation," and "of achievement." An old meaning of *abstract* is, after all, "absent in mind."

Of course abstraction has its uses. The unfortunate thing about abstraction is that its *abuses* don't lead to anything beautiful or interesting. For example, disorganized strings of concrete phrases can be wonderfully ludicrous, as in "The Browns returned this morning from their vacation in the mountains on a bus," in which the suddenly miniature Browns spend their leisure time amidst the little mountains situated atop a bus. In this example the scale of things fluctuates wildly, releasing a surrealistic humor. By seeing the imaginative possibilities in such ludicrousness, creative writers can use confused strings of prepositional phrases to good advantage.

I've always been attracted to the lankiness of long strings of prepositional phrases: "in the city of Cincinnati under an enormous elm in the summer of 1942. . . ." This series of phrases generously opens up and extends itself, like a carpenter's rule. It has a midsummer sense of timelessness built into its syntax. It exudes ease and flow and relaxation, something like the rhythm of using the extra "and" in the first half of this very sentence. Carried to extremes, such lankiness can create elongations that, like Giacometti sculptures, instill in us a new but oddly familiar mood: "in the light of the moon in my bed at midnight in the late summer in Oslo." Pushed far enough, some mysterious or at least amusing image emerges, not despite the confusion, but because of it. The moon gets in bed with you.

Other types of phrases—verb phrases, participial, gerundive, and infinitive phrases—don't have for me the strong physiological associations that prepositional phrases do. Verb phrases are really just verbs, no? Participial phrases are perpetual motion machines: the *-ing* keeps them going forever. Gerund phrases are perpetual motion machines that stopped and became frozen in noun form. Infinitive phrases are Platonic versions of verbs and their accoutrements. Also, these all lack the attractive simplicity and particularity of direction of prepositional phrases.

A phrase of an entirely different order, the dangling phrase, sometimes has a comic effect similar to that of the misplaced prepositional phrase, as in "Being in a hurry to leave Denver, the dented fender was not repaired then." Dangling phrases are reminiscent of the comic dislocations of what the Germans call *Grotesktanz,* or "eccentric dancing," and of the consciously misplaced and witty phrases of contemporary dance.

So much for the confused, misplaced, comic, or surreal phrase. What about the graceful, articulate, adroit use of phrases? What about the periodic sentence that flows from beginning to end like a big river? Is it not related to the classical ballet, its nineteenth-century counterpart?

The graceful dancer has (too) often been described as "poetry in motion." This is flattering to the dancer, at the expense of poetry, for what it overlooks is that poetry already has motion. It does, though, refer to the relation we feel between poetry and dance. The phrase in writing and the phrase in dance don't seem all that different to me. Given the somewhat grammatical structure of dance and the kinetic nature of syntax, it might be useful to see how they could strengthen and develop each other (something like the "body syntonicity" Seymour Papert discusses in his book *Mindstorms).*

Here are some exercises toward that end:

1) Have each student invent a dance phrase: a brief gesture or movement of any type, using any part(s) of the body. Then have the student write down a prepositional phrase suggested by the dance phrase. Prepositions involving directions (*behind, under, through, around,* etc.) are the most physical. E.g., a student whose dance phrase involves taking a backward step might write the corresponding "behind the bear."

2) Do the same as in 1, but reverse the order: prepositional phrases first, dance versions of them second. "Abstract" prepositions (*of, at, by, for,* etc.) are more challenging to translate into dance phrases.

3) Have three or four students perform their dance phrases at the front of the class, as their classmates "read" them from left to right and translate them into prepositional phrases that read consecutively.

4) Same as above, only reverse the order: have students read aloud a string of three or four prepositional phrases and have a corresponding three or four students at the front spontaneously translate them into dance phrases.

Rosalind Pace and Marcia Simon

Image-Making

At Poughkeepsie Day School a group of fourteen students (grades 1–12) and teachers worked all day every day for a week with pens, pencils, scissors, printers' and India inks, rollers, magnifying glasses, shells, leaves, feathers and other found objects, glue, and words. Each student and teacher designed and created an individual book of his or her own poems and visual images, as well as a large communal book. In the process, they realized that inside each of them is an endless source of rich personal imagery that can be articulated, developed, and enjoyed by others.

In 1976 the two of us developed Image-Making, a workshop in creative bookmaking based on a series of simple, carefully structured, parallel verbal and visual activities. Our goal is not only to stimulate creativity, but to make workshop participants aware of the sources of their creativity so these sources can be tapped again and again.

During our week at Poughkeepsie Day School, mornings were devoted to individual projects, and afternoons were spent working on the communal book.

On Monday morning we began with an introduction to the book as a unique format. We talked about what existed before books— Assyrian clay tablets, Egyptian wall paintings, and Hebrew scrolls, for example. By becoming aware of what a book is *not*, students become more aware of what a book *is*. We told the students that inherent in the book form is a beginning, a middle, and an end. The turning of pages creates possibilities for anticipation, memory, surprise, and resolution.

We then gave out the materials for the first visual project: one large sheet of white paper, two smaller sheets of black paper, and white glue. (We use 65 lb. Mohawk cover stock, cool white, 26" x 40"; 19" x 25" black pastel paper; and Elmer's Glue-All. The big sheet of white paper must be large enough to allow for a range of book sizes, and heavy and opaque enough so that what is glued onto it will not show through.) We told the students to fold the white paper in half three times, making books of sixteen pages (counting both sides of each page).

With the students holding their folded sheets, we told them to decide on the size and proportions of the book they would create. This choice was the first of many intuitive decisions they would make. Students then cut their books to size, being careful not to cut off the book's spine. The only rule we imposed regarding size and proportion was that the book must be rectangular. This rule eliminated books shaped like butterflies or hearts, or books with scalloped edges—designs that impose too rigid a content and elicit preconceived ideas.

By this time, students were wondering what their books were going to be about. This is what we said: "The content of your book will be one black rectangle—or less—per page. The rectangle may be cut, or torn, or both. It may be any size, any proportion, and may be placed anywhere on the page. Begin with the first page (front cover) and work consecutively through the book. Do one page at a time, one rectangle at a time." We said that the centerfold is a special place, and can be treated as one page or two. Students will often ask if they can break the rules. The answer is always yes, as long as the black shape can be recognized as a rectangle. For example, rectangles can get crumpled up and smoothed out again before being glued onto the page. Some students project rectangles over the edges of their pages, fold rectangles so they pop out when the page is turned, or cut or tear rectangles into tiny pieces and reassemble them. We never give examples of what might be done because we don't want to influence the students' impulses. The possibilities within a limited framework are endless, and that is precisely the point.

We did not say how much time students had for this project until they had been at work for about fifteen minutes. Then we said that they had about twenty minutes more. (Young children can work more quickly). A time limit does what our other rules do—it encourages quick, intuitive decision-making. We propelled the students through this activity by insisting that they did not have to know what their books were "about." "Just pay attention to what you want the rectangles to do on each page," we said. "This book is only about rectangles." We made sure that students understood that a blank page—a page without a rectangle—is not nothing, but signifies something when viewed in the context of the total book. We also told students to save all their scraps.

The parallel verbal activity, which was done on Monday morning immediately after we "read" the rectangle books as a group (more about this later), was to build poems from "word blocks" drawn at random from a common pile of words. Each student contributed to the common pile by writing ten nouns and ten verbs on small slips of white paper (about 2" x 3"). We introduced the activity by talking about words as concrete things that have not only meanings, but also resonances and implications, just as the black rectangles do. We talked very briefly about what is unique about poetic form, about what a poem is and is not. We emphasized that a poem is not necessarily a preconceived totality, but a discovery—line by line by line. We read a few poems with startling images: "Two athletes / are dancing in the cathedral / of the wind" (James Wright, from "Spring Images") or, "gritty lightning / of their touch" (Mary Oliver, from "Starfish"). We reminded students to use specific verbs (*stroll* instead of *walk*) and nouns (*trout* instead of *fish*). We told them to write down words that they like—that they like the sound of, or that have special personal associations for them. The only rule was that students must use concrete nouns and verbs. The two of us also contributed to the word pile.

The common pile was then mixed up, words face down, and each student drew out ten words, no more than two of which could be ones that he or she had contributed. These words then became the raw material for building a poem. Our instructions were: "Use as many of these words as you can; use as many other words as you need to. You may repeat words if you wish, and you may change the form of the word if you need to (*dream, dreamed, dreamer*, etc.). Write one line at a time, and don't plan ahead. Don't try to rhyme. Resist the temptation to put obvious words together (like *horse* and *gallop*). Allow for surprise."

Each morning session was about three hours long, divided roughly two-thirds and one-third between the visual and verbal activity.

*   *   *

On Tuesday morning, we began with a brief history of the alphabet, paying particular attention to how the letters *A* and *B* evolved from images of concrete things—an ox's head, a house. We showed alphabets in various languages to help students begin to see letters as visual delights. We told students that the most beautiful letters were designed to please the eye, and that efforts during the Renaissance to design letters according to mathematical formulas were not entirely successful. Then each student selected a letter from a variety of alphabet styles. (We use *The Alphabet and Elements of Lettering* by Frederic William Goudy as a source book.) Without telling the students what they would be doing with their letter, we asked them to examine it closely, using a magnifying glass and mirror, and to measure it carefully with a ruler. When they were familiar with their letter, students were told to draw it in pencil on black paper, making it at least four times larger than the original so it would be big enough to cut out. We told students to pay close attention to proportions, relationships of height to width, and the spaces in or around the letter. We assured students that this was not an activity requiring scientific precision (which is beyond young children) and that they could, in addition to measuring carefully, trust their eyes. The students drew the letters, cut them out, and glued them onto heavy white paper—half the sheet of the Mohawk cover stock mentioned earlier—of which students could use as much or as little as they wished, since the relationship between the letter and the space it occupies is another important intuitive choice. We tacked the mounted letters to the wall for viewing.

The parallel verbal activity was to make an acrostic poem, using the letters of a student's first and last names as the spine of the poem. (Students used thin black markers and ordinary white paper without lines.) "Write your name vertically down the left margin of the paper. Then, in a few seconds, write on another sheet of paper as many words as you can think of that begin with the first letter of your name. Now choose one of those words—any one. This is the first word of your poem. Write it on your first sheet of paper, using the first letter of your name as the first letter of your first word." We told students to be aware of all the white space to the right of each letter of their name, and to use as much of it as they wished—the lines of a poem do not all have to be the same length. The words of the lines can form sentences, but each line doesn't have to be a sentence; if they wished, they could write one sentence running down the whole length of the poem. We told them, "Even though this is a poem held together by your name, it doesn't have to be about yourself; you don't have to consciously think about yourself as you write the poem. Just let the letters of your name—the letters of the spine—propel you through the poem." When the poems were finished, we read them aloud, slowly and clearly, much to the delight of even the shyest students.

Before leaving school on Tuesday, we asked the students to bring in on Wednesday morning a bag of found objects—anything with a surface that could be inked and pressed to paper.

*   *   *

Students always bring in interesting things. This time they brought a wonderful variety of objects, including leaves, shells, flowers, feathers, paper clips, letters carved out of wood, thread spools, cut potatoes and carrot slices, lemon halves, lace, string, and a flyswatter. All of the found objects were placed on pieces of large white paper in a communal pile. Before introducing the day's visual activity, we presented a very brief history of the invention of printing with moveable type, and emphasized that this made commonplace and accessible what was previously considered magical and inaccessible except to monks, priests, and scribes. We pointed out that the printed word, however, can still carry with it a power beyond its literal meaning.

Students were then invited to help themselves to the found objects in the communal pile, and to an assortment of water-soluble printers' inks (black and not more than four colors), and to a variety of papers (black pastel paper, sumi or rice papers, plain white paper, etc.). We then explained that the purpose of the activity is simply to explore the printing process—to experience the magic of the printed image emerging as an object in itself, which may or may not look like the original object. Repetition of an image automatically creates rhythm and pattern. We told students not to create pictures or "finished" pieces but simply to have a good time printing, and to do at least five sheets of prints, including at least one on black paper. After they had finished, we cleaned up the rollers and inks, spread all the prints out on the floor, like a beautiful carpet, and looked at them.

Then we told the students to pick up their own prints and examine them closely, using a variety of picture mats, as well as right angles cut from mat board or heavy white paper (which can easily be moved around to form temporary "frames" for sections of the prints). We asked students to explore their prints until they found a particular section they liked. This can be a hard choice because students usually become very excited about everything they find by "framing" sections of their prints. We told them: "Don't worry about your choices. Anything you choose will work." As the students looked at their framed "pictures," we told them to let their minds go and to jot down their thoughts on a separate sheet of paper: what they see, what they are reminded of, what is happening in that space, what it might feel like to enter it.

These notes formed the basis of the repetition poem, which we then introduced. We talked briefly about repetition as an organizing principle of a poem, and we read a few examples: repetition of sound (e.g., "soundless as dots on a disc of snow"—Dickinson), repetition of word (e.g., D. H. Lawrence's "Bavarian Gentians"), repetition of phrase and syntax (e.g., Whitman), or repetition of image (e.g., Stevens's "Thirteen Ways of Looking at a Blackbird" or James Wright's "Spring Images"). Students then wrote poems, looking at their notes and their print "pictures," open to whatever else came into their heads, and using as many of these various modes of repetition as they wished. We ended Wednesday morning with a group reading.

★   ★   ★

On Thursday and Friday, students composed and assembled their final books from the mass of material that had been generated during the previous mornings' activities. We introduced this final project by talking again about the book as a format for designing in time and space, which has inherent in its structure a beginning, middle, and end, and the possibility of anticipation, memory, surprise, and resolution. Each page is both complete in itself and exists in relationship to what comes before and after. We looked at several examples of beautiful books, including Horace Rackham's *Sleeping Beauty*, Kenneth Patchen's hand-painted poem-books, and individual pages from *The Complete Graphic Works of William Blake*. We pointed out how graphic images and words relate to each other not only in terms of content, but also in the way they look. We then told students that their first task was for each of them to discover the theme of his or her own book.

With all of their work (including their collection of scraps) spread out around them, students then began this search. They spent a lot of time looking at everything, rereading their poems, fingering their scraps. Slowly, they began to notice commonalities and echoes, the threads that ran through all of their work. We told the students that what they had before them was raw material, and that nothing they had done so far should be considered either finished or inviolate. Poems could be cut apart and reassembled, copied over. Their rectangle books, enlarged letters, and prints could be cut or torn to make whatever visual image they desired. The point is that the final book is *not* a scrapbook. It is not a container for the previous days' activities. It is a new invention, made from the raw material already generated. More black paper could be cut or torn as needed, but no drawings or other material could be added. We assured the students that once they had discovered their theme, they would be amazed at how everything would become relevant to that theme. We also assured them that the titles of their books already existed somewhere in their verbal material—all they had to do was find them.

We gave them a deadline—the end of Thursday morning—for deciding on their titles, and on the size and shape of their books, and folding and cutting the blank pages, approximating the number of pages needed to present their material in sequence. Friday morning was devoted to completing the books and viewing them.

It is during the assembling of the final books that the teacher needs to provide the most encouragement and exhibit the most restraint. The teacher must believe that this process works.

*   *   *

Afternoons at Poughkeepsie Day School were spent working on a collaborative book, *Seasons and Seconds: A Book of Days* (fig. 1). In a mirror image of the mornings' activities, in which the theme of each book was discovered *after* the poems and visual materials had been produced, the afternoons' activities began with the class's agreeing on a theme for the communal book, selecting the title, and deciding how the verbal and visual material would be produced. Each participant had a special task, following the division of labor of monks in a medieval scriptorium, in which one monk did the illuminated letters, another the minuscule letters, another the animal drawings, another the portrait miniatures, and so on.

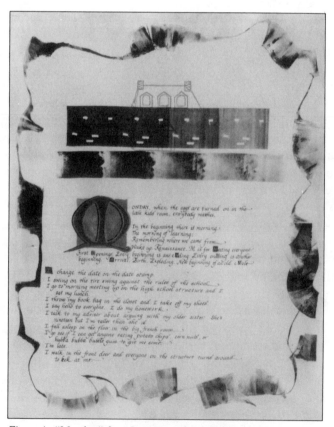

Figure 1: "Monday" from Seasons and Seconds

We had designed the afternoon activities especially for the Poughkeepsie Day School workshop. The situation at Poughkeepsie Day School was ideal for several reasons. First, the school had already demonstrated its belief in creativity by freeing teachers and students for an entire week. This helped set the tone for the workshop.

Second, the amount of time allocated was crucial. The continual involvement of the participants, without distraction, allowed time for maximum individual concentration and time for the group to look at work together. The director of the school, Richard E. Hanson, Jr., commented on the high level of concentration that he observed whenever he entered the classroom. In fact, his presence, as well as that of two newspaper reporters, was largely ignored. Some students needed quiet and solitude in order to maintain the level of concentration that their work demanded. Joan Scott had to hide out in the school's darkroom to do her calligraphy. Adrian, a first grader, was able to concentrate intensely while lying flat on his stomach on the art room floor, with everyone stepping over him as he drew a toucan, a sea monster, a yak, and other marvelous creatures in the medallions of one of the pages. "Students get a lift," Hanson noted, "from seeing someone else totally involved." It was time that made this level of concentration possible. Forty-five minutes a week, or even forty-five minutes a day for a week, would not have done it.

Third, the diversity of the participants created a wider audience for the work than the usual homogenous class, and thus provided a wider "outside world" to validate each person's work. Everyone did the same activities in the mornings, using the same materials and approximately the same amount of time. Everyone contributed something different to the communal book. Often a first grader, a sixth grader, and a teacher would be working on the same page at the same time, doing jobs of equal importance. Hanson felt that the age mix was important: "It works, and it emphasizes that one is a learner always, and that learning is a human activity."

Fourth, the participation of teachers as equals allowed for the possibility of carry-over from the workshop into regular classroom activities. Teachers can hardly be expected to foster student creativity unless they know how to foster it within themselves. Maggy Sears, the fourth grade teacher, said that it was important, as a teacher, to be in the position of the student. She was already doing many creative things in her classroom, especially with poetry, but she said, "If you experience it yourself, it makes you *sure* it's the right thing to do."

Establishing the conviction within a student that he or she *is* creative is the critical first step in nurturing creativity, just as making students realize that they *can* master a given task is at the heart of all effective teaching. In the Image-Making workshop, this belief in one's creativity emerges in two ways: when the student sees his or her own personal style or "signature" emerge in the verbal *and* the visual work, and when the student sees that the work has meaning and significance to others.

The student's signature emerges when work is produced intuitively—that is, without a preconceived idea. Therefore, the first activities are designed to circumvent the preconceived idea. In both the rectangle book and the word-block poem, students are forced to deal with the materials themselves—the papers and the words—rather than with any conscious plan.

For intuition to operate effectively so that the individual signature can emerge, the students must begin with the act of choosing: choosing the size of each rectangle, choosing where to place it on the page, quickly writing down any five nouns on the five pieces of paper. If choices are made for the sake of choice, rather than for a specific "goal," the choice will automatically be intuitive. And no intuitive choice can be a mistake, because it automatically is a reflection of the chooser.

A student's artistic signature will manifest itself in a characteristic use of space, patterning, repeated images, and quality of line or edge. It can be seen in the way the words look on the page or the relationship of the rectangles to the edges of the page. When verbal and visual activities are presented back to back, as parallel activities, and the same characteristics appear in both, the students cannot escape themselves and call what they did an accident.

The two of us teach, as it were, after the fact, as opposed to the conventional practice that begins with the goal (or the rationale) followed by examples. In the Image-Making activities, the students work *first*, so intuition can operate freely, and learn the why afterwards. We give simple instructions that allow students to work directly with the materials—e.g., use one black rectangle (or less) per page. Then, only after the work is done, do we respond to it.

Our responses are always based on finding the uniqueness in each work—not on what we think it ought to be, but on what is there. Students learn that everything counts, that every tear, wrinkle, and cut matters, whether they meant it or not.

And it is because everything has significance that we insist the students keep all their scraps—their leftover cuttings, their first drafts, everything. By the end of the week, they learn that what they ignore can be as important as what they pay attention to.

The conviction that everyone can do unique creative work began to be established on Monday morning when we "read" the rectangle books of the group. First, everyone looked at the books in silence. This allowed everyone to experience the books intuitively, or emotionally, first. Then we, as teachers, set the pattern for the language to be used to discuss the work, and quickly the group also began to develop fluency in this way of looking and articulating. Rectangles flew and fell, exploded from centerfolds, or slid off pages into space. We pointed out the sequential nature of each unfolding drama—how particular pages anticipated or recalled other pages.

Each morning, we reinforced the students' confidence in their ability to create work intuitively that not only bore their own signature, but also had meaning for the rest of the class. For example, on Tuesday morning, we observed how Scott Frisco's big letter *M* (fig. 2, center letter) was impressive in its grace, with its balance of thicks and thins, and its serifs waving gallantly. Placed in the center of a large white space, the actual center of the letter is slightly to the right, making the letter look as if it were moving across the page. The delicacy of the thins make the letter seem fragile, more brave than assured. A little later, when we were looking at Scott's poem,

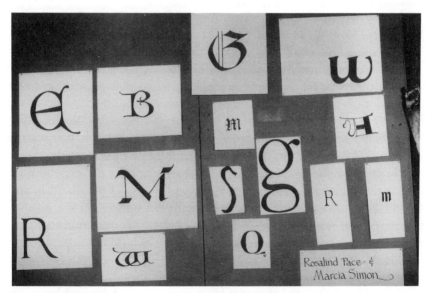

Figure 2: Initial letters

several things were immediately apparent. In his handwritten poem, his tiny writing was strung out over long lines and echoed the delicacy of his big letter *M*. His poem was surrounded by a lot of white space. And the subject of his poem—moving through space, reaching, yearning—the soft echoes of sound, and the precise and sophisticated use of enjambment and internal rhyme, echoed the shape, movement, and intricate design of his letter. *M* for motion. *M* for melody. *M* for moon:

> S o there are green, red and maybe blue, people will cry all over this
>> place.
> C ome with me. I am going to more than just the moon.
> O n this, from here, I will go, places, people, I see them all.
> T he end is near, not very far, yes, we'll go to the moon just
> T he two of us.
> F or if we don't we're sure to go to a place of
> R easons where you'll never return. We must get away
> I fear soon, we'll go away to the moon.
> S o come with me I can't go alone just us two and the
> C hrome-plated place where nomads dwell, where the
> O cean is red and the sky is green, come with me to the moon we'll
>> go to the moon.

The first and last lines of the poem repeated the colors of red and green in the same way that the top serif was repeated by the bottom serif of the letter. Turned sideways, the shape of the poem itself echoed the shape of the letter. Scott made none of these correspondences consciously—we had presented the verbal and visual exercises as distinct rather than illustrative of each other. All of these correspondences served to make Scott and the others in the group aware of the coherent, rich personal imagery that informed his work every step of the way.

When Scott saw that he wasn't the only one who was convinced—that his work also had significance for others—his belief in his creative power took root and began to grow. It is interesting to note that Scott is a high school student receiving special attention for dyslexia. In spite of his initial fear of writing and his shame about his penmanship and spelling, he revealed himself as a natural poet with a gift for musical language and startling images. His final book had more text than any of the other books in the group. It was very helpful for Scott to hear his poem read aloud, so he could hear its music. It was even better for him to experience the group's favorable response to his work because he had always believed that this kind of work was beyond him.

There are always two parts to the creative act: the artist's creation of the work, and another person's re-experiencing the work. Until this communication takes place, the creative act is incomplete. This is why it was important to allow enough time for group viewing and public response to each activity.

Because there are two of us teaching, the process of convincing students that their work has meaning to others was accelerated. The two of us created an atmosphere of a community of artists, working together without a single authority figure, sharing our visions, insights, and also our frustrations, and stimulating each other. When both of us, as individuals whom the students knew to have different personalities, responded in a similar way to a student's work, the students saw that it was the work that had elicited this response.

Nowhere was this more important than in the case of Brandon, an eighth grader and self-proclaimed anarchist, who wore the long, black gloves of the political assassin and put up considerable resistance to completing his book. When he finally took off his gloves and finished his book, he showed it to one of us. Everything he had secretly hoped would be seen *was* seen—all kinds of reverberations and transformations that expanded his theme. He could hardly believe the excitement he had generated or the praise that was heaped upon him and, though he blushed for a moment, he pretended not to care. But he insisted that the other of us look at his book immediately. When it elicited the same response from the second viewer, with the same subtleties noticed and admired, he then permitted himself to believe that he had not betrayed his defiant, anarchistic self, but had actually advanced his cause by making a coherent and meaningful book *about* anarchy—and peace. His immediate response was to seek out another student, to check the accuracy of the French he had used in his text.

Throughout the week, we were able to demonstrate, during the relatively generous amount of time allocated for the group viewing, that each student's work had a content beyond that which was expected. And thus, each student became convinced that his or her work, as well as the work of others, was successful and had distinction and meaning, vitality and character, and because the work arose from each individual's imagery and bore each person's artistic signature, was unlike any other. Thus, we accomplished our first goal as teachers, which was to provide activities that convinced the students that they could do it, that they do have within them the power to create.

Our second goal, as artists who also teach, is to be sure that the work the students do is good—that the work itself is convincing as art. A convincing work of art is a work in which the form and content are one. The exercises we use and the way in which we discuss them are all geared toward this fusion.

Therefore, how we talk about the students' work becomes an important part of our teaching. This articulation contains two elements: first, the intuitive response ("The 'A' looks like it's dancing"), which is a statement about the *content*. Students see that their work has an effect. Then we tell why their work has that effect ("because of the way it is placed at an angle and, therefore, freed from the horizontal and vertical edges of the paper, and because of the way this serif points delicately into the corner")—this becomes a statement about the *form*. This two-part articulation helps the students see the work more fully. It goes a long way toward dispelling the myth about creativity that says that it's whatever I want it to be and whatever I see in it and my guess is as good as yours, an altogether too typical response to art, poetry, or anything else that is not immediately understood.

By teaching verbal and visual art together, not as one kind of art simply illustrating the other, we further encourage the fusion of form and content. We "read" the visual material as well as look at it, and we "see" the verbal material as well as read it. If a work's form and content are only loosely related, the work will be weaker and less satisfying. When one looks only at form, one can then say, "If it rhymes, it's poetry"—no matter how trite the message. When one looks only at the content, one can then say, "It has mountains and a rainbow, therefore it must be art"—no matter how badly it is painted. Mere illustration, as in drawing a picture to illustrate a poem, can allow content to take over. Similarly, mere decoration can allow form to take over. Both can be nice to look at and fun to do, but they should not be confused with deeper creative activity, which expresses the voice and vision of a unique individual.

If a student understands the relationship between form and content, even intuitively, then that student can allow the materials to have their own life. Being able to do this comes from the belief in oneself: "I will play with these things. Something exciting is bound to happen." As teachers, of course, we never tell the students that they are going to do exciting work, that it will be a lot of fun, and that they will learn important things about themselves—nothing would be more intimidating. Instead, we focus their attention simply on the task at hand, and the possibilities that they must consider in order to do it. The excitement comes afterwards, when we help them to see what they have done. When students begin, on their own, to see possibilities in the material that they had not seen before, they cross the line from being doers to becoming makers.

Perhaps one of the most dramatic examples of this is when someone dares to cut up the big letter (from Tuesday morning) for use in his or her final book. When Joan decided to put her carefully copied, meticulously cut fourteenth-century Lombardic *E* in the paper cutter (fig. 2, upper left), everyone gathered around to watch. Joan had become convinced that her book needed a certain shape, which cutting the letter would produce. She sliced it with understanding and enjoyment, sacrificing a beautiful form in order to create other forms that the content of her book (*Shadows from the Moon*, fig. 3) demanded. With

Figure 3: A page from Joan Scott's book

less fanfare, but with the same understanding, six-year-old Adrian incorporated the form of his *S* into his final book as startling new content: an elephant's trunk twisting right off the page (fig. 4).

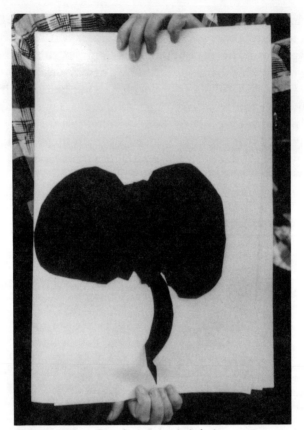

Figure 4: Adrian Brougher's S-trunked elephant

A further stage is reached when the maker is able to use new material to discover even more new material. This stage can incorporate the use of "accident" as a means of discovery. Heather's experience demonstrates this second stage. She had finished her book, except for the title. The book had coherence and theme, but she kept saying, "I know what my book is about, but I can't find the words to say it." We insisted that she come up with a title, and kept asking her questions until she did. It is important to note that we never gave her suggestions, we only asked her questions, so that both the insight and the language to express it came from her. It was simply a matter of getting her to say out loud what had been floating around in her head as feeling. "It's about wishing," she said. She then looked at her cover with the big *B* in the middle. "What is the *B* for?" we asked. "Beginning." "Then what is the title of your book?" "*Wishing and Beginning*." But she was not satisfied. Then, because she had not abandoned her pursuit, the title came to her in a flash: "*In the Beginning, I Wish*." She was thrilled. So were we.

Heather then decided to cut out the large letters of her title. She asked if she could make the small letters with ink and white-out instead, since it would be too hard to cut them. We said yes. However, after she had cut and pasted the big letters, it was her own decision to cut out the small letters as well. She spent intense, agonizing minutes cutting out very small letters with a large pair of scissors. After she discovered that scissors produced the right shape, rather than a brush or pen, she made a further discovery. Notice how the *I* in "Beginning" (fig. 5, right) is half black and half white. This was not planned; it came to Heather when the *I* landed on the edge of the black border as she glued down the cut-out black letters, one by one. It was the invention of the *I* made of positive and negative, black and white, one half the reverse of the other, that led Heather to the concept of the back cover (fig. 5, left). Here, the negative space of the *B* is used in the center and becomes a new, positive space, and the reverse of the title becomes the conclusion. Heather discovered how these pages could be designed; we see how "Beginning" is born out of the belly of the *B* like an invitation to turn the page into the future. We see how, in the end, there is no end but rather a seed that has taken root and is growing. Heather was fully in control of her materials to the extent that she had allowed herself to be led by them. She worked with utter intensity for about an hour and a half. She had become a maker.

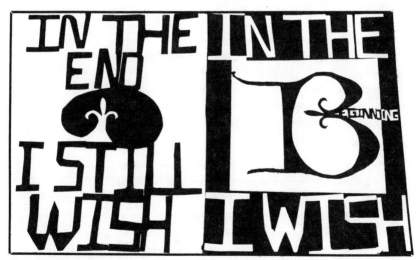

Figure 5: Heather Borachuk's book covers, front (right) and back (left)

Similarly, when Joan came to the last page of her book, she related the following experience. "I had it all planned, but when I turned the page, the pieces of black paper fell onto the facing page, ruining my plan. But I saw immediately that the new position was right, more right than I ever could have planned. This realization was the most important thing that happened to me. It was the realization that I had the freedom to take risks." She, too, had become a maker.

The group developed the phrase "doing a Matisse" to acknowledge the incorporation of a mistake or accident into the work. We had looked at Matisse's book *Jazz*, in which he makes "mistakes" in his hand-written text and crosses them out. These cross-outs are like improvisation in jazz. Tenth grader Scott Frisco was upset when the letters of his first poem bled through the paper onto his cover, but he quickly saw how the new blots could add to the visual design of the cover. He, too, had become a maker.

What we look for in our students' work is evidence that a discovery has been made, that they have gone beyond the expected and the previously known, and that both their language and their vision have taken them to a new place. We facilitate this by insisting that they stick as closely as possible to both the materials and the task at hand. If the focus is narrowed, the vision expands. The more precisely we look at a big letter, the more we see. The more we look at fewer words, the more resonance those words have, as in Brian's poem:

I can smell the rain, I can
feel the rain, it comes down
one by one.

The slant rhymes of *can/rain/down/one* are happy poetic moments, but the real discovery takes place in the last line when we are suddenly thrown into a new awareness of rain by the way in which the repetition of the language itself becomes rain. In Caroline's acrostic poem, discovery occurs when unexpected words are linked together, as in these lines:

I magination that curls like a ribbon woven into a
N est of hidden secrets, around a newly hatched
E gg.

Occasionally, the materials will declare themselves to such a degree that a strong self-revelation takes place. The force of the fusion between the form and content of the materials produces a stunning emotional response in the reader as well as the maker.

Of all the group, Maggy, the fourth grade teacher, was probably the most affected by the discoveries she made in her final book, and the one most deeply aware of what she had achieved by allowing her materials such a strong voice. Maggy's rectangle book had as its centerfold a black rectangle that unfolded by itself to become a three-dimensional black box. Some people reacted to this as a comic image; others found it frightening. Her word-block poem had as its central image a basket full of eggs. As the week progressed, Maggy's work continued to present contradictory, unrelated images, both verbal and visual. She wrote a terrifying poem, with images of rattling bones and a witch doctor, about the recent death of a friend. When it was time to put together the final book, Maggy came to class intending to make the book a memorial to her dead friend. She even brought a photograph of the friend to include in the book. However, through our persistent efforts to have Maggy try to include all of her materials in the final book, not just the material that obviously related to the death, she was able to make an enormous leap into unknown territory. Once she saw that her black box, which opened by itself, was both basket *and* casket, and that her eggs were not only symbols of shame for her public display of grief (she used the phrase "egg on the face") but also stood as symbols of rebirth, she was able to relate the previously unrelated and, ultimately, to reconcile herself to the previously unreconcilable. As she commented to us later, "I was finally able to accept what had happened." It wasn't that she had blotted out her rage and despair, but that she had incorporated them into a wider, healing vision.

All of this was accomplished through an intense involvement with each of the poems and the visual materials that Maggy had produced during the week. For the centerfold of her final book, she made a second black box that opened by itself (fig. 6). In this basket/casket she arranged carrot looked like rosary beads. Other common objects, printed, evoked images of relics and the bones of saints. This was all material we had seen before, but here it was used in a new way. However, it was on the next page that the great leap took place. By playing with the negative of her big black *R*, Maggy suddenly created an explosive, light-filled page. Using darkness, she created light. This transformation had the power of an epiphany. On this light-filled page, the white half-*R* shape points toward the resolution of forms and images on the final page. There the objects inside the centerfold casket reappear, arranged in rhythmic patterns of organic forms. This last page has at its top a black circle that partially extends beyond the upper edge of the page and is visible even when the book is closed. This ominous black

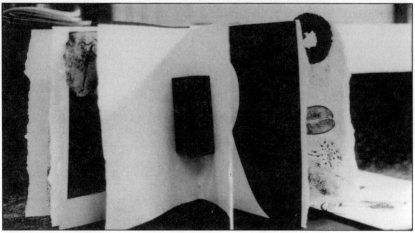

Figure 6: Maggy Sears's book

circle, which now for the first time is seen to contain a radiant inner circle of white, seems to be rising off the page, out of the book itself, transformed into an image of resurrection. Maggy saw that she did not need to include the photo of her friend. The book itself is not only a memorial to the friend, but also a testament to Maggy's own struggle toward faith, which repeats itself every time the book is opened.

Maggy told us that in college she had been intimidated when required to write. "Reveal myself? Impossible. But in this class, because we were given a structure to work within—specific tasks and clear rules—I had something to hold onto. I could work without thinking about whether I was revealing myself or not. The anxiety was gone." And because the fusion of form and content was so complete, Maggy's book was intensely moving as a work of art both to its maker and to its wider audience.

★   ★   ★

When all of the books were finished, we took them to an empty room that had carpeted risers built into the floor, where we displayed them on large pieces of black or white paper. For about half an hour, the fourteen members of what we should now call the Poughkeepsie Scriptorium read each other's books. There was absolute silence. Often the most comfortable way to look at the books was to kneel before them on the bottom riser. It was an appropriate posture for the atmosphere in the room—the awe, the rapt attention, the amazement. We didn't give any directions for looking at the books; it just happened.

When everyone had read all the books, we sat in a circle and discussed them briefly, this time with specific references not only to the works themselves, but also to the works of well-known artists and writers whose themes, structures, forms, and genres were related to our handmade books. We had made our own journeys into the unknown—the jungles, the forests, outer space. We had our own three-part night/sea journey book, and our own political manifesto. Each of these handmade books was unique because each had grown from intuitively produced material. Their makers, whether first graders or experienced teachers, had entered into the community of artists, having created rich and complex work from their materials.

★   ★   ★

The value of nurturing creativity in a school setting is enormous. Attitudes toward self, toward school, toward work, and toward others often take a great leap forward. At the start of the workshop, Beth, an extremely shy sixth grader, clung to one of the other students. Later, her teacher told us that during the week of the workshop she walked in the door every morning and lit up. "She was thrilled each day because she was doing something that was hers." During the afternoons, when we were working on the communal book, she contributed more than anyone else to the group acrostic poem. She stood up while most of the others remained seated, and moved closer and closer to us. Her enthusiasm and her imaginative, often funny contributions inspired the rest of the group.

In the afternoon work on *Seasons and Seconds*, each individual functioned as part of a community of artists working toward a common goal. From their experiences each morning, the students brought with them a sense of themselves as artists.

Our assignment on Monday afternoon was for the class to make a contemporary Book of Hours based on some theme as common to them as Christian prayer was to the makers of the original Books of Hours. The common theme they decided upon was life at Poughkeepsie Day School. The form they decided upon was to have one page for an introductory acrostic poem, followed by one page for each day of the school week. We discussed various measurements of time—years, hours, seconds, seasons, and so on. Because the students had looked, that morning, at rectangles as more than just rectangles, as shapes that imply an emotional and dramatic content, they were immediately able to look at Monday as more than just Monday. The first page grew to encompass many kinds of beginnings—September, primary grades, the founding of the school, the individual's first moments in the morning. The students were quick to grasp the relationship between the page as a complex space and the sequence of pages as a metaphor for time. Every detail in the final book participates in this overall metaphoric structure. The book's wide margins signify the psychological wide margins enjoyed by the students at Poughkeepsie Day School. Even the progression of illuminated letters has significance: the Monday letter is medieval in style, while the Friday letter looks like airbrushed graffiti (fig. 1).

We were surprised and gratified to see everyone, including the youngest students, use the Book of Hours we had looked at in the morning as a reference for the communal book project. The students checked to see how illuminated letters were done, what kinds of animals were drawn, what range of colors was used. They looked not because they were told to (we didn't tell them), but because they were curious. One of the advantages of working with the book form is that books tend to have a beginning, a middle, and an end, creating feelings of anticipation, surprise, memory, and resolution. Just by turning a page, one is inescapably caught up in a particular structuring of time and space. In this sense—because our lives are the stories we construct from the time and space we inhabit—the book form automatically becomes a metaphor for life.

At the end of the workshop, director Hanson made this comment: "The book," he said, "is the least important part. The workshop could be done with science activities or in social studies. It is a workshop in creative thinking."

The purpose of teaching creativity in the schools is not to train book designers or poets, or even to improve reading scores (although these may happen), but to develop people who can think creatively, find solutions to problems, and go beyond the boundaries of the expected, people who trust their instincts, who dare to make connections between seemingly unconnected things, and who see the infinite data of the world as raw material that increases rather than decreases the more it is used. The purpose is to develop people who can act as purposefully as Joan slicing her big letter; as tenaciously as Heather cutting her little letters; as energetically as Adrian inventing a plastic lizard to tape to the back of his book; as intuitively as Scott, dancing his ink roller around the border of the Monday page; and as hopefully as Maggy, daring to confront the darkest questions. The purpose of teaching creativity is to influence the students' attitude toward learning. They learn that they matter, that what they look at matters, that other people matter, that everything matters. In the structure of true education, in schools such as Poughkeepsie Day School, creativity is the foundation, and not the ornament.

Bibliography

Blake, William. Any facsimile edition of a book he himself designed.

Evans, C. S. *Sleeping Beauty*. Illustrated by Arthur Rackham. New York: Dover Publications, Inc., 1971.

Goudy, Frederic William. *The Alphabet and Elements of Lettering*. New York: Dover Publications, Inc., 1963.

Hunt, Walter Bernard and Ed C. Hunt. *101 Alphabets*. Milwaukee: Bruce Publishers, 1968.

Jean, Georges. *Writing: The Story of Alphabets and Scripts*. New York: Harry N. Abrams, 1992.

Levarie, Norma. *The Art and History of Books*. New York: James H. Heinemann, Inc., 1968.

Matisse, Henri. *Jazz*. Munich: R. Piper & Co. Verlag, n.d. Printed for members of the Museum of Modern Art, New York.

Narkiss, Bezalel. *Hebrew Illuminated Manuscripts*. Jerusalem: Encyclopedia Judaica, The Macmillan Company, 1969.

Sullivan, Sir Edward. *The Book of Kells*. New York: Crescent Books, 1986.

Bernadette Mayer

Science Writing Experiments

The following writing exercises are designed to blur the boundary between imaginative writing and science, to bring out the intuitive, associative side of the mind, and to develop a sense of play and pleasure in writing.—Editor

Experiments with Dailiness

Have students write on subjects such as the science of cooking (both at home and in the laboratory); how guns work; what ballpoints are; how jets go; what languages are; how color TV works; how a flash bulb works; why a ship floats; what glass is; how gas and water meters work; how an automatic transmission works; what a quartz clock is; what the difference is between a compression refrigerator and an absorption refrigerator; what plexiglass, enamel, rubber, and porcelain are; why and how toilets and door locks work and don't work; and what a differential gear is. Good references for such subjects are *The Way Things Work* (no author credited) and *Extraordinary Origins of Everyday Things* by Charles Panati.

Everyone can present subjects in the form of questions, answers or suggestions, then research and write about them in the form of essays or poems that are both ruminative and factual.

Experiments with Sound

Echo was a nymph in Greek mythology. Because of her unrequited love for Narcissus, who had fallen in love with his own image, Echo pined away until only her voice remained. Another version of the myth says that Hera, Zeus's wife, deprived Echo of her power of speech unless Echo was spoken to first, and then Echo was compelled to reply with the same last word that had been spoken. Hera did this because Echo was trying to distract her, by incessant talking, from Zeus's dalliances with the other nymphs.

Echoes, sonar, and radar are forms of reflection and repetition, ranging from bats to whales to poetry to mountain yodeling. *Echo ranging* is the generic term for obtaining data about distant objects by the transmission of energy and the reception of its reflection.

Excellent and mysterious poems have been made by humans (and maybe whales and dolphins!) using echoes. Here are some examples by humans:

> If I address the Echo yonder
> What will its answer be I wonder?
> (Echo) I wonder.
>
> O, wondrous Echo, tell me, bless,
> Am I for marriage or celibacy?
> Silly Bessy.
>
> If then to win a maid I try,
> Shall I find her a property?
> A proper tie.
>
> If neither being grave nor funny
> Will win the maid to matrimony?
> Try money.
>
> If I should try to gain her heart,
> Shall I go plain, or rather smart?
> Smart.
>
> She mayn't love dress, and I, again, then
> May come too smart, and she'll complain then?
> Come plain then.

> —*Excerpt from anonymous seventeenth-century poem*

★   ★   ★

From "An Echo"

Ah, will no soul give eare unto my mone? one.
Who answers thus so kindly when I crie? I.
What fostered thee mat pities my despair? aire.
Thou babbling guest, what know'st thou of my fall? all.
What did I when I first my faire disclos'd. los'd.
Where was my reason, that it would not doubt? out.
What can'st thou tell me of my ladies will? ill.

> —*Lord Sterling (1604)*

★   ★   ★

Heaven

O who will show me those delights on high?
> *Echo.*   I.

Thou Echo, thou art mortall, all men know.
> *Echo.*   No.

Wert thou not born among the trees and leaves?
> *Echo.*   Leaves.

And are there any leaves, that still abide?
> *Echo.*   Bide.

What leaves are they? impart the matter wholly.
> *Echo.*   Holy.

Are holy leaves the Echo then of blisse?
> *Echo.*   Yes.

Then tell me, what is that supreme delight?
> *Echo.*   Light.

Light to the minde: what shall the will enjoy?
> *Echo.*   Joy.

But are there cares and businesse with the pleasure?
> *Echo.*   Leisure.

Light, joy, and leisure; but shall they persever?
> *Echo.*   Ever.

—*George Herbert (1593–1633)*

Here's a contemporary and deliriously whimsical example:

From "The Echo"

Violets! No flower can compare
> Pair

With your frail beauty
> Yooty

As I bend down to sniff you
> If you

I must declare
> Air

That such frail power
> Hour

Resides in your frail beauty
> Ooty

That like a frail bunny
> Unny

I must beware
> Where

Lest by some chance

                    Ants
I too beguiled
            I'ld
Should rest, should stay
            A
Here by your fragrant bosom
                    Uzzim.

 —Kenneth Koch

Some classroom experiments could include:
• Write an echo poem from the point of view of any combination of the following: an average person, a nymph deprived of all but echoic speech, an alien, a scientist, a whale, etc.
• Write a brief essay on what sound is and how it returns to us. Also, write about noise.
• Write about the noises you hear right now.
• Listen to them and imitate them vocally and on paper. (Echo them.)
• In an essay, attempt to communicate with other species.
• Visit an aquarium (or buy a record) and listen to eels, whales, and dolphins. Translate their speech. What time is it for them? Do they know you? Who is visiting whom? Can whales' language be heard by us more clearly than ours by them? Do we interpret emotionally or scientifically? (P.S. Let's make ourselves the subjects of ranging. Let's let the experts—the other mammals who can speak—study us.)

Permutations in Writing

What we hear is often random, and in terms of astrophysics the universe is quite unpredictable, even chaotic.

Have everyone reorganize or reorder science or mathematics material at random, as an attempt at the total transformation or complete (chance) rearrangement of any given, based on the idea of interchanging. This is an experiment in discovering whether permutations create new ideas. If 1, 2, and 3 taken two at a time can be 12, 21, 13, 31, 23 and 32 (six combinations), then words, lines, phrases, and sentences put together in random combinations might do something different too.

In music, John Cage and other composers have made use of random methods that include computers; the throwing of dice; the methods of the ancient Chinese text, the *I Ching*; incorporating everyday sounds in composition; and chance techniques to determine, on stage, in what order and way a work is to be performed. Painters such as

Jackson Pollock also used randomness by splattering canvases with accidental dots, splashes, and patterns of color reminiscent of the visual data of electronics and of astronomy. The poet Jackson MacLow incorporates chance into both the reading and writing of his poetry, through the random introduction of words and phrases from outside sources, as well as different reading methods, rendering the work different every time it is seen or heard. Of course, at the moment of the creation of a such a work, its new meaning may not be apparent.

Writing techniques that can be used in the classroom include: making the last sentence be the first, the penultimate the second, etc.; numbering a poem or essay's sections from 1 to 6 (or 12) and throwing the die (or dice) to determine a new order; combining the first word and the last words of each typed or written line to discover what new combinations of thoughts eventuate; cutting pages in quarters and replacing one quadrant with another; finding clues from numbers that appear at random, such as the temperature; taking all the words and phrases that "stand out" in a given piece of writing and making a list of them to discover why they seem important; repeating things that "stand out"; combining two or more people's writings on the same subject by interspersing paragraphs, phrases, or ideas; reading a text backwards; and inventing new chance methods of one's own.

When dealing with the operations of chance, simple methods create results as magical as more complex ones. And what about 11, 22, and 33? Repetition can be explored mathematically and verbally.

Here is an excerpt from a verbal example of repetition called "If I Told Him, a Completed Portrait of Picasso," by Gertrude Stein:

> If I told him would he like it. Would he like
>   it if I told him.
> Would he like it would Napoleon would
> Napoleon would that he like it.
>   If Napoleon if I told him if I
> told him if Napoleon. Would he like if
> I told him if I told him if Napoleon.
> Would he like it Napoleon if Napoleon
> if I told him. If I told him if Napoleon
> if Napoleon if I told him. If I told
> him would he like it would he like
> it if I told him . . .
>
> Presently.
> Exactly do they do.
> First exactly.

Exactly do they do too.
First exactly.
And first exactly.
Exactly do they do.
And first exactly and exactly.
And do they do.
At first exactly and first exactly
      and do they do.
The first exactly.
And do they do.
The first exactly.
At first exactly.
First as exactly.
At first as exactly.
Presently.
As presently.
As as presently.
He he he he and he and he and
and he and he and he and and as and
as he and as he and he. He is and as
he is, and as he is and he is, he
is and as he and he and as he is
and he and he and and he and
he.

Repetition automatically jogs us into thinking of words and ideas in new ways.

A History of One's Own Ideas

When Albert Einstein was asked to write his autobiography, he wrote little about his personal life and mainly about the history of the development of the ideas that led to the general and special theories of relativity and to his other conceptions in physics. Students and teachers can set aside a day or a week or a year for students to write a history of the development of the scientific ideas that have influenced them most, how and why, and what might happen in the future. Such histories or autobiographies of ideas most often will be written in the form of discursive prose, which may be interspersed with diagrams, equations, illustrations, and other visual data. Occasionally a history of an individual's ideas has been written in poetic form, for example Wordsworth's *The Prelude* and R. Buckminster Fuller's *How Little I Know*, two long poems. The work need not be long, however. When Einstein wrote his history, he spoke abstractly about the concepts of thinking and wonder, and about the feelings of awe experienced in childhood. In writing such a history, it's vital to recognize that the ways we think, learn to think, reach conclusions, and create questions are as much the stuff for analysis as what we know (and what we do not know). A good way to begin this project is to discuss childhood memories, especially those that relate to wonder and awe.

Mutual Aid

This involves writing and thinking about the evolutionary concept of the sociability, mutual protection, and shared struggle for existence of ants, bees, birds, and humans in tribes and in cities. It's fun to begin this experiment by bringing an ant colony to class and then asking "Why do we live in cities?" The writing exercise can be based on direct observation or on memories of mutual aid among human beings. Here is an example:

> Organisms help each other so that they may survive and evolve faster. Yesterday I had to babysit in Manhattan. I had to take care of two kids, one is four years old, the other twice her age. I had a problem getting them to go to sleep because they both refused to go to bed on time. Both of them fell asleep at about ten thirty and I went to bed an hour after that.

This is a good experiment to use after discussing Darwin, since, in high school today, the concept of mutual aid creates a spirited set of disagreements about human nature, akin to those the theory of evolution create about the relationship between religious and scientific belief.

Peripatetic Scientists

The word *peripatetic* comes from the Greek *peripatein,* "to walk around," and from the Indo-European base *pent,* "to step" or "to go" (related to *find* and *bridge*). It refers to the followers of Aristotle, called "peripatetics," who walked about in the Lyceum while he was teaching. Have students take a walk together, talking, observing, and making notes about everything. The scope of discussion can be limited to the sizes of things, the colors of things, types of trees, questions concerning the construction of cities, kinds of materials and stone observed, the weather, and so on. Written records can be gathered and compared in the classroom. The ambience of this experiment can be either intently serious or lighthearted and hilarious: it seems to work either way. Stress the importance of detailed observation.

Science Acrostics

The acrostic is a poem in which the first letters of each line, read downwards, form a word, phrase, or sentence. The subject of each poem can relate to this vertical "spine-word," or not. In the first three acrostics below, the vertical word is "science":

Science seems to
Come into every
Introduction to
Every last
Notion at the Manhattan
Center of
Entropy

Science places
Calm clams
In
Every ocean
Nothing is
Critical but
E=MC²

Science is
Corrupt yet maybe
It is not.
Everything
New
Contains
Everything

    —Anonymous

Here are some examples for "atoms," "math," "philosophy," "absolute value," and "factorization."

All
Tiny
Objects
Make
Sense

    —Rodney Pink, high school

★　　　★　　　★

Maybe the most
Astonishing subject,
Terrorizes and
Hard.

　　　—*Yesenia Ramos, high school*

★　　　★　　　★

People
Have
Incredible
Love
Of
Space
Other
People
Have
Yaks

　　　—*Eurik Perez, high school*

★　　　★　　　★

Absolutely un
Believable the way
Some people understand the value
Of math just
Like adding of integers it's really
Unbelievable
The way you know what you're saying
Even if you don't

Valuable math
And
Like addition of integers
Understanding a person's language
Even in English

　　　—*James E. Rivera, high school*

★　　　★　　　★

Fast
And
Complicated
The
Others say
Really not hard but not easy either
I think the way they think
Zooming around around
And
Thinking
It
Over and over again
Nagging about the things they know

> —*James Rivera, high school*

Acrostics can also have the vertical word at the end of the line or in the middle. This is an especially useful form for developing verbal inventiveness. In science classes, it is marvelous to see metaphor lead to new ideas and speculation about scientific subjects through the use of the acrostic.

The Use of Etymologies

In class, make frequent use of the origins of science words such as "atom," "decimal," and "epiphysis." Students and teachers should rapidly get out their dictionaries to find the unique clues to understanding that etymologies often provide.

Here are some examples:

• muscle: from the Latin *musculus*, meaning "little mouse."

• science: from the Latin *scire*, "to know, to cut; to divide, to separate" (related to "skill" from the Swedish *skäl*, meaning "reason," and the Icelandic *skilja*, meaning "it differs"; also related to "sex" from the Latin *secare*, "to cut or separate"); also from the Indo-European root *skei*, related to "scissors."

• mathematics: related to the Greek *manthanein* ("to learn, to be alert"), the Indo-European *meudh* ("to pay attention"), the Persian *mazda* ("memory"), and the German *munter* ("cheerful").

No wonder mathematicians have such good memories, while being cheerful, alert, and attentive. No wonder scientists are always dividing things with their reasoning scissors!

• technology: from the Greek *technologia*, "a systematic treatment," which in turn derives from *techne*, "art or artifice" (from Indo-European *tekth*, "to weave, build, join," whence the Greek *tekton*, "carpenter") and *logos*, meaning "word or science."

An "engineer" (a producer) means much the same as "poet" (a maker), but etymologically speaking, the engineer has the better of it, being derived from the Latin *ingenium*, related to "genius."

Basic etymologies can be found in most editions of *Webster's Collegiate Dictionary*, in Eric Partridge's *Origins*, in *Skeat's Etymological Dictionary*, and many other etymological dictionaries.

Epistemology

Epistemology comes from the Greek words *episteme*, meaning "knowledge," and *logos*, meaning "word or science." Though it seems for-midable to experiment with the origins, nature, method, and limits of knowledge, this becomes the simplest of writing exercises, and works equally well for people of all ages.

Invite students to write a series of ten questions on any or all subjects, and then to write a second series of ten questions about the subject of the class. Then, in a third exercise, have them write about how to find the answers. For instance, What book or library would contain the information I need? If I don't know, whom could I ask? Where is the nearest bird sanctuary? What means of transportation do I use to get there? Can I call the public library or the natural history museum to find the answers to my questions? Can I call a professor at a college or university? Can I call someone who works in a private business? Can I call or write the author of an article or book to get answers? Or even, How do I obtain the money to buy an expensive book I need? Finding answers often leads to further questions.

Though the questions need not be answered, a further experiment could be to exchange questions and attempt to answer each other's, then to return them to the questioner for comment.

If there's time, a good summary writing could involve the idea of the questions themselves: How do we know what we know? Can we know everything? Do we know everything just by the fact of existing? Is it important to know the names of all things—rocks, minerals, fish, birds, mammals, stars, flowers, elements, trees, etc.?

A brief example comes from a ninth grade student:

I know everything I know
Such as
Education
My religion
The danger around us.

—*Herman Zarate*

Complexity of Thought

Here's an attempt to create writing that reflects—yet does not speak "about"—the complex nature of thought. Invite everyone to write about the most complex scientific or personal topic they know of, one they feel cannot be understood. Give a variety of possible forms for writing: freewriting; discursive writing; poetic forms; using a visual image, as if one were drawing a dream; using a design of words on a page singly or in phrases or sentences that seem best to reflect thought. Encourage both the visual and verbal creation of transitions between aspects of a thing or things, an idea or ideas. Subjects for this experiment have included death, disorder, advanced algebra, nucleic acid, cute guys, philosophy, calculus, the news, and white dwarfs. Here are two examples:

> The square root of 2 to the decimal comma by $E=MC^2$ to the supposed interest of man to space if a dehydration to the skin and to mind biology and biochemistry hhhhhhhh/do not mix with each other has me to the waterplow to a toilet bowl to a field of gumdrops up and down all around jump hop skip don't matter where you land fall up throw down dog meow and a cat barks he can they do because of me to he of me you see. The dreams of an unknown turtle to me to be again you see if we dream of monsters, creatures and things that'll go bump in the night a mouse dreams about a cat a cat dreams about a dog what does a dog dream about it's come to Christmas time for humbug and time for taking do you think I'm going to jump low, walk low, that's the way to do it. Pretend in a dream just jump into someone's hair and be in a forest.
>
> —*Eurik Perez*

> Dis ain't da way I should rite
> I should bee more intelligent
> Maybe I Should learn more to make da world better
> Or should I stay da same and cauze more
> DisoRder
> I Did not mean to hurt u, i didn't know
> Excuse me if i cry.
> Remember mee cauze i'm not
> important but two me I'm
> quite brite.
>
> —*Hank Bueno*

An Attitude of Silence to the Stars

This poem by Walt Whitman expresses the simultaneous doubt and wonder of the student (and teacher) of any science:

When I Heard the Learn'd Astronomer

When I heard the learn'd astronomer,
When the proofs, the figures, were ranged in columns before me,
When I was shown the charts and diagrams, to add, divide, and
    measure them,
When I sitting heard the astronomer where he lectured with much
    applause in the lecture-room,
How soon unaccountable I became tired and sick,
Till rising and gliding out I wander'd off by myself,
In the mystical moist night-air, and from time to time,
Look'd up in perfect silence at the stars.

Study the poem, thinking of the beauty of natural events and of the gorgeousness of scientific ideas, then imitate the poem by writing a piece that begins, as the poem does, with four "when's," followed by "how . . ." and "till. . . ."

When preparing to write, think of the idea of silence in combination with studying and teaching and writing. Think of why we choose to express some things and not others. How much do we know? What have we seen?

Should we then not investigate, put things into words or formulae? Is science dull and unrelated to the stars, the clouds, the weather, the fruits and vegetables we eat, to sex and love, to evolution, to the complex matters of death and wealth, to the daily matters of where our water and electricity come from?

The piece could end with a sentence about silence—how it can be "perfect."

Robert Hershon

Lawrence Stazer

The Use and Pleasure of the Hoax

There have been many poets whose writing lives were brilliant, but brief—Chatterton, Marlowe, Keats, Shelley, Rimbaud, Burns, Stazer.

Lawrence Stazer's public career was the shortest of them all. It lasted about an hour. Here's why.

A few years ago, I was teaching two high school courses for Saint Ann's, a private school in Brooklyn. One course was a poetry workshop, an elective in which the students presumably had a particular interest in poetry. The other was a senior English class, mainly concerned with contemporary European novels. I don't think most of the students in this class actually hated poetry, but they weren't crazy about it either. Their occasional attempts to write it were, at best, reluctant; they did not pour forth.

For the past few years the school had provided a generous budget for poetry readings and the students had become a discerning and enthusiastic audience. Among the many poets who had read at the high school was Bill Zavatsky. He had read his memorable Roy Rogers poems, written in homage to the Cowboy King by a fictitious young Japanese and painfully transcribed from short-wave radio broadcasts by their translator. The poems had provoked a certain amount of discussion. This, in turn, had led me to introduce a similar work, correspondence between "Dr. Thalo Green," Director of the Design Conceptualization Institute of Brooklyn, and a group of Harley Elliott's poetry students from Kansas Wesleyan College. The letters were detailed responses by Dr. Green to student assignments which had been carefully destroyed before he could read them.

The week after Zavatsky's reading, during those odd moments of time usually reserved for baseball talk or the teacher's life story, we talked about Piltdown Man and the Cardiff Giant, the epic poems of Ossian and the one-word poems of Joyce Holland. My poetry class was momentarily diverted but eager to get on to more serious matters. The English class, though, accepted the invitation: a student named

Danny Rosenblatt said, "Let's invent a poet." The other eleven students in the class agreed. I think some of them thought it would be fun and the others saw it as some sort of revenge for having had to sit through all those damned poetry readings.

We named him Lawrence Stazer. Stazer is an anagram for *ersatz*. We invented quite a detailed biography for him. He was young, which was why he wasn't terribly well known. He hadn't yet published a book, which was why one couldn't be found in a store, but a manuscript had recently been accepted by a Very Big Publisher, which was why he deserved everyone's attention. All we needed was his life's work.

Stazer's poems were written in a number of ways, some in class, some at home. There were group poems and game poems, tender poems, angry poems, poems that had to contain the words *ashtray*, *Portugal*, and *savings bank*, short poems, long poems, poems that parodied other poems, poems that stole from other poems, poems designed to be opaque, poems written at blinding speed. In short, any kind of poem we could think of.

It was spring. The weather had grown sweet and tempting. It was the time of year when high school seniors, many of whom already have enough credits to graduate anyway, start becoming restless and then invisible. I had thought that Stazer would at least keep them indoors, but then something even nicer began to happen. As the persona of Stazer grew bigger and more solid, the kids were more and more comfortable hiding behind him. Students who wouldn't write a poem of any sort a few months before were now writing, as Stazer, with ease and delight. They were saying things they would never venture in their own voices and, with a sense that none of this counted as "real" writing anyway, they were saying them in a wonderfully relaxed, what-the-hell style. They were also reading more poetry and talking about it more.

The students had discovered what many poets had discovered before them, that it's sometimes easier to discuss painful or revealing feelings if you're using someone else's voice. A class could develop a persona—or maybe two or three—and simply use that voice or voices to write various kinds of work. A good school library should be able to produce some models. A few that come to mind include John Berryman's Henry poems and Robert Peters's *The Gift to Be Simple*—an entire book written in the voice of Ann Lee, founder of the Shakers—which prompts me to note that the adopted personality could certainly be that of a real figure, celebrated or not. Writing in another voice isn't exactly synonymous with perpetrating a hoax, but I found that the hoax added a further element that helped sustain the students' interest over the months; it may be revealing that the class that stayed with the Stazer hoax was not the class that started out with much interest in poems.

★   ★   ★

Stazer's first name, Lawrence, was the result of a promise I had made to the class: if Stazer's work was good enough, I'd see to it that he got the chance to give a full-scale reading. I even had an impersonator in mind. Poet Larry Zirlin had all the necessary qualities: he was young, he was unknown at Saint Ann's, he could think fast on his feet, and he always looked sort of bad-tempered.

The head of the English department wasn't wild about scheduling yet another reading—even some of the English teachers may have been getting poem-weary—but he agreed to it. A couple of weeks later, about 150 high school students and the English faculty gathered in the Harcourt Room. I gave Stazer a fulsome introduction. Larry cleared his throat several times and began to read the poems, with conviction and intensity. The audience was polite. As the reading went on, they stayed polite, if a bit confused. Occasionally, a lone, unsure laugh would start up but, in the face of Larry's total gravity, it would soon trail away into nothingness. Afterward, there were questions about when he started writing and who his major influences were. He didn't miss a cliché.

Stazer had a two-month gestation period and a one-hour life. During all that time and for weeks afterward, I don't believe that a single person who was in on the creation revealed the secret to an outsider. If you've ever worked in a high school, you know that's a remarkable record, for students and teachers alike.

★   ★   ★

A STAZER SAMPLER

Awaiting the Auditor

the security and exchange commission
splits open like an oyster
there are no pearls

the day holds still and the
steam of life runs white

bums steam open like rotting wallets

★   ★   ★

Sun Up

the sun's up to the fourth slat in the blinds
the cat stretches and lies on my lover's legs
the clock ticks slowly toward six o'clock

when i was a boy, grandpa
your shiny grey beard, your wise blue eye
and the way your nostrils flared at dinner
when my little league team had lost
you were a lighthouse when the dark days came
now your mangled body, the foundations of my heart

★   ★   ★

Cisco

he was tired that morning
a sleepy texas town
with tumbleweed in the streets
and barmaids with lace garters
didn't tempt him at all
only vodka and milk
to bring out the stars
a little in his clouded head
and last night was there a last night?
Caramba

★   ★   ★

A Continuity

The rainbow falls down, hung over
And the birds, stripped of their feathers
screaming in the wind

She fell on the ice
and the bells were ringing softly
The chair slid across the room

and I looked for you in Gimbel's

The floor sat promptly on the spot
The pencil had no point

His nose fell off his ears his elbows

and I looked for you in Bloomingdale's

The flatness was too much for me
Once that snow was white

Orange! Orange! Orange! he shouted
How he loved the word

Flying bugs eat my eyes
but beneath the stars, the barking dogs
an empty quart of ginger ale
and the shoes marching by themselves
the despairing gestures of the empty gloves

And I looked for you in Macy's

An L. L. Bean shoe seen
through the crack in the door
and the things we said mattered

Now I can't keep my matches from going
out

★ ★ ★

Like a Chocolate

Like a chocolate bar melting
in the pocket of a heedless child
your love is wasted on me
a cold stone round and flat
warm room damp fire

Like a hard candy that will not melt
even after days of the tongue
tongue melts candy melts
warm tongue cold room

★ ★ ★

Monday Nights

I hate Louise, I hate red hair, what's left?
Fat bears eating jelly donuts

The roof shingles are falling
And just whom are they falling on?

★ ★ ★

Algeria, 1972

i hear nothing, for my ears are blocked
i see all for my eyes are open
i speak not for my mouth is stuck
i shit not for my bowels are blocked
wander in the everlasting night
a stranger to this town
and stop just stop
and be absolutely still
and gather dust until i might be
a chair a boulder a toothbrush

★   ★   ★

A Day in the Country

O dogshit, nothing like a sweet red rose
O shit, how unreflective and unlike
the cool still pond

Why don't sidewalks flow like green hills?
Why don't cars move silent as cows?
Why don't buildings burst into leaf?
Up the plow, down the jackhammer

To be buried alive!
To feel the root of the
blueberry bush
tickle my nose

★   ★   ★

Homage to Thomas Hardy

And I saw dunes as high as mountains
The lovely lovely lovely little lilies

And boxes of windows, pockets filled
with doors. Everything knocking knocking knocking

The oval out of plumb, the biting cold
biting her cheeks   the birds

flew like dying dogs
My hands are wings

My foot neatly in my back pocket
I rode in the wind

My head bounced softly

★   ★   ★

Editor's Postscript

There is, of course, a difference between hoax and fraud. Literary fraud (such as Clifford Irving's "biography" of Howard Hughes) is rarely interesting or literature. Hoax can be both. Two good examples are the Spectra hoax and the Ern Malley hoax.

The Spectra hoax (see the book of the same title, edited by William Jay Smith and published by Wesleyan University Press in 1961) involved the creation of a fictitious literary movement, complete with aesthetic statements, articles, letters and a body of work by three mysterious (and talented) poets.

The Ern Malley hoax was less good natured, but the joke turned out to be on the perpetrators, as Kenneth Koch explained in the special collaborations issue of *Locus Solus* magazine (No. 2, summer 1961):

> *The Darkening Ecliptic* was a collection purporting to be the complete works of Ern Malley, but actually written as a hoax by two Sydney (Australia) poets, James McAuley and H. S. Stewart. McAuley and Stewart sent Ern Malley's works to Max Harris of *Angry Penguins,* who was so taken with them that he declared Malley one of Australia's greatest poets and forthwith published his entire *oeuvre* (in 1944). Though Harris was wrong about who Ern Malley "was" (if one can use that word here), I find it hard not to agree with his judgment of Malley's poetry. The following "confession" by McAuley and Stewart may help to explain some of the profundity and charm of Malley's poetry:
>
> "We produced the whole of Ern Malley's tragic life-work in one afternoon, with the aid of a chance collection of books which happened to be on our desk: the *Concise Oxford Dictionary,* a *Collected Shakespeare, Dictionary of Quotations,* etc.
>
> "We opened books at random, choosing a word or phrase haphazardly. We made lists of these and wove them into nonsensical sentences.
>
> "We misquoted and made false allusions. We deliberately perpetrated bad verse, and selected awkward rhymes from a *Ripman's Rhyming Dictionary.*
>
> "The alleged quotation from Lenin in one of the poems, 'The emotions are not skilled workers,' is quite phoney. The first three lines of the poem 'Culture as Exhibit' were lifted as a quotation straight from an American report on the drainage of breeding-grounds of mosquitoes."
>
> Their three rules of composition were given as follows:
>
> "1. There must be no coherent theme, at most, only confused and inconsistent hints at a meaning held out as a bait to the reader.
>
> "2. No care was taken with verse technique, except occasionally to accentuate its general sloppiness by deliberate crudities.

"3. In style, the poems were to imitate not Mr. Max Harris in particular, but the whole literary fashion as we knew it from the works of Dylan Thomas, Henry Treece and others."

In recent years, there have been at least two reprints of Ern Malley's work and several studies of it, most recently *The Ern Malley Affair* by Michael Heyward.

Marvin Hoffman

The Pleasures of Parody

Everybody has a favorite literary form. It may be poetry rich in natural observation. Or confessional, introspective autobiography. Or sociological examination of a community or group. Or writing bristling with wordplay. This does not exhaust the possibilities by any means, but it's a fair representation of the central thrust of work particular writers and teachers tend to elicit from children. My students and I have explored all these genres in class with some success and pleasure. Often one form seemed to mesh perfectly with the style and interest of a particular child.

But we found ourselves turning to parody with increasing frequency. Nothing matched it for the pleasure it gave to the kids. It comes naturally to most kids and, in fact, constitutes a good portion of the play and conversation of older pre-adolescent children during their out-of-school time: imitating teachers and other adults, particularly those who are "weird," i.e., distinctively idiosyncratic; mimicking TV commercials and favorite shows; making up irreverent lyrics to current pop songs.

Kids are often surprised, relieved, and a bit suspicious about the opportunity to "make fun of " (read: parody) things in school: it seems like the kind of thing they're supposed to get into trouble for. But when you think about how weak and powerless children are as a group, how few weapons are available to them in their confrontations with adult society, it makes good sense to me to hold out parody to them as a relatively safe and satisfying way of holding their own.

Young children play the role of mother, father, teacher, doctor, etc. as a means of learning about the world. At a later age, parody carries this process one step further. In order to do parody one must first come to some basic understanding of the thing or person being parodied. One teacher, who did a good deal of simple typesetting and printing with his young students, told me that he was amazed by how well they were able to read: they seemed to have no difficulty reading the lines in their composing sticks which were, after all, upside down and backwards. There's an analogous process of transformation at work in parody, an ability to grasp certain elements of style well enough to stand them on their heads. Children's ability to create a parody contains its own built-in test of their understanding of the subject matter at hand.

My exploration of parody had begun with my colleague Dick Murphy's initial work on his imaginary worlds project with students in New York City. Dick discovered that the social studies class with which he was working was united in their distaste for the textbook they were suffering through. He hit on the inspired idea of enlisting the students in the task of writing their own textbook about a non-existent country. This textbook would duplicate the tone of the original and would preserve its structure—those ubiquitous section headings in dark type that read: NATURAL RESOURCES, CLIMATE, THE LAND AND ITS PEOPLE, COMMERCE AND INDUSTRY, FLORA AND FAUNA, etc. The result was funny, insightful, and, I dare say, therapeutic.

Dick and I used this same tactic with upper elementary students in Fairlee, Vermont. Here the villain was a geography textbook, but this time of a more "hip" variety. It was constructed around a flimsy fiction involving a kindly old gentleman, owner of a Boeing 707 jet, who spent his time flying groups of children around the world with him. As they passed over Holland he would exclaim: "Look, there are the dikes of Holland! As you can see much of the land of this little nation is below sea level, and in order to make farming possible. . . ." The kids' contempt for this text inspired the following introduction to their own book:

An Introduction to the Kawinee

Our plane took off from Friendso, where we had just gathered 250 grapes, at 3:40 A.M. Ann said, "I'm tired." She turned around in her seat and noticed Mr. Wilson sitting with fifty-one martinis in his lap. He was tubing those martinis right down. Mr. Wilson was looking out the window with his telescope. He said, "We are now flying over Miami. All take note of the pretty young lady in the bikini." Bob pressed his nose against the glass and said, "Duh." Jane said, "Mr. Wilson, stop tubing those martinis or you'll get drunk."

Too late. Mr. Wilson was already drinking another. Mr. Wilson looked out the window again and said, "I wish I was the man with that young lady out there." Jane said, "Man, are you drunk. There's no man with that lady. That's a cocker spaniel." Bob said, "Duh." The plane left the land and began to take off over the Atlantic Ocean. Suddenly Mr. Wilson piped up, "Hic. Is that a killer whale down there?" Bob said, "Duh." The pilot said, "This is the last time I'll ever fly a Sabena. We're running out of gas!"

Mr. Wilson said, "All take note. We're getting closer and closer to the water." Bob said, "Duh." Jane said, "Help!" Then the plane crashed. We were in Kawinee. Mr. Wilson said to the pilot, "You idiot. You spilled my martinis."

—*John and Lori*

Our classroom storage shelves were crammed with other antiquated texts the school board could never bring itself to part with, although they had been of questionable educational value even when new. One of these battered old books had a series of illustrations that caught Maura's fancy. She and Dick decided that it would not bring down the wrath of the gods if they cut these illustrations out and used them as the basis for a new text. The result (reproduced at the end of this essay) was a visual parody that comes close to Donald Barthelme's quirky commentaries on the Victorian drawings in several strange pieces in *The New Yorker*.

Parody isn't reserved for objects of contempt. Anything or anybody with a sufficiently distinctive style is open to the same elbow in the ribs. We spent a number of weeks in our class viewing the twelve films on the life of the Netsilik Eskimos that were made as part of the Educational Development Center's social science curriculum, "Man: A Course of Study." The later, re-edited versions of these films have a soundtrack and standard narrative opening and closing: they zoom in on an old man in front of an igloo saying, at the beginning and end of each film, "And that was the way things used to be."

All of us were entranced by the scenes of seal hunting, kayak building, igloo construction, etc., but from the second film on, the kids began to repeat the refrain, mimicking the old man, and finally ringing their own irreverent variations on his litany.

The playful parodying process was at work. Instead of trying to squelch it, we acknowledged it and suggested a channel for it. The result was the production of an ambitious movie, the thirteenth film in the Eskimo series, made under top secret conditions by four boys who worked with us after school and on weekends for as long as there was snow on the ground. It was shown without explanation during a regular social studies period and became favored viewing for countless recess periods and lunch hours thereafter.

Writing was involved in outlining and blocking each of the film's scenes. For me the film was glorious good fun first. At the same time, it gave me an unexpected glimpse into the extraordinary visual illiteracy of our kids. They were ultimate TV viewers, yet they had no sense of how the illusions on which they thrived were created—or that they were illusions at all! Here are some of the scenes that constituted their introduction to illusion:

SCENE: *The Eskimos Break Camp and Set Off on a Grueling Dog Sled Trek to New Hunting Grounds.*

Chris, the biggest kid in the class, owned Chocolate, the smallest dog in town. The museum in Hanover owned a lovely scale model of a sled which we hitched to Chocolate. Hence, shots of Chocolate headed across the snowy tundra of our baseball field, lured (off-camera) by tidbits of food. These intercut with shots of a determined Chris, wielding whip as he, presumably, rides along behind. Then the final denouement as camera pulls back to reveal tiny dog, tiny sled, and huge boy headed across field in that order.

SCENE: *Seal Hunters at Blowhole.*

Two hooded hunters set out across ice, find blowhole, dig it out, set cowhide alarm that jiggles as seal approaches hole. Many shots back and forth from one hunter to another to connote passage of time. Finally a sighting, a tugging, great struggle, and up from under the ice emerges an old inner tube (some clever editing here). Hunters, full of mutual congratulations are seen in long view, trudging back to village dragging their prize. (These long shots made with camera stationed on roof of school, pointed in a direction that avoids views of houses, woods, powerlines, and so on.)

Here is one final example of the pleasures of parody. Several of the girls became interested in the whole genre of do-it-yourself, how-to, fix-it books. (I no longer remember how this came about. It seems to me that they puzzled over the absence of such books for women.) What emerged was the *Do-It-Yourself Manual* by Maura, Sandy, Cindy, and Sue—a twenty-section volume for women that included advice on how to fix your tile floor, sink, dishwasher, cracked mirror, and your face; how to get rid of bugs, take out the trash, buy the right kind of tomatoes, etc. Here are a few selections:

How to Fix Your Sink

Sooo you got your sink clogged up again! What happened? Did your son throw up in the sink again? You really should teach him to throw up in the toilet. Well, let's get down to work. First you've got to make sure nobody's going to throw up. Then you get your utensils: ammonia, noseplug, turpentine, Top Job, vacuum cleaner, and a comb. The ammonia and the Top Job is to set on the counter to keep your kids out of the kitchen. The noseplug is to plug your nose so you don't faint. You use the comb to comb your hair and make a good impression on your sink and if you make a good impression on your sink the stuff will come out easier. The turpentine is to slick down your hair to look better. Now you're all set. You turn on the vacuum cleaner and if it explodes you just take the Top Job and clean it up. You always thought unclogging the sink was hard. Now with the easy-to-do method there's no work or worry.

—*Sandy*

★　　★　　★

How to Paint Your Wall

Sooooo you want to paint your wall. Now this is how you do it. Get some chopsticks, toothbrush, Silly Putty, ladder, umbrella. Use the chopsticks to make some Chinese food and eat it so you won't have to paint on an empty stomach. Use the toothbrush to scrape off all the old paint. Use the Silly Putty to stick in your holes in your wall. If there's any left after, give it to your kids. Use the ladder to get to the top of the wall. Then you take the umbrella to balance on the ladder. Then you start to paint. Make sure you don't get stuck to the paint. If you don't use the umbrella, you will fall down and crack your head open. If you don't use the chopsticks, your stomach will growl. And if your stomach growls, you will get an ulcer.

—*Maura*

★　　★　　★

How to Put Up Your Drapes

Soooo you got new drapes and you want me to tell you in my book how to put up your drapes. I just want to ask you one question: Why can't you keep your old drapes? I know your kid splattered paint all over your drapes. Well, let's get down to work. You will need a bikini, fish hooks, window cleaner, and a branch from a tree. Now put the bikini on. If you have a horrible figure you can't use this method. Now clean the window so everybody can see you working with your bikini on. When the men see you they will come around and offer to help. Now it's smooth sailing. All you have to do now is to tell them what to do. Now just tell them to take two fishhooks and hook the tree branch to the wall. Now tell them to hook eight fishhooks to the drapes and take the other ends of the fish hooks to the tree branch. If you have a horrible figure, catch your husband in a good mood and ask him to help you. SOOOOO DO IT YOURSELF!!!! . . . Almost.

—*Sandy*

ME AND HENRIETTA
by Maura Rafferty & Dick Murphy

Me and Henrietta retired to the country with our life savings. We bought the house of our dreams. It was panelled with people. There was lots of work to do. I had to shinny up each pole and dust off the animals, while Henrietta held a net in case I slipped. After dusting, we had to sleep on the floor, and, of course, we had to install central heating. Finally, our work was done, and we decided to have a party.

People came from all over. They brought presents and lots of good things to eat. We found our new country neighbors very attractive. But we were worried because at first they didn't seem to like us.

But then Henrietta told some of her favorite jokes. Soon she was the center of conversation. Everyone wanted to talk to her.

But I was still lonely. I spent too much time at the bar, dipping into the big punch bowl. The three women bartenders started luring me on.

My head started spinning. My eyes began to play tricks: our visitors began to look like animals: fishy birds and scaly dogs. They had to put me to bed.

Meantime the party was getting really wild. Maybe our house (with its new central heating) was too hot, because people started running around outside naked.

Henrietta was flabbergasted.

Someone must have called the police because, about an hour later, we heard bugles and horses and the sound of marching feet tramping over our bridge. The chief of police said, "Hand over all those naked people." Henrietta said, "If the chief of police finds out what's going on here, our reputations will be ruined."

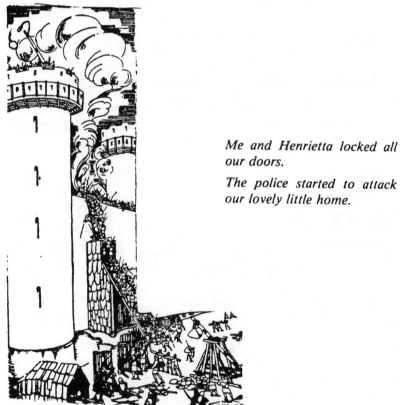

Me and Henrietta locked all our doors.

The police started to attack our lovely little home.

They got inside and treated us real mean. Then they set the house on fire.

Henrietta was outraged and miserable.

She screamed at the police. She got so mad she clawed and bit the five police sergeants.

But nothing stopped the police. Finally they smashed down the living room door. Our guests ran for their clothes. But it was too late. They were caught in the act.

They carried us off to a prison camp in the mountains.

Life in the prison camp was pretty hard. They made us pound rocks just for the heck of it. And we had to cook our meals outside over an open fire.

We had to live in caves, crowded in with another couple. We never had any privacy because the other couple had four noisy, naughty kids. We learned that all the other prisoners in the camp had had wild parties that got out of hand. Henrietta started to lose her figure and her beautiful complexion.

They kept us at the prison camp for three years. We thought we'd never get out. Then one morning a messenger with a torch came running through the field, yelling out our names. He told us to put all our rocks away in a neat pile, pack up our few belongings, and run with him to the courthouse.

When we got to the courthouse, they introduced us to the judge. The judge looked as though he had just fallen out of the clouds. He read from a big law book, and he kept on shaking his head and yawning. Henrietta kept falling asleep and I had to pinch her. His final verdict was, "Not Guilty....If you invite me to the next party!" Then he started snickering.

Henrietta said, *"We wouldn't dream of having a party without you."* And we were free at last! They carried us out of the courthouse as if we were kings and queens.

So once again me and Henrietta retired to the country with our life savings. We bought the house of our dreams. Henrietta said, *"Let's not put in the central heating until after the party's over."*

So we started to plan our party.

Our party was a great success. People came from all over, and there was lots of food and drinks. And this time, nobody got too hot from the central heating so nobody took off their clothes.

*Only there was one problem. The judge said, "This party's boring!"
And he sent us back to the prison camp.*

Joyce Dyer

Imitation Hemingway
Making Literary Analysis Fun for Students

I began getting the idea for a writing assignment when I heard some of my high school sophomores laughingly greet each other one day with this line from Hemingway's "Big Two-Hearted River": "I like to open cans." Students, about midway through *The Nick Adams Stories*, begin to see the potential for humor in Hemingway's repeated patterns and in the trademark conventions of his style.

Their impulse to chuckle at Hemingway now and then, however, in no sense diminished their respect for him. On the contrary, it made them far better readers than they might have been otherwise. For parody can also be a pleasurable form of literary analysis. During our class discussions, students had acquired a lively and vigorous understanding of Hemingway's style. Their laughter came not from thoughtless derision, but from the pleasure of recognition.

Before I wrote up my final assignment for *The Nick Adams Stories*, I tested the extent of my topic's appeal. I told students about the annual International Imitation Hemingway Competition sponsored by Harry's Bar and American Grill. I read the requirements of the award to them: "Write one really good page of really 'bad' Hemingway. It can be funny. It can be very funny. It should be a parody—an action scene, dialogue, character sketch, etc." Silence and attention. Next I added the description of the award itself: "Round trip airfare for two from winner's home to Florence, Italy, plus dinner for two at Harry's Bar and American Grill in Florence, Italy." Cheeks immediately began to brighten, eyes opened wide, and pens seemed to vault into students' hands, ready to go.

The next day, I brought in the writing assignment:

There is, as you now know, an international award given each year for the best parody of Ernest Hemingway's writing style. A parody is "a literary work that broadly mimics an author's characteristic style and holds it up to ridicule." You certainly know enough about Hemingway's style by now to be able to write a story that humorously exaggerates (and makes fun of) his particular trademarks. Your assignment, then, is to write a short story that parodies Hemingway's style (and themes as well, if you choose).

I didn't want to exhaust the topic's possibilities in our prewriting session. If students hear too much, they sometimes have difficulty thinking of ideas other than those mentioned in class. But I did think it was important to make sure that they understood parody and Hemingway's style, so I briefly tried the topic out.

For several minutes, it was impossible to maintain any order. One suggestion toppled into another. This was their opportunity to get at the sacred Hemingway.

"I know!" giggled one student. "You could have people who are depressed or resigned to fate turn against the wall. Have all these people keep turning against a wall, again and again, over and over."

I asked her where she remembered this gesture in *The Nick Adams Stories*. She vividly recalled the husband in "Indian Camp" who had rolled over to slit his throat, unable to stand an instant more of his wife's labor screams. Students eagerly cited other examples: Ole Anderson in "The Killers" had turned toward a wall after telling Nick he would no longer run away from the thugs who haunted his past; Carper in "Night before Landing" had rolled toward the wall, drunk, afraid of the war he was returning to.

They moved from laughing about significant gestures to considering the humor of Hemingway's having characters engage in the same activities over and over. Just a phrase made our entire group smile broadly. "Trout fishing!" "Bullfighting!" "Making camp!" "Boxing and boxers!" "Skiing!" The list that students came up with could only have been Hemingway's.

"How about the way your sentences are going to look?" I interrupted. They were ready for that as well, although it took a minute before anyone volunteered anything specific enough to be helpful. "Reticence!" someone shouted. This was a word they hadn't known before Hemingway, but certainly understood after twenty-four stories. "Sentences that look simple but have special meaning."

"Like what?" I asked.

"For instance," one boy began, "the way Nick made camp in 'Big Two-Hearted River' showed a lot about how nervous and cautious he was after coming home from war."

"Remember the beans and spaghetti in that story?" another student asked in the same way a familiar group of friends might reminisce together, "Remember the one . . . ?" They remembered the description of the frying pan, the bubbles the beans and spaghetti made as they warmed, the dousing with tomato catsup. They had loved sentences like this one: "Nick got out a bottle of tomato catsup and cut four slices of bread." (Closely related, of course, to "He liked to open cans.") But they recognized that all such sentences, though potentially very funny and, at times, nerve-fraying for the reader, were often hints from Hemingway about Nick's need for method, pattern, order. And when we had arrived at the sentence, "His tongue was very sensitive," they knew that Hemingway was talking about more than beans and spaghetti. Hemingway could put all of human experience—its pleasure and anguish—in a taste bud.

They remembered, too, how ironic Hemingway's prose often was. We recalled the seemingly docile Bugs telling Nick in "The Battler" why he had been in prison: "I was in for cuttin' a man." Suddenly Bugs's efforts to keep the cooking knives in his own possession seemed more than precautionary. They mentioned, as well, Alice's use of profanity in "The Light of the World." Or Nick's father, after somewhat perversely informing his son about Prudie's sexual disloyalty, looking at the pie and asking Nick, "Have some more?" Students thought of Nick in "An Alpine Idyll" complaining about the hot May sun and the boredom of skiing, while Olz, a poor, hard-working peasant, uncomplainingly shoveled dirt over the body of his wife who had been dead since winter but whom he had only now been able to transport to town for burial.

After this, students began thinking more and more quickly of specific ideas for their own parodies. One student, for example, had earlier been exasperated by Hemingway's incorporation of significant book titles into his stories. The mention of *Wuthering Heights* in "The Last Good Country" hints that Nick and his sister Littless would have to resolve their vaguely incestuous attraction to each other. That in "The Three-Day Blow" Nick "couldn't get into" *Richard Feverel* quietly lets us know that Nick was not yet ready to admit his true reason for breaking up with Marge: in his arrogance, Nick, like Sir Austin Feverel, fears the consequences and "look" of a marriage between people of very different social and economic backgrounds. This particular student had read none of the books referred to except *Swiss Family Robinson*. He vowed, sneering malevolently, that he would figure out a way to work every book he had ever read into his parody.

Another student began to imagine a symbolic introductory segment, much like that of "Big Two-Hearted River." In the Hemingway story, the fish Nick looks at in the second and third paragraphs immediately defines his own condition: it, like Nick, is trying to keep steady in the brisk current, "with wavering fins." The student considered absurd alternative images, such as a fluttering sparrow with a broken wing or a half-baked worm in the afternoon sun.

Enough. Now I was certain that students were not only eager to begin, but also ready. They were as familiar with Hemingway's style and themes as I had hoped. After weeks and weeks of careful textual study (where all successful literature-related topics begin), they were ready to dream about sampling Italian cuisine at Harry's.

All week, each day before class, I heard students laughing about twists they had thought of, or giving one another ideas. This was clearly a good assignment for these tenth graders. At this age, they must begin developing analytical skills, but also be allowed opportunities to enjoy writing and to laugh. Parody is a perfect format for all of these.

The results were superb. They confirmed that the students really did understand Hemingway. And nearly every paper displayed wit and imagination.

There were, of course, touches I had expected to find after our prewriting session. A lot of cans were opened, and a lot of Nicks/Dicks/Ricks turned against walls. But even here were surprises. One girl, for example, made her hero look especially ludicrous. After "Mick" burned his marshmallows, he panicked and tensed. "He looked around," she wrote. "There were no walls. Mick turned against a tree." She added, before proceeding with her narrative, "It was a while before Mick would turn around again."

But many papers represented powerful extensions of our discussion in class and a careful reconsideration of the points we had raised. Titles, to begin with, offered strong invitations to the essays. "A Farewell to Trouts." "Eighty-five Shots." "An Alpine Idol." "Dick Builds a Snowman."

The author of "Dick Builds a Snowman" remembered the importance of psychological associations in Hemingway. In a work such as "Now I Lay Me," even the recollection of fishing bait and jars of snakes triggers harsher war memories for the vulnerable Nick Adams. The student who wrote about Dick making a snowman trivialized the associative power of her hero's mind:

> Quickly, Dick shaped the snow into a ball by rolling and patting it with his hands which were really numb and cold, but he did not mind it because he liked it. When the snowball was finished, Dick threw it high into the air. The snowball spun towards the sun and the sky, flashing

brilliantly, turning and spinning. Then it began to fall, making Dick think of the fish swimming in the big stream on the Black.

The author of this parody also made fun of another prominent feature of Hemingway's fiction: the quietly significant ending. Like Nick in "Big Two-Hearted River," who can't complete his fishing, who is afraid of the tragic adventure that lay ahead in the swamp, Dick could not finish constructing his snowman. "Walking all around the frozen, stacked balls," her final paragraph began, "Dick thought it looked like a snowman. He named it Yemedge. Dick had forgotten to put a face on Yemedge. He would do it tomorrow, maybe."

The creator of Dick and his snowman also elaborated on the idea of a character's ordinary gestures providing psychological insight. She showed Dick eating breakfast before the ordeal of the snowman began:

> Dick went downstairs. He shivered in the early-morning chill of the air. There were two eggs on the table. They had been fried in butter. Dick ate them and two pieces of toast which he had spread with margarine. It was a good breakfast. He did not eat any bacon. He did not like to eat meat. It was too painful.

Dick has become, we learn, a vegetarian. We smile at the author's ability to keep our understanding of his conversion excessively vague. A little later, pain again presented itself, this time in the form of the wool scarf Dick wrapped around his neck.

> Dick walked back downstairs. The boots made pleasant clomping sounds on the wooden steps. In the kitchen, there were two hooks by the back door. On the right hook hung a long, wool scarf. Dick took the scarf. He wound it around his neck, going counterclockwise, careful not to wrap it too tightly. He wrapped it around his neck two more times.

Poor Dick. This is surely no normal winter he is preparing for so cautiously.

Other stories parodied Hemingway's choice of scene and descriptions of movement. One student had Rick Musselbaum, owner of a World War I ambulance, drive to a tavern, then to a boxing ring, next to a bullfighting arena, and finally to a river to fish. The quick progression was humorous and outrageous. Still another student made fun of Hemingway's tedious descriptions of minute movements:

> He gathered the coffee beans and flapjack mix and put them in his tent. He came out of his tent.

One boy mocked the convention of the model hero. He added to our sizable list of exemplary figures (Alice, John Packard, Ole Anderson, the major, and so on) the name of Ernest Noway. Ernest was a very dull, middle-aged man who smoked cigarettes while drawing graffiti on the wall toward which he was always turned (of course). The student's Nick Adams figure found Ernest Noway in a hotel lobby somewhere in Northern Michigan. Nick's face brightened up as he saw the man facing the wall, spirals of yellow smoke seeming to float from the top of his head. He quickly approached the man, and the following conversation ensued:

> "At last," Nick cried. "I've found someone who can help me!"
> Ernest Noway stared at the wall.
> "Please," Nick begged, "can you kindly tell me the causes of the Protestant Reformation?"
> Ernest Noway continued to stare at the wall. "Get lost," he finally muttered in a gravelly voice.
> "Gee," said Nick. "I thought I could *learn* from you. I thought you could . . . O just forget it. I . . . I . . . I . . . I'm speechless."

One girl enjoyed focusing on Hemingway's word choices. She decided to exaggerate her hero's use of the word *swell*. We had discussed Hemingway's incorporation of such terms (in stories such as "The Three-Day Blow" and "Cross Country Snow") to emphasize Nick's naïveté. The student's hero, Brick Adams, began the story by drinking tomato juice.

> "Gee," said Brick as he opened a can of juice, "this tomato juice sure tastes swell. Swell as that tomato juice Roy used to give me. Boy, was Roy swell. Swell juice that swell Roy gave me. Just swell. Gee."

She returned to the word after she got Brick to a trout stream:

> Brick was at the river.
> "All is swell!" said Brick. The sun went down.
> He hurried to the river. He stepped on a thorn. His foot began to swell. "Swell!" he cried. "It can't swell. All is swell and now it's swelling. Oh, I wish things would never change. I wish all would be swell."

Larger and larger the list of parodied conventions and techniques grew. After I had read all the papers and made suggestions, students read them to one another in class. We took two days for this. Students eagerly made follow-up recommendations about their classmates' work, constructively trying to explain where any opportunity for humor had been missed. And, as others read out loud, they heard things that would improve their own work. They were then given a week to revise.

Students worked carefully on sections that needed a little more crafting. The student who wrote about Nick's movement into and out of his tent, for example, added a sequence. The new paragraph looked this way:

> He gathered the coffee beans and flapjack mix and put them in his tent. He took the pot and pan back in his tent. Soon he came back out. He had forgotten the syrup. He wiped off the syrup and carefully carried it inside his tent.

The Nick Adams figure here might be mistaken for a sight-gag comedian.

Next, I gave them a choice. They could submit their parodies to *Bufo,* our school literary journal, for consideration. Or, they could cross their fingers, dream about Italian villas, and gently slide their manuscripts into envelopes addressed to Harry's Bar and American Grill, 2020 Avenue of the Stars, Los Angeles, CA 90067.

Frances Reinehr

Storyteaching

Before education became an item of national concern and national politics, I had begun to experience a haunting. Not the haunting in ghost stories, but a haunting of the heart. The haunting grew out of a fear that my students and I were not connecting. The seeds of the haunting were planted a number of years ago when I was teaching in an inner-city elementary school in Lincoln, Nebraska.

One particular fourth grade class exhibited just about every behavior problem possible as individuals and as members of a group. Not one of the children felt welcome, let alone wanted, on this earth. They had no self-esteem; they operated daily with a good deal of rage, expressed in verbal and physical assaults upon one another, often racially motivated.

My response was "adult." I chose one of their problems—"prejudice"—and conducted a series of lessons to help them confront it. My abstract method was inappropriate. This was a group of angry children expressing their rage. They did not need indirect approaches to their estrangement. They did need nurturing. They did need to hear some good things about themselves. They did need to hear stories that could offer them escape, consolation, and hope.

I should have begun by reading them myths, legends, and fairy stories from diverse cultures, for these kinds of stories contain inevitable lessons about decent human behavior. I have since learned that my students and I are secret relatives bound by our ability to recognize one another through a story. I believe in the power of a story as a principal way to fill children with hope, for, as Sam Keen says in *To a Dancing God*, "Storytelling raises a person out of the randomness of the moment and inserts him into a larger framework." When we tell stories, we "retell ourselves." The stories we choose to tell illustrate our beliefs, fears, attitudes, hopes, and how we see ourselves in relation to others. Raised by storytellers, I have in some sense kept myself alive through stories. In my family, we entertained one another and ourselves with a great many accounts, hilarious and sad, of "what if" and what actually had been—all with a good deal of embellishment.

Through storytelling, I believe, we transcended a sense of randomness and came to a place of belonging in the long, continuing story.

Now more than ever, children need stories. They need to hear stories of every genre, and they need encouragement to tell their own stories. In this age of a floundering sense of commitment, of the attitude of looking out for Number One, and of the general state of unsafety in the world, we need the consolation of stories that serve as models to strengthen our perspectives on our own stories. We need stories, too, that end with the consolation of "happily ever after." We need those stories, told and retold by every culture throughout time, because we all need redefinitions of what it means to arrive safely after difficult journeys.

What we teach—the curriculum—is important in all its variety, but it all comes alive when one area of it becomes radiant, illuminating the rest. The area of light for me, now, is stories. Stories help us make connections with the lives of others. When I tell my students a story to illustrate a point, they listen, because through storytelling I become real. I become real because the stories reflect a way the students and I are similar.

How and why good talk produces good writing and art that in turn becomes stories is the central passion of my teaching. When children become participants in a story—their own or another's—they respond with spontaneity and excellence. They talk. They write. They read and they express a joyful pride in their accomplishments. Life in the daily round of the classroom can be lived with some measure of grace, can reflect a creative hope, can be arranged so that each student realizes a wondrous part possible in the long, continuing story.

★ ★ ★

All too often, teachers of writing express a multitude of inadequacies about their own writing: "I don't have time to write much." "I can't write much of anything, but if I do write, I like to write poetry because it's shorter." "My third grade teacher, thirty-five years ago, froze my writing ability." "Creative writing is not my thing." These, of course, lead to: "I can never think of anything to get my students to write about in creative writing."

But each day, children come to school bringing a wide range of experiences and the language to describe them. They have come to school by car, on foot, on rollerskates, on bikes. They have noticed the weather, animals, pets, siblings, friends, parents, and others. Since yesterday they have slept and dreamed. They have played games and (maybe) tricks on someone else. They have watched TV and have heard neighborhood gossip. Some of them have read something. Once in a while one will have witnessed a street tragedy. Some have heard arguments or taken part in them. Some of them are anxiously anticipating the next chapter of the book being read in class. There are spelling words, scientific experiments, and math to work with. There are all sorts of people to learn about in social studies. There may be a play or dances to rehearse. Children come to school brimming with experiences to write about.

I had one class particularly interested in gothic horror tales. The school was in the middle of an active neighborhood: supermarkets, furniture stores, bars, bookstores; to the north a lovely park; to the west an older home; residential neighborhoods to the south and east. Some of these older homes were elegant, with wooded back yards, connected by alleys. My students and I did a great deal of walking in the neighborhood to investigate.

On one particularly orange October morning, one of the boys came in quite excited and asked if we had a camera ready to go. We did, so he proposed a writing group be selected to go on a photo-taking jaunt because he had discovered, on his way to school, an old tree with a knife stuck in it. So seven gothic horror fans and an aide went out to take photos. They found the tree stump, an old garage with all its windows in various degrees of brokenness, alley cats in various positions lurking about, a clothesline filled with billowing white sheets, and a man rummaging through some trash. While the children were taking his picture, the aide took notes of what they were saying in response to their excited discoveries. Some of this found its way into *Goodbye, Chris Ann,* the story that these children wrote in collaboration when the photographs were developed:

Goodbye, Chris Ann

The old house with the tall chimney was dark and creepy and you never saw anybody who lived there. It looked like it was watching you. (*Photo of the house.*)

One day Chris Ann was walking by the house. She thought it looked pretty nice, so she went to the yard. She saw watermelons, big, juicy, and plump, lying in the garden. Hearing her mother calling her, she left, but she decided to come back later that night to get a watermelon. (*Photo of the house from a distance.*)

While Chris Ann was walking home, the day got foggy and sort of gloomy. After dinner, Chris Ann told her mother she was going over to Cindy's, her friend's, house to do some homework. She started toward the old house. Walking up the dark, long driveway, she thought she'd never get to the watermelons. She started to roam around the yard and she heard a door slam. She started to run, but when she turned around, the fence gate was closed. She was trapped. (*Photo of the fence.*)

Hearing footsteps coming closer and closer, she turned and saw an ugly-looking man. He came toward her. With a start, she screamed, but the man said, "Come in and have some juicy, plump watermelon." Chris Ann thought to herself, "Oh, I guess it will be all right." So she followed the man into the house.

"I'll go into the kitchen and prepare the snack. You make yourself at home." When he went into the kitchen, he put instant sleeping drugs into the watermelon. When he came back to the living room, both of them ate watermelon. Chris Ann's was full of sleeping medicine. The man's was not. Chris Ann fell asleep and dropped to the floor.

The man sneaked Chris Ann down the ladder and out the back door. He tied her neck to the stump and took the knife and do you know what happened next?

Goodbye, Chris Ann.

The blood streaked down her neck. He took a handkerchief out of his pocket and wiped the blood off the knife. He replaced the knife back in the stump. Then he sucked the bright red blood from his victim. (*Two photos: the stump and knife; an old garage.*)

Then he cut off her hair and went to the old garage with broken windows and chipped paint. The trees growing nearby looked like hands reaching down, and bloodthirsty bats flew overhead. He took Chris Ann's head and threw it through the broken glass. It crashed and the head fell into the garage for his pet bats to eat. He went home laughing to himself. Then he took the body and wrapped it in white sheets for later.

At 10:00 P.M., Chris Ann's mother called Cindy and asked, "Where is Chris Ann?" and Cindy said, "I haven't seen her since school is out."

Her mother immediately called the police. The police looked all night but found no clues. In the morning the papers, radio, and the TV were all full of Chris Ann's description. An old lady, neighbor to the spooky house, called the parents of Chris Ann and said, "I saw your daughter going toward the old house." (*Photo of the garage with a foggy overcast.*)

So the parents went up to the house. In the garage they saw bloody things sticking into the floor and the walls. "Oh, Chris Ann, did that happen to her?" Across the alley they saw another garage, the one with the broken glass. (*Photo of the stump and knife.*)

They looked and there they saw their daughter's head bald and bloody. They saw a man wiping something off near the stump. They had noticed her math book near the gate, so they told the man, "That's our daughter's math book. You haven't seen her, have you?" He said,

"Yes, I have, but I don't know where she is now." He said this with an evil eye.

They rushed home and called the police and told them that their little girl was dead. The police came to the house and handcuffed the villain and put him into prison. The house was torn down. The man and the house were never seen again. Moral: No trespassing.

I am not about to analyze this from a psychological point of view. My sense is that this kind of story helps children relieve some of their anxieties and fears, much like the original fairy tales do. *Goodbye, Chris Ann* remained in the school library for five years. It was in constant circulation until one child noticed its degenerating, fragile condition, and wrote on the inside cover, "Be Careful of this Book. It is very Old." When student writing is made available—in class books, individual books, and posters, or printed in some way other than handwriting—it becomes more worthy of time and energy. There is no writing my students do (except journal writing) that is not transformed in some way and made available to an audience. We write every day and publish at least once a week. During the school term, every student writes and illustrates at least one individual story and puts it into a bound book.

Good talk generates good writing. I also think careful listening results in successful teaching. For me, there has to be a time each day when the children and I just talk. It is essential for me to know what they're thinking and feeling. If classroom time is lacking, I eat with the children in the lunchroom, or at least rotate myself into their writing and art groups so I can get into the interaction.

★　　　★　　　★

Reading to my students is one of the most important things I do. What follows are examples of what kinds of things happen when we "live through" *The Lion, the Witch and the Wardrobe* by C. S. Lewis, *Harriet the Spy* by Louise Fitzhugh, *The Hobbit* by J. R. R. Tolkien, *Book of Greek Myths* by Ingri and Edgar Parin D'Aulaire, and a selection of Sioux myths and legends.

Before I begin reading *The Lion, the Witch and the Wardrobe*, I post a map of Narnia on the wall. Narnia is an imaginary land beyond this earth with time occurring concurrently with earth time. On the door I put a huge poster of a lion, with this quotation printed in large letters on the lion: "Safe, who said anything about safe? Course he isn't safe. But he's good. He's the King. I tell you." I also happen to have some newspaper clippings and coverage of the actual "wardrobe," a type of

great oak closet that held clothing in huge British homes and that inspired C. S. Lewis to write the story. I also post this challenge on a
closet door: "What if you opened this door and found yourself in a
totally different world? What goodness would you find? What bad
creatures might there be? What kind of an adventure could you have
in a land that was quite different from the one in which you live each
day?" In response to this, the children write adventure stories. Here's
one example.

My Adventure

I walked into the closet, pushed the paper aside and suddenly I was in a
jungle. There were strange noises in the jungle, but I decided I was not
going to let noises stop this adventure. It was very dark in the jungle, but
luckily, I had my flashlight. Then I spotted something on the ground. I
picked it up. It was a piece of paper that had words and a map on it. Below the map it said, "TREASURE MAP. BEWARE OF MONSTER."

I figured it was a treasure map and I decided to follow it. The map
showed there was a cave about three miles ahead. It was late at night and
I was very tired and I soon fell asleep. In the morning I found myself in
a cave. The cave had electric lights. I thought that was very strange. I
wondered how I got to the cave without knowing it.

The cave was huge and it had a whole bunch of hallways and two
elevators. I went in one of the elevators and saw a picture of this thing.
It had a dragon head, eight arms, and a body too weird to describe.

Suddenly I remembered the map and I don't know why I remembered it either. I looked at the note on the paper. When I read "BEWARE
OF MONSTER," I figured the picture on the wall of the elevator was
the monster. The elevator suddenly went up. I stopped on the second
floor of the cave and got out of the elevator. There were weapons hanging on the wall. I took a sword, and a net fell on me. Then something
knocked me out. I found myself tied to a chair and the monster was
boiling some water. I figured it was going to COOK me.

I tried to get out of there, but the ropes were too tight. Then I saw
the sword I had taken off the wall. It lay right beside me. I picked up the
sword with my feet and cut myself out of the ropes. Suddenly the sword
started to glow. I pointed the sword toward the monster and it shot the
monster dead. I ran all the way out of the closet and never told anybody
about my adventure.

—*Randy Christopher, age ten*

Before we get to the part where Edmund is eating the Turkish
Delight, I tell the children, "I know the professor and will call him to
see if I can get a little bit of the Turkish Delight for you to sample." I
have a tin exactly like the one in the book, and I load it with just

enough of a wonderful chocolate-covered marshmallow and nut candy for each student to have one taste. I tell them the professor came through, and, after reading about Edmund's gorging on Turkish Delight and wanting more and more, I pass out the candy. Some of the children are so caught up in the magic that they refuse to eat the candy, sensing some hold in it they care not to address. Others want more and more. I ask the children what they feel about the candy, and later I write their responses on balloons and post them about the room: "I wanted more and more." "I know how Edmund felt. I wanted more." "It tasted funny, like maybe it had a little poison on it." "I thought it would be some kind of turkey."

Lewis's clear description of the White Witch is a fine lead-in to descriptive writing:

> On a much higher seat in the middle of the sledge sat a very different person, a great lady, taller than any woman Edmund had ever seen. She also was covered in white fur up to her throat and held a long straight golden wand in her right hand and wore a golden crown on her head. Her face was white—not merely pale, but white like snow or paper or icing sugar, except for her very red mouth. It was a beautiful face in other respects, but proud and cold and stern.

After reading this description aloud, I ask the children to draw a portrait of what they see in their minds, urging them to stay as close as they can to Lewis's description. Their inner pictures of the White Witch are often wonderful. The next phase is to have each child write a description of a witch so clearly that another child can conjure up a drawing to match it. This writing always creates a lot of excitement. All kinds of witches—from Halloween versions to terribly evil-looking creatures the children draw—verify for me that their image-making machinery is ready to go to work when we provide the oil. We post these all over the room, along with a large printed copy of Lewis's description.

Another writing activity derived from this story involves the list of terrible creatures surrounding the Stone Table when Aslan is killed. I have the children verify this list through dictionary definitions: wraiths, boggles, ogres, ettins, ghouls, wooses, hags, cruels. (We have had to call the city library to verify a few of these creatures, but we've always gotten them all.) For the final step in this lesson, each child receives a card with the name of one of the terrible creatures. On large sheets of butcher paper, we draw our interpretations of the creatures, first in bright crayon and then with a wash of black tempera over the whole parade. The effect is eerie. The children definitely capture the evil in these creatures.

When we come to the end of the book, we are surrounded with writing, quotations, and art that evolved out of our living the story.

As I read to the children, they often ask, "But it isn't real, is it? There really isn't such a place as Narnia. There isn't really any magic, is there?" My reply is, "Yes, there is magic. Yes, there is a Narnia. The magic is within each of us. And we usually do not know we are in Narnia when we're there, because it is only when we've left that we remember where we've been."

★   ★   ★

Louise Fitzhugh's *Harriet the Spy* is a perfect book to use as an invitation to journal writing. Before we start that story, I make up a blank journal for each student. They are simply stapled booklets with oak tag covers.

Harriet, the principal character, keeps a journal. She writes to record what she has seen during her wanderings through her neighborhood. She also includes a great many thoughts about what she has seen. Her observations are heavily dosed with humor. After we get into the book, I pass out the journals, telling the students that this time their writing is simply for them: I will never see it, but they have the option of showing it to others. We talk about the difference between diary writing and journal writing: instead of just recording what we observe, we also write about what we think about what we have seen. Some of the journals started during *Harriet the Spy* continue long after we have finished the story.

★   ★   ★

There are different ways to read a story to children. One is the reader's theater presentation. This approach requires several readers who can alternate reading the narrative parts and dialogue. Several years ago, my friend and fellow teacher Pat Kurtenbach and I returned from the winter holidays with the feeling of gray. You know the feeling. And there were endless days with no sun. The school was surrounded by a moat of ice, so we were pretty much schoolbound. To redeem the January blahs, Pat and I decided to read *The Hobbit* to our collective seventy children each day, right after lunch.

We gathered our children into one room and began by playing "what if": "What if a wise person came to your home on a calm summer morning and told you that you had to leave your home to go on a trip that would include dangers and risks, but also some adventures. If you survived the trip, you would return a richer person. What adventures and dangers might you anticipate?"

Giving the children an opportunity to write about what they sensed as dangerous and exciting brought them right into the story of *The Hobbit*. Pat and I took turns reading and acting out the story. While we read, there were all sorts of activities going on. The only restriction was that there had to be absolute quiet for the listeners who really did want to hear every word. Some of the children drew parts of the story and wrote about it. Others redrew the Middle Earth maps we had brought in, and asked us where Middle Earth is on the globe. We didn't tell them it is more than likely within each of us in our struggles to keep from giving in to the ring, a thing of such power that only love and freedom can keep us from the final relinquishment. We just let them draw the maps, telling them it's a real place.

When we got to Beorn's, we stopped and had a feast of classroom-baked bread, honey, butter, and Koolaid (our substitute for mead).

After we had met Gollum, whom the children were fascinated with but never liked, we played the riddling game, always giving the children a chance to guess first between Bilbo and Gollum. The joy in the right guess was inexplicable. Naturally, this led to more riddling games by the children, who played them spontaneously during recess and lunch hour. Others went to the media center and checked out books of riddles, trying them out on Pat and me.

By the time we got to Smaug's cave, we were all more afraid of dragons than ever before. I posted this quotation of mine on a large piece of paper: "Everyone knows a dragon, but everyone's dragon looks different." We had lively talks about dragons, especially when I would announce I had again seen one just the night before. The children would quiz me and I would relate some terrible thing I had had to do the night before, or I would tell a story about someone afraid to give for fear of losing something precious. My dragon metaphor was becoming clearer for them. They began to draw dragons, which seemed to put them in closer touch with the metaphor.

Pat and I brought in felt, yarn, cloth, needles, and thread so the children could make puppets while we read to them. Others pasted scales on the outline of the huge paper Smaug we had made.

When we finished the story, we held a splendid celebration. The children showed their drawings, acted out parts of the story with their puppets, and told about the characters they remembered best. Gandalf and Bilbo always get top billing with this story. One child said he liked

Gandalf best because "he was so filled with justice and good magic."
Another liked Bilbo because "he did not know how to be a hero, but
learned how in the adventure." There are children who admit to not
liking *The Hobbit*. When I hear remarks such as "I don't know. I don't
like stories like *The Hobbit*. Bilbo seems silly to me," I feel as if my
mother has been attacked. But most of the children wanted to have
been along on the journey with Bilbo, the dwarfs, and Gandalf. By
the end, the halls, walls, and cafeteria were all one large collage tribute
to the story we had lived through together.

In this experience the skills developed all merged: listening became art that became writing that became talking that turned into
reading material for others. Listening also found form in puppets that
retold parts of the story.

Pat and I wanted to teach *The Hobbit* because we both held a deep
affection for the story. We also wanted to "live through" the book with
enthusiasm and fun, so we planned every activity to engage even the
most reluctant reader. As Bill Martin, Jr., said, "When I read a good
book, I just want to do something with it." You come to the end of a
book that has been a total joy, filled with energy, and now it is over.
This regret or loss is probably why I have come to try to "live through"
stories again with children.

There are some stories, like *The Hobbit,* that almost always work
with children. The students find something worthwhile in them, they
listen to them, talk about them, draw scenes and characters from them,
and write in response to them. Because this story is a fantasy, it readily
provides image-making possibilities. It liberates the imagination.

Also, *The Hobbit* is comforting because it is the kind of story where
"all rules are fair and there will be wonderful surprises." Children want
so desperately to be members of a world they can trust. I believe this
is a major reason that stories like *The Hobbit* and *The Chronicles of Narnia*
issue an invitation of hope to them. Some children value little because
so little of real value has been offered to them. These are especially the
children who have no responsibilities and too much pocket money. It
doesn't take them long to see the world as a place of things, a place as
disposable as a styrofoam cup.

Some years ago, Madeleine L'Engle wrote, in the April 1978 issue of *Language Arts:*

> Now we're approaching the 1980s and we've discovered the hard way
> that the real world isn't very real after all; the joys of technology are
> smothered by the stupidities of technocracy. Technocracy has provided
> us with vegetables and meat smothered in plastic packaging; tomatoes

are being grown so that they can be picked by machines instead of human hands and there's no way to make them tough enough without sacrificing taste; and there are some people who have never smelled the aroma of freshly brewed coffee.

And we're rebelling. We're going back to baking our own bread . . . and so once again people are writing fairy tales and reading fairy tales, because the fairy tale world is the real world, the world of the whole person, where we aren't limited to our intellect at the sacrifice of our intuition.

When we read fairy tales to children, we're opening up the world of reality to ourselves, as well as the child, because we all, grown ups and children, contain within ourselves all the elements of fairy tales.

Madeleine L'Engle is right. As we proceed into this more developed technological world, we will have to find more and more ways to keep in tune with ourselves and each other, or we will suffer further estrangement. Consoling stories, fairy tales, and fantasy bring adults and children encouragement and hope, and to a deeper search for what is real.

One of the central questions we all ask ourselves—in one way or another—is "Who am I?" Bruno Bettelheim maintains that fairy stories are expressions of our cultural heritage and provide some of the answers. He describes a fairy tale as "a gift of love to a child." Tolkien saw the function of the fairy story as threefold: recovery, escape, and consolation. As a parent and teacher and someone who remembers some of the time what it is like to have been a child, I want to preserve the tradition of fairy stories with the children I teach.

When my mother or grandmother told or read me a fairy story, I distinctly remember thinking, "Why, this story is about me." Those princes and princesses who suffered as I did were sorting out their greed, selfishness, and sibling loathing just as I was. I remember the actual book of fairy stories read to me long ago. We kept it in the piano bench. It had a dark blue cover with a lovely illustration of the Frog Prince on it. The very memory of this book comforts me.

To listen to fairy stories is to listen to our names being called. In the quest of finding out who we are, we discover that we are always more than we thought we were. As Madeleine L'Engle says, "We begin, somewhere along the quest, to see ourselves as the younger son, the true princess and the true prince, the stepmother too, at times, and the enchanted beast." This is what I mean by "hearing our names called" when we participate in a fairy story or fantasy.

These stories are also important because they have a healing power; they are about confidence and dragon slaying. "In the fairy tales, the cosmos goes mad, but the hero does not go mad. In the modern novels, the hero is mad before the book begins and suffers from the harsh steadiness and cruel sanity of the cosmos," wrote G. K. Chesterton a long time ago. This is one of the main reasons many modern novels bore me. I prefer children's stories because the heroes and heroines in them refuse irreparable loss.

★　　　★　　　★

But Where Is Zeus Now?

Reading the myths of different cultures is a broadening experience for children, and a knowledge of mythology certainly helps children understand other literature. But I like the six weeks we spend on myths during the school term because they're just plain exciting.

I read the D'Aulaire translation of the Greek myths to my students because, although the originals are adapted for children, the integrity of the stories is preserved. When the children come into the room and see posters of monsters, the names of the major gods and goddesses on big cards hanging from the ceiling, maps of Greece, pictures of gods and goddesses on the walls, books of myths and about myths on the reading tables and chalk trays, they plunge into a sense of high excitement. For the fifth and sixth graders I have worked with over the past seventeen years, the myths have brought us to intense writing and art work. My copies of the D'Aulaire books have been worn out and rebound many times.

Embedded in the myths are transformation stories, how one thing became another, such as "How Arachne Became a Spider" and "How Argus Became a Peacock." These transformation stories are read and retold by my students in various forms, including comic books. Recently my sixth graders produced an 18" x 24" comic book of their interpretations of their favorite transformation stories. It is filled with humorous insights into their understanding of *hubris*, the Greek word for pride, which caused the transformations. The gods did not tolerate any human presumptuousness or boasting.

One student adapted the story of the goddess Artemis and the hunter who dared to look at her while she was bathing after a hunt. The illustrations and captions demonstrate this student's sense of humor. The first frame: "One day, after a long hunt, Artemis, goddess of the hunt, decides to take a bath." (Artemis is decked out in hunting gear, near a pond.) Frame two: "So she took off her clothes and got into the water." (Artemis, bathing, singing, "La, de, da, da.") Frame three: "Meanwhile, farther down the road. . . . " (Hunter appears: "Hi, ho, I am a hunter.") Frame four: "Then the hunter saw Artemis: 'Wow!'" (Artemis throws up her arms, with a bar of Tone soap flying.) Frame five: "Since no mortal can look at her taking a bath, she turned him into a deer." (Explosion, with Artemis wielding a zap gun.) Frame six: "The hunters, thinking he was a real deer, ate him." (Piles of bones and bloated dogs, bellies up.)

The children also write new transformation stories, showing pride as the source of downfall for those who dare to try to surpass the gods.

Meanwhile, our vocabularies grow as we identify words from the stories, defining and illustrating them and putting them into bound class dictionaries: *hygiene, Promethean, echo, narcissistic, nemesis, macho, morphine, tantalize,* and *panic.*

Although I do not work as a bibliotherapist—except in the sense that anyone presenting literature to children is allowing them opportunities to match what goes on inside them with what goes on in stories—it is apparent to me that the myths open up for children new ways of looking at power. The Greek myths are about power, and in the D'Aulaire translation the message is strong and clear: the real power source is Zeus. He is the favorite of most students, no matter what socioeconomic group they come from: "I like all the gods and goddesses, but Zeus is the best of all because he is so strong" and "Zeus, man, is the baddest god of all."

Children also respond strongly to hero stories, particularly those of Hercules. When we finish reading about him, we brainstorm heroic qualities, male or female. I've done this with at least ten different groups of children, and the list characteristically looks like this: 1) heroes must be strong physically or have a special talent; 2) heroes must be attractive; 3) heroes must have class; 4) heroes must be able to do things better than anyone else could do them; 5) heroes must be willing to take risks no one else will take; 6) heroes must be the best at what they do; 7) heroes are always protectors of their people; 8) heroes must have the trust of their people.

Once the list of qualities is compiled, I ask the students, "Do you have any heroes? Do you know anyone who has any of these qualities?" Sometimes children have nowhere to go to identify a heroic person except to the pantheon of current TV shows. However, most find a heroic figure in their familial pantheon. Many children write heroic tales that exemplify some of the qualities we've identified. Here are two pieces by ten-year-old students.

My Hero Is My Brother

My brother can do all those things. He can jump over big wheels and over six of them at a time. He is not that good looking, but I love him. He has a clean-cut class. Some people believe in him, too, like his girl-friend and me. He is good at what he does. He can and does protect me when I get in trouble with big kids. He can jump one truck when he tries. He can lift sixty pounds, twenty-one times, up and down.

      ★   ★   ★

John Dutton, My Hero

My hero is John Dutton because his team is the Colts. He came from Nebraska and you know, if they come from Nebraska they are tough. Sometimes, John takes a risk by charging the quarterbacks. Sometimes John is attractive when he is playing. John does his part on the team so good that his coach thinks he has a lot of class. People believe in him a lot and so do I.

Another way we come to know the gods, goddesses, heroes, and heroines is to trace our own shapes on large pieces of butcher paper and transform the shapes into the characters we've just learned about. We use paint, magic markers, and collage. For example, a recent Dionysus was decked out with leaves entwined in his hair and around his feet, holding a large collection of wine bottles cut from magazines. Theseus wore a button, "The Minotaur Slayer." Hera is always the least admired goddess. The children detect too many qualities they dislike: her pettiness, her distrustfulness, and her constant nagging. One child pasted pictures of Comet, soaps, and other cleaning materials onto Hera's hands. Zeus, of course, held huge thunderbolts dramatized with a good deal of Reynolds Wrap. The halls were alive with this big paper collage of the characters the students had come to know about and admire. Each group of students comes up with fresh interpretations of the stories.

The children do some rather sophisticated work, but when we come to the end and read, "Everything must come to an end, and so did the rule of Zeus and the other Olympian gods. All that is left of their glory on earth are broken temples and noble statues. Also, the Muses fell silent, but their songs live on to this very day, and the constellations put up by the gods still glitter on the dark blue vault of the sky," many children lament, "But where is Zeus now?" Some of them come to believe that if they could just get to Greece, they would get at least a glimpse of Zeus. Others say, "There really is no Zeus. He's just a character in some stories." The argument over what is real and what is "just in some stories" comes up year after year.

The stories never fail to excite and entice children into a new way of looking at things and expressing those perceptions in writing, art, and lively talk. Their enthusiastic entry into these stories confirms, for me, that children today are still quite ready to put their image-making machinery into action. As one four-year-old said to me not long ago as we sat on a dock, early one morning, "See that fish? He jumped out of the water and woke the sun up." Piaget has pointed out that children and myth makers share similar ways of explaining natural events. That child on that particular morning perceived the fish acting as a cosmic alarm clock for the sun as a natural event. It was, for him, the way things happen naturally, if one but observes. So it is with the Greek stories and other mythic tales available for use with children.

I present the myths year after year because the children love them. They identify with the weaknesses of characters like Arachne, Niobe, and the others who dare to boast. The heroic episodes hook them because there is in those stories a challenge of great proportions held up for them to contemplate. When the children say the hero is always the protector, they are seeing a correlation between their own sense of the hero and that of the hero of the classics, the one who is responsible for fighting great battles, the one who places the needs of the community above his own needs and desires, the one "who takes risks no one else would take."

*   *   *

I also work in detail with the mythic stories and legends of the Sioux Indians. Because I teach in Nebraska, I choose the Sioux because they represented a dominant culture in this geographic area and I want the children to know what has gone on, historically and socially, on the very ground they walk on. I want them to recognize the heroic Native American chiefs who placed the needs of their community above their own personal needs. It is also my goal to help the children understand that although the great legendary chiefs were heroic, they were real people with their own personal dreams, visions, and goals.

We begin by learning about the buffalo, how it was an important source of the Sioux economy and spiritual beliefs. There are some superb films available for this study, but the best is *Tahtonka*. This film conveys the Sioux's reverence for the buffalo, and it gives a fair historical survey, ending with the battle of Wounded Knee. We also do a lot of reading, visit the local Indian center with our questions written out for discussion, and invite members of the Sioux tribe who live in Lincoln to come to the classroom to talk with us, to tell us stories, and to listen to ours.

Next, I give the students some titles of Sioux myths: "How the First Buffalo Came to Be," "The Legend of the White Buffalo," "The Great Flood," "How the First Rainbow Came to Be," and others. I ask the children to write the myths, trying to imagine themselves living here long ago, in touch with the land and the buffalo. Here are children's pieces on "How the First Rainbow Came to Be."

> With the beginning of time, there was a God, a happy God. He loved sunshine. He loved clouds. He loved snow, but most of all, he loved rain. It helped the plants grow and gave animals ponds to drink from. It gave a fresh smell of pine from the forest. Because the rain helped everything, he would do something. Something that would please everyone. So after each rain, he made some paint and painted a rainbow for everybody to see. Everyone who saw the rainbow thought it was beautiful. So after every rain, the happy God has painted the rainbow for many, many centuries.

★   ★   ★

> The first rainbow came to be one beautiful day in the month of May. The Lord would cry because the picture he was painting looked wrong, so he cried all over the painting. The paint dropped into place in the sky and that is what the Indians believed was true.

★   ★   ★

> Once upon a time there were some Indians and some different people from China, brown, red, yellow, and blue. The China people were all kinds of different colors of all sorts. Then the Mighty Spirit thought about this and decided that they should not die when winter came. So now after a refreshing shower we may look up in the sky and see all the colors of the flowers and it will be a rainbow.

After they've written and illustrated their stories, we compare them with the original Sioux myths. It is uncanny how closely my students' stories relate sometimes to the originals.

Mythic stories are retold in all cultures. I want to make these retellings available so that my students begin to know the stories that people everywhere, throughout time, use to teach their young the rules for human conduct, through metaphors for bravery, greed, faithfulness, envy, change, pride, order, lust, and laziness. Myths and legends teach us what happens to people when they attempt to overcome the weaknesses that are in all of us. These stories belong to each and every one of us. Children can look deeply into myths, see themselves, and make connections between themselves and all the other people who live and have lived. Children enjoy myths, because way down inside, they experience in them the stirrings of self-recognition.

Bibliography

Bettelheim, Bruno. *The Uses of Enchantment*. New York: Alfred A. Knopf, 1976.

D'Aulaire, Ingri and Edgar Parin. *Book of Greek Myths*. Garden City, N.Y.: Doubleday, 1962.

Fitzhugh, Louise. *Harriet the Spy*. New York: Dell, 1964.

Keen, Sam. *To a Dancing God*. New York: Harper & Row, 1970.

L'Engle, Madeleine. "What is Real?" *Language Arts*, Vol. 55, No. 4, April, 1978.

Lewis, C. S. *The Lion, the Witch and the Wardrobe*. New York: Macmillan, 1968.

Tahtonka, Prairies States Life Insurance Co. Made by Nauman Films, distributed by ACI. 1966.

Tolkien, J. R. R. *The Hobbit*. Boston: Houghton Mifflin, 1966.
—————. *The Tolkien Reader*. New York: Ballantine Books, 1966.

Bill Zavatsky

Morphology of *Goodbye*

This afternoon I wrote *goodbye*
on the blackboard. I wasn't going anywhere.
But in my self-appointed role
as History of the English Language
in my seventh-grade class
a pleasure like none I have experienced
flooded my whole body.
I laughed a bit maniacally
as I crossed out
the word's final *e*.

"You see how a word changes, eh?"
I said to the children
who quietly stared from their desks.
"The *e* in *goodbye* is going.
You see it spelled the old way less and less.
You leave it off in your papers
and only this morning in the *Times*
I saw it spelled without its *e*.
What once meant 'God be with thee'
has lost some of its history
since I was your age in school."

Unbelievably the children
did not fall to the floor
dead in horrible positions.

Maureen Owen

Circa

For years I thought   "Circa" was a place
and when I read the word followed by its dates
"Circa 1903"   "Circa 1812"   I assumed these were
just times events occurred in Circa   And
I was amazed continually that so much had happened
in one tiny pinpoint of geography   And to myself
I said   "It must be in France"

Ron Padgett

Problems with Words

Although a grapefruit looks nothing like a grape and a pineapple has nothing to do with either a pine or an apple, I always knew perfectly well what those fruits were. I had grown up eating them at home. But at a certain point—in my early twenties, I think—I began having trouble discriminating between the words *pineapple* and *grapefruit*.

When the actual fruits were before me, I had no trouble. But in conversation I was mysteriously unable to differentiate between them. "Honey, at the store why don't you pick up a fresh grapefruit, to go with the ham." Wife: "A grapefruit? You mean *pineapple*, don't you?" So I began simply to guess: the odds were that I would be right half the time. The other half I pretended was one of those perfectly ordinary slips of the tongue: "How silly of me, of course I meant *pineapple*." Eventually I began to dread using those two words at all. One day, after ten years of this confusion, my wife stated flatly, "You have trouble with those words, don't you?"

The simplest solution, which I used for a while, was to avoid using them. I would look up the road of a particular sentence and see one of those words approaching, then I would veer off onto a service road and go around it, using some clever circumlocution. This mental agility pleased me privately, but also caused me to wonder about my condition.

Now, seeing those words up ahead in a sentence, I no longer veer away. I arbitrarily pick one of them and call up a mental picture of it. After a moment the picture appears, something like a dictionary illustration. Then I match the picture with the place the word is to occupy in the approaching syntactical slot: if it matches up, I go ahead and say it; if it doesn't, I automatically say the other word. As I say the word, a little smile comes to my lips and I laugh inwardly at what a strange person I am and how peculiar it is that someone supposedly so articulate should have to resort to such a clunky mechanism, just to say "grapefruit" or "pineapple."

★   ★   ★

I've always had trouble with the word *atavism*. I can never re-member what it means, no matter how often I look it up in the dictionary, and its context never seems to provide a clue to its mean-ing. Its Latin root was one I never came across, so I can't decipher it etymologically. Furthermore, I can never invent quite the right mne-monic device for it.

Instead, as soon as my eye hits the word, I freeze. Then I tell myself to relax and just think for a moment, just let my mind go: surely its meaning will come to me. I begin to free-associate. In my mind's eye I see a large jungle clearing, at night, with a group of primitive people hopping up and down in front of a bonfire dedicated to the carved image of their deity, a totem pole with pointed head and almond eyes that curve upwards at the outer points. The muffled guttural growl of their tribal chant goes out into the darkness around them. Their blood sacrifice is being delayed because they have no victim, yet. Will they see me?

I open my eyes. In my hands I am still holding the book. I reread the sentence in question, projecting my fantasy onto the word *atavis-tic*. It never fits, so I look it up in the dictionary and then reread the sentence, which makes perfect sense. Within ten minutes its meaning begins to fade again.

Tony Towle

Typing Test (2 minutes)

By the time the thick brown box encloses the xenophobic fog,
the two halves of the brain should be working together: the left,
with its nose to some rational grindstone, and the right,
which was probably off gathering wool somewhere. That is,
the *reasonable* letters of h, j, k, l, n, m, y, u, i, o, & p
will be interacting with the illusory, or "off-the-wall" letters
of a, s, d, f, g, b, v, c, x, z, q, w, e, r, & t. One's own name,
for example, might start out with letters that are logical enough
and then get a bit screwy toward the end. But do you remember
when the human race had to write "by hand"? Certainly a great deal
of irrational nonsense was dashed off by right-brained left-handed
authors (Blake and Dostoevsky, for two), before the typewriter
imposed the practice of having the two brains cooperate, thus
insuring the intelligent balance of the modern movement.

To be sure, whether the writer was right- or left-handed,
there was always the issue of the unused digits in those far-off days.
They could help keep the parchment from moving for a while,
until the inevitable boredom would cause them to wander off,
most often to the writer's lap, an unwholesome situation that released
a centuries-long torrent of superfluous erotic imagery,
infiltrating even the composition of religious disquisitions,
as in St. Augustine. John Donne had the good fortune to lose an arm
in mid-career—resulting in the abrupt elevation of his concerns.
Milton, of course, classical as always, went literally blind from
this phenomenon: "a sinister hand in the nether land," as he tellingly
mumbled on his deathbed, and took the precaution of having his daughters
take his dictation with both hands at once. Thomas Aquinas
strapped the left hands of his monkish scribes painfully behind
their backs and so forth, the two minutes by now being up.

Ed Friedman and Kim MacConnel

The Frontiers of Language

JAU TU IUZ ZDIS
(How to Use This)

1. Covur zdi grameticel-reten inglesh sentenz uiz c card. (Cover the grammatically written English sentence with a card)

2. Sei zdi saunds ov zdi fonetical-rendurd inglesh sentenz *aut laud*. (Say the sounds of the phonetically rendered English sentence *out loud*)

3. Luk et zdi picchur tu jelp huiz sentenz mineng. (Look at the picture to help with sentence meaning)

4. Oncovut zdi grametical-reten inglesh sentenz end covur fonetical-rendurd huan. (Uncover the grammatical-written English sentence and cover phonetical-rendered one)

5. Nau rid grameticel-inglesh sentenz aut laud. (Now read the grammatical-English sentence out loud)

shi suipz lik no
bodis beiznez

She sweeps lik
nobody's busi-
ness.

ji is aur big djis
en zdi cumponi

He is our big
cheese in the com-
pany.

ai em flotin on
clauds

I am floating on
clouds.

ai em en e fok

I am in a fog.

zDi man jas aibols

The man has eye-
balls.

ai jav salaiva in
mai mauz

I have saliva in my
mouth.

iu enturfir pipols
praivetz

You interfere
peoples' private.

iu cip zdet iespi
iuatself

You keep that ESP
yourself.

campiuter sez jis klin

Computer says he's clean.

ceir tu sain iuar yon jencac tuet

Care to sign your John Hancock to that?

jelo skai zeitur ken iu reiserv tu beks tals itz for banzogoztucaledj

Hello, Sky Theater? Can you reserv two back stall seats for *Bonzo Goes to College?*

luk huat e biutefol gerl zdi illant vevianliuaz

Look what a beautiful girl the young Vivian Leigh was.

Stephen Vincent

In Class

Azuonye sits in front. He's tall.
He loves to raise his long arms
to discuss literature. Yeats. Achebe.
Wordsworth. Okigbo. Shakespeare.
An ear for two worlds, and more. I
change the subject. We speak
about how the children
are named. That in his village,
six weeks after birth, it is
the grandmother who visits.
If there is a dimple in one place
and not another, the grandmother
says it is this uncle or greatuncle
or cousin and not another. He demonstrates.
He points to his neck. He wears
an open-collared shirt.
There is a large birthmark, purple,
almost black, under the jugular.
Its wide diamond shape
cuts a sharp angle
down to his chest. "I am named
after a distant uncle," he says.
"The man was assassinated
with a machete
in an act of revenge."
The class—many of the students
are from the village—
suddenly ricochets into laughter.
Even Azuonye, as if already
divided by fate, breaks into
an odd smile. Only gradually
can I turn the class back
to a poem by Yeats.

Sheryl Noethe

From *Salmon Diary*

The second graders show up at school in the morning as if they had spent the night in a den or a nest. Their hair explodes off their heads in wild sprays, their glasses crooked, shoes untied, mysterious substances around their mouths and on their fingers. When they sit at their desks things fall off of them and out of their desks. The things have patches of fur and bubble gum on them. They have curious, inexplicable smells. They are at the stage between baby animal and law-abiding human being. Suspecting they know something I don't, I assign the old "My Soul" poetry topic to write about. They take minute pencils in hand and laboriously sketch out things like:

> My soul is a chicken dancing with a rug
> My soul is a chicken dancing with my cells
> My soul is a snowman dancing with the end of the world

and I grab the child and ask him, "What does the chicken mean? How do you mean, 'end of the world'? Who is the snowman?" and he looks back up at me with crayon breath and bottle-thick glasses and shrugs. Grins impishly. Elaborates with, "Dno."

My High School
English Teacher

In my junior and senior years in high school in Paterson, New Jersey, the outstanding, classic, Sherwood Andersonesque character was a Miss Frances Durban, who was a huge lady weighing perhaps 250 or 300 pounds, of immense girth and humor, who dressed in blue dresses with lace around the neck. She taught Walt Whitman by reading him aloud with tremendous enthusiasm, in particular the lines, "I find no fat sweeter than that which sticks to my own bones . . ." (and I have to paraphrase the rest: "the odor wafting from my body . . . admire my own armpits . . . breasts . . . feet . . .").

I still remember Frances Durban's smell wafting across the classroom on hot May days. There was an awful body odor from such a sweating mass of fat. Somehow, repulsive as that was, her cherubic round face, half-smile, and huge-girthed laughter were miracles of pleasure and energy that imprinted Whitman on my head forever. Her presentation of his humor and self-acceptance was decisive in turning me on, not merely to his sympathy, not merely to his empathies, not merely to his range, but also to his humorous intelligence.

I had home teachings of all poetry, including Whitman, from my father. Whitman was on the curriculum in high school, too, so I knew something, particularly "When Lilacs Last in the Dooryard Bloomed." But Frances Durban specialized in the self-acceptance poems in "Song of Myself."

—*Allen Ginsberg*

*   *   *

Knowing what I know now about writing, I'd say to my high school English teacher Jon Beck Shank then of Friends Seminary, New York City: Thank you for the marvelous, spirited reading of the poems of Wallace Stevens in your slightly nasal, persnickety voice. I've not forgotten the "poem of the act of the mind" and how "it has to be living, to learn the speech of the place" or "Tom-tom, c'est moi. The blue guitar / And I are one . . . ," thinking this is what poetry's to do, to be ordinary (natural) and yet give a kick, a shiver of excitement because it's full of surprise. It's fun to be a drum and a guitar and in a painting by Picasso, and speaking French too! This immediate oral "hit" made me want to try to make poems myself, and I did, terrible serious girl poems with colors and laundry and animals in them, and I also wanted to read them aloud (they were, after all, my soul's songs) and did, earnestly and shyly, and indeed doing this repeatedly was getting somewhere near that first shiver and then I guess poetry became a habit with me.

—*Anne Waldman*

★   ★   ★

I had a very lucky situation. One of my high school English teachers, Mrs. Flood, was really terrific. She inspired me to go ahead and do whatever I wanted to do. When my sophomore English teacher, Mrs. Gullett, refused to read a book report I wrote on *Raise High the Roof Beam, Carpenters* because it was written by J. D. Salinger, who used dirty words, Mrs. Flood stepped in and said that she would read it and grade it for me, which was approved. No one believed how bad a teacher Mrs. Gullett was until several years after I left, when she showed her cards by giving the students who flunked a test the choice of taking an F or kissing her feet to pass. That was her last stand.

Mrs. Flood had me do an assignment in which I rewrote *The Canterbury Tales* using contemporary types. That was something that really got me started in the different forms of poetry.

In my freshman English class, my teacher, Mr. Bolton, Barney "Barnyard" Bolton, who was a conservative religious fellow, as a lot of my teachers were, read "The Bells," by E. A. Poe. He stood in the back of the class and read it with great fervor while no one in class was allowed to turn around and look at him. He caught me sneaking a peek, and once again Mrs. Flood stood up for me.

This was in New Richmond, Ohio, a little river town twenty miles upstream from Cincinnati. It was a rural school that consolidated three schools (grades 1–8) to form a class of about a hundred students. My junior English teacher was Miss Todd, who was wonderful, except that twice in one year she made me come up and sit beside her because I was an acknowledged agnostic. She wanted to talk to me about "How can there be no God when you can see a flower grow?"

She thought this would be a difficult question for a poet to answer. That was the year I read Amy Lowell's poem "Patterns." This poem was very moving to me. I really believed her when she said, "Christ, what are these patterns for?" At that time the use of the word *Christ* in a textbook was extraordinary. It really grabbed me that someone could use that kind of vocabulary and get away with it.

Afterwards, when I was in college and read a lot of Amy Lowell and the Imagists (or, as Ezra Pound called the other American writers, "The Amy-gists"), I never could find a poem to equal "Patterns." I should read it again and see if it's all that good.

My advice to English teachers would be, "Let people turn around and look at you when you read "The Bells," and grade papers on J. D. Salinger yourself."

—*Bob Holman*

★   ★   ★

Dorothy Latski. I've always believed, these past seventeen years, that she was the pivotal person in my development as a writer and appreciator of literature. Fiftyish, thin, almost anemic, with fluffy grey hair. Now and then she was absent from school, suffered from some mysterious ailment that kept her at home, in and out of hospitals. Cancer? A disease that infects middle-aged lovers of literature? I never learned why.

She was of Polish extraction, had lived many years in Brooklyn working as a nurse in a psychiatric hospital before moving to Florida. She would not elaborate on her past, simply toss her head, murmur some ungraspable remark about those tough years in New York (I visualized a less frail Dorothy trying to put a straitjacket on a brawny sailor or administering an injection to a howling patient). And what made her even more mysterious was the fact that she lived with a woman named Tito—an elementary school teacher twice her size, but extremely loving and protective in nature—who had left New York with her. I never said it, no one else did, but I suspected that these two aficionados of wine, theater, and French cuisine were lovers as well as household companions. In white, southern Baptist Miami Springs, where Dorothy taught, news of such an illicit bond would have created a public scandal. But Dorothy was special. Our lips were forever sealed.

Her approach hypnotized me. Something about the way she read *Beowulf* in Old English made Grendel take on monstrous physical form before my very eyes. She forced us to learn facts—the Angles, Saxons, and Jutes; William the Conqueror, 1066 A.D.—but then she would throw herself entirely into *Macbeth* and mimic the three witches: "Double, double, toil and trouble, / Fire burn and cauldron bubble." She had that rare ability to transport the mind and heart away into another age where passion, alliances, and betrayals ruled the day; in a second the two-car garages, the spiffed-up Firebirds and Camaros, the ludicrous pink three-tiered fountain in the heart of Miami Springs vanished into the witches' smoldering cauldron.

Literature, for her, was a rich seedbed, the stuff of life, that bore fruit amidst the tangle of thorns. She read Joyce's *Portrait of the Artist As a Young Man* every year, religiously. Dylan Thomas's poetry, the subject of her hefty master's thesis, was her all-consuming passion and she was quick to point out the differences between his mellifluous lines and what she considered to be the crazy ravings of Allen Ginsberg. I memorized the fifty-four lines of "Fern Hill" for her, an offering she was never made aware of, up to this very day. Simply, I was in her power.

B.D.—before Dorothy—I was a superior math and science student who awaited, albeit half-heartedly, the opportunity to study structural engineering at the University of Florida in Gainesville. But she opened a door to a world in which trigonometric functions simply didn't exist and a broader, much more vital reality did. I gravitated towards literature, as if learning English for the first time. I began to look at words in a special way, admiring the sounds as well as drawing pleasure from their effects. The word *surf. Petty pace from day to day.* Language affected my life and if I succeeded in my apprenticeship I, too, could be a Creator.

Dorothy, this woman with blue, almost floating eyes belied the reality around me which, till then, I had accepted as the only truth.

—*David Unger*

★   ★   ★

The teacher who was variously the most respected, feared, and loved in my high school was all of these because, for her, words were equal to actions. When Mrs. Snowden asked a question, we often squirmed in our sweaty plywood chairs because she didn't ask to hear parroted some pat response. She wasn't asking us to give back a flattering reflection of her own thoughts. She was asking us to think. And she needled us until we did, or tried to. This was highly risky business, thinking on our own. At the very least it laid us open to twitters of ridiculing laughter from our classmates, which was roughly the same as being pilloried.

But just as often as her questions struck fear in our hormone-pumped-up teenage blood, they also caused hands to shoot up. Somewhere in the body there crouched, tiger-like, an idea ready to leap out and devour the classroom. Sometimes we had original thoughts, or thought we did. But often we learned that our thoughts were readily connected to a long history, and that was all right too. We found out that our ideas could be connected with other ideas. So it didn't hurt that we were learning more through Shakespeare than we'd ever thought we'd want to. Of course it was easier to read the current stuff, in our language. But once we came to know that there might be some connections with our feelings and our thoughts, the forms that the words took—antiquated, poetic, funny, even embarrassing—became as welcome a part of our lives as lunch. The hours in that class were time alive.

I remember sitting in Mrs. Snowden's class when classmates came in late. On such occasions a few students used to bring notes of dubious origin to excuse tardiness or absence. All quiet on the eastern front. We knew these notes were a sham but Mrs. Snowden did not deliver lectures on the evils of forgery. She made us take responsibility for ourselves, even though we sometimes didn't want to. It seemed that much school experience up to this point had been directed at getting us students to jump through hoops. "You're jumping through hoops, why?" Mrs. Snowden was brave enough to ask.

—*Arthur Dorros*

★   ★   ★

Concerning English teachers, I have two moments of reference:

The first involves the Reverend Matthew Conlin, O.F.M., freshman composition teacher at Siena College. I wrote an essay on a subject long forgotten, but what I cannot forget is the profound humiliation I felt when he read excerpts of my essay out loud and, to the vast amusement of the class, mocked its pretentious language. I have been enormously grateful to Father Matt ever since on three counts: one, for not naming the pretender; two, for making me aware of the importance of commonplace language; and three, for instilling in me a respect for exalted language only when it's thoroughly under control.

The second instance has also faded from memory, but only in the particulars. In high school Brother Eugene, F.S.C., taught me senior

English. I can't recall any of the books we dealt with or anything specific that he said, but what I remember is his continuing enthusiasm for literature, and the importance of it to our lives. He was very astute in his critical response to books, but the importance of what he said was not in that as much as it was in his joyful appreciation of, and gratitude for, good and great writing. Brother Eugene made me want to read, Father Matt made me want to write well.

—*William Kennedy*

*   *   *

I went to high school in San Francisco. We had very good English teachers, and a separate poetry class with a dreadful, pompous teacher, who stands out as being very destructive. I don't remember Mr. X's name, but I can see his face. He was like a cliché, very dramatic, with sweeping gray hair. You can imagine him with a scarf around his neck and the wind blowing. He was a hypocrite and a cultural imperialist. He taught only one sort of poetry. To him Dylan Thomas was the height of the moderns. He didn't go beyond that. He encouraged us to see poetry as a mothball art form, a cornball, boring, dreamy, highfalutin thing you do because you have a lot of time. Yuck.

He was condescending and cruel to students: "Well, you kids, you could never possibly understand Keats, but let me throw some at you anyway." This was a very progressive high school with a good academic reputation, so there was no reason to be teaching this way. I am not one to stress that you teach only contemporary writers. I think that American students in particular need a sense of history. But the connections must be shown quickly, so that when students go back to the old writers they see the points. Mr. X bored us to death with how great and inaccessible poetry was. It was like studying museum pieces.

For a person like me he was very bad news. I already knew I wanted to write. My grandfather was a writer and he was responsible for my love of books. I had to shut myself off from this teacher to protect myself, and as a consequence I flunked the class. I wonder if he's still around. He wasn't an old person. He may still be in that school.

Of the other English teachers there were two who stood out: Mr. Lombardi and Mr. Gamble. I respected them and they respected me. They appreciated my writing and had a respect for language. They made the students perk up. They encouraged students to give feedback. Students knew they had to produce. In Mr. Gamble's class we studied Dostoevsky. *Crime and Punishment* became an exciting detective story with metaphysical areas. We all got involved with why Raskolnikov was running. If I were Dostoevsky, I would feel good about being taught that way. Mr. Lombardi was very strict; but even though he terrified everyone, including me, I could sense he really loved literature and he wanted the best to come out of us.

There is a basic difference between Mr. X and Mr. Lombardi or Mr. Gamble. The latter encouraged us to look inside ourselves, use our imaginations, take our time, and make an effort. Mr. X made poetry exactly what it shouldn't be. I've seen a lot of his type in college studies too. Students continue to be exposed to this pretentious academic posturing. That, to me, is incredibly destructive, especially to poetry. It creates schools of writers who produce endless, boring poems. It really worries me.

If only I could think of Mr. X's name. I think: "Revenge!"

—*Jessica Hagedorn*

★　　★　　★

It wouldn't be bad for young writers if their teachers did as Miss Lobsenz did for me. I sat in the front row, right in front of her desk, because I was a deportment problem. Too much benzedrine when I was a kid. The doctors gave me that for my metabolism. I was fat and they wanted me to be skinny. They thought the bulbar polio I had got over affected my metabolism, so why not speed, they thought. I wanted to be skinny, but even more than that I wanted to be a writer. This was in junior high school. I was going to be a short fat writer. Miss Lobsenz taught *The Red Badge of Courage* with all her spinster passion. She was a small woman with long arms and a skinny neck, and she had many of the mannerisms of a chicken on a farm; particularly, she had the clucking down pat, which she did after the pecking. Although she had a great nose to peck with, she liked to peck with her hand, thrusting it out like a blade on the end of her long arm to make her point about *The Red Badge of Courage*. She had many points to make about that book, though I don't remember what they were. I did read the book and was impressed, but what I remember most was dodging and ducking Miss Lobsenz's hand. She was quick as a bullet, and the training I got in that classroom served me well in my later years as a writer, when I understood you've got to be able to move your own head if you want to move anyone else's. Pardon me.

Mrs. Makarof would sit on your desk and show you some inside thigh. I sat in the back of her class writing my first novel. This was about tennis bums. I didn't know what a novel was, I was too young, but I liked the way the word sounded. I wrote it secretly in the back of her class. She let me do it. Once she sat on my desk and looked at the notebook. She smiled, touched my face, and let me do it. I was going on thirteen the first time I had to slip my writing out from under to let her sit on my desk. I loved that class from the back of the room, but it wasn't English, it was science. She was the perfect science teacher. I suppose this isn't relevant to English, but there is something teachers of English can learn from Mrs. Makarof.

I was always a deportment problem in junior high school, and I think it was the bennies, although even without bennies these days I'm still a deportment problem. Mrs. Clayf hated me. She looked into my corner of the room from the blackboard where she was diagramming her sentence, and no matter what it was she picked on me, no matter who else let a fart, yelped, or threw chalk. She narrowed her eyes and started her "oooooooooooo" growl that almost always culminated in her favorite expression, "The booold impertinence of the buhrazen lot." By this time she'd be shaking her wattles, and this lady's chins were the definition of wattles, at least three chins and other stuff hanging from her neck, flapping around like pj's on a clothesline. If you want to impress your students, learn to use that expression. It has a certain rhythm. As a curse it is not unflattering, and the writers among them will come to terms with words like "brazen," "impertinence," and the special meaning of the word "lot." They might even notice how the redundancy cops can shut one eye to allow the alliteration of the *b*'s.

My high school teachers made less of an impression, though they were impressive. Dr. Shipley (he was actually a Ph.D.) was hard at work on his dictionary of slang, and hardly noticed his class. I spent most of my time with him working on the literary magazine, which meant cutting out for the 14th Street Billiards, where there was always a rumor that Willy Hoppe was going to show up. Now there was a guy, you might say, really understood the effects of English. I got another year off from English just to work on the literary magazine, and that was useful. My senior year was spent with Mr. Astrachan, about whom I remember very little, except a certain pomposity, expressed with his belly, that he thrust out above the class as he spoke, so he looked, when giving us Whitman or Frost, as if just a little more wind—say a jab of Dylan Thomas—and he would start to rise. He was actually jovial as a balloon. He wrote me a recommendation that got me into a special freshman English class in college. His nephew published a novel in the same year I published my first, 1968, that had a startling image in it that still sticks with me, describes the shadow of his Russian grandfather lengthening through time at his death to shade himself, the writer, as he attempted the book. Mr. Astrachan's recommendation for me described the "startling imagery" of my poetry. That made me try to figure out what imagery was, and look back through the few poems I had written, and notice that by no definition I could manage could I find a real image in any one of them. That too was useful.

So teachers of today, hello. All I can suggest is that you leave the writers alone, those of you savvy enough to recognize who they are. You can't teach them. They'll invent their own teacher out of the writers they love, and they'll appreciate all the space you manage to give them. Teach the readers instead. Leave them alone too, but teach them to read. That's my advice, respectfully submitted by a former, ongoing, and hopefully future serious deportment problem.

—*Steve Katz*

★   ★   ★

My favorite high school English teacher did say I had a talent for writing; but what I remember best was his dry, cynical way of saying that what the Church needed was a good persecution, to weed out the weaklings. I would say to Fr. Skiffington, "God bless you, wherever you are."

—*Elmore Leonard*

Christian McEwen

Four Women

At the Beginning of Teachers & Writers Collaborative

When Grace Paley was still in school, she cut a picture of a young woman out of the anthology of *Best Poems of 1943* and stuck it up on her wall. "I thought, 'Well, there it is, a girl and a poet, it's a possibility at least—' and I went back to not doing my homework very much." The woman in that picture was Muriel Rukeyser.

Years later, in the fall of 1967, both Grace Paley and Muriel Rukeyser came to work for the newly founded Teachers & Writers Collaborative (T&W), part of an eclectic group that included Donald Barthelme, Jonathan Kozol, Richard Lewis, and Ishmael Reed, as well as two other women writers, June Jordan (then June Meyer) and Anne Sexton.* Apart from Muriel Rukeyser, none of the four women had ever taught before. But by the time they left, their strategies and assignments, their personalities and politics, had become embedded in the very fabric of the Collaborative. Fanciful as it sounds, for me they stand like four caryatids, one at each corner of the "house" that is T&W: June Jordan, the black activist and poet; Anne Sexton, the WASP self-investigator; Muriel Rukeyser, the androgynous philosopher; and Grace Paley, "the chubby dark-haired woman who looked like a nice short teacher" (as described in one of her own stories), everybody's favorite grandmother and friend.

June Jordan

June Jordan was born in the Bedford Stuyvesant section of Brooklyn, and as a young woman worked in film and as a freelance writer. By 1967, she was technical housing assistant in an anti-poverty program, Mobilization for Youth. T&W's first director, Herb Kohl, remembers

---

* The complete list of writers who went into the schools in the fall of 1967 includes Elaine Avidon, Donald Barthelme, Jonathan Baumbach, Robert Clawson, Robert Cumming, David Henderson, Florence Howe, June Jordan, Herb Kohl, Jonathan Kozol, Richard Lewis, Mark Mirsky, Grace Paley, Ishmael Reed, Muriel Rukeyser, Anne Sexton, Peter Sourian, and Jay Wright.

her as "an incredible translator of moral values into action." She in turn remembers Kohl, for whom she had considerable respect, as "a crazy dynamo of a man. He was high and crazy, but he knew what he wanted to do." But as the lone black woman writer, she was less engaged with the other members of the Collaborative. Her heart was with black people and black poetry. "So when Herb told me he had found a woman for me to work with—a white woman from Mississippi—I was incredulous. I thought, 'You're kidding!' But that was Terri Bush, and in time I came to love her very deeply."

June Jordan and Terri Bush ran a Saturday writing workshop in the Fort Greene section of Brooklyn for the best part of four years. Their "Voice of the Children" project was one of the most successful that Teachers & Writers ever sponsored. From the start, Jordan brought in books by contemporary black writers, poems by Langston Hughes and Gwendolyn Brooks, and anthologies of modern African poetry. The children devoured them. Here, for example, is part of Jordan's teaching journal for October 21st, 1967:

> Around the table a fantastic thing was happening.
>
> One [child] would show another a particular poem—secretively, with extreme delight, nervously, giggling, furtive—as though they could not really believe what they were reading. . . . It got to be like the most beautiful kind of neo-Quaker meeting: there would be this extreme silence, and then somebody would just start reading a poem aloud.

Reading poems led to copying them out in longhand, and copying led to more ideas, until by the end of the session the children knew they wanted to write poems of their own. By December they wanted more books, and records too, and a record player. They wanted a place to dance and mess about and talk and browse. They wanted something simple and at the same time almost unimaginable to them, "to board a Saturday subway and get off at a place like home is supposed to be."

Their own homes were not often very home-like. From Jordan's point of view, "the proliferation of crises was staggering." Some of the kids were dyslexic. Others had parents on drugs or alcohol. Then, "so-and-so's sister's boyfriend would beat her up. Someone would get pregnant." There were problems with housing, with abandonment, with rape. And the streets of course were far from safe. As a child in Bedford Stuyvesant, Jordan had belonged to a gang called the Royal Bops. She had learned how to fight and to defend herself. "I was a girl gangster of necessity. I had a street baptism and training. It was a good thing my mother was a nurse, because she could patch me up." But as an adult, as someone who was building a life for herself outside of what was then inevitably called the ghetto, Jordan wanted to model other methods of coping. She and Terri Bush "tried very hard to put out fires." They also taught the kids to find words for what was troubling them. "Sling it on the paper!" Jordan would say. The children grew used to writing from "an urgent passionate place." It was a skill that was to prove especially useful in the coming year—"that unspeakably brutal year of 1968."

Martin Luther King, Jr., was assassinated in early April. As soon as the children heard the news, they asked for pencils and paper. That night, while Jordan read at Washington Square Methodist Church, they all sat through the reading, working on their poems. One of the poems, by twelve-year-old Michael Goode, was later published in the *Village Voice*:

Untitled

April 4, 1968
war war
why do god's children fight among each other
a great man once lived
a Negro man
his name was Rev. Martin Luther King
. . . .
it's funny it's so you can't even
walk out in the street anymore
some maniac might shoot you
in cold blood.

what kind of a world is this?

I don't know.

In the cab on the way home, the children were still burning up with words. One girl asked the driver, "Can you keep the light on please? I'm writing a poem." The light stayed on, and when the cab arrived at Bedford Stuyvesant, the driver refused to charge them for the ride.

At times, the children gave voice to a sense of panic that many black adults also shared. June Jordan remembers one student, Wayne, a streetwise adolescent all hung about with silver chains. When Dr. King was killed, Wayne kept fooling with his chains as if they were a rosary. Finally he looked up at Jordan. "Do you think they're going to kill *all of us*?" he asked.

Even without the edginess added by the assassination, such terrors appeared again and again in the children's poems, from Vanessa Howard's "I am frightened that / the flame of hate / will burn me," to Linda Curry's "My Enemy":

My Enemy is the world
The world hates me   it is trying
to get rid of me   Somebody
up there don't like me.

But it is important to say that the children wrote other kinds of poems too. Freedom to write meant freedom to dream, to enjoy, to celebrate, as well as freedom to rage and mourn. When Deborah Burkett started a poem, "I would like to go / where the golden apples grow," she was learning from Robert Louis Stevenson as all young poets learn from their predecessors. But the "rainbow clear in the sky" and the "red flamingos" were entirely her own:

Travel

I would like to go
Where the golden apples grow

Where the sunshine reaches out
Touching children miles about

Where the rainbow is clear in the sky
And passersby stop as they pass by

Where the red flamingos fly
Diving for fish before their eyes

And when all these places I shall see
I will return back home to thee.

The end.

As the first year came to an end, and then the second, The Voice of the Children began to attract increasing external support. Teachers & Writers stood back, and Jordan and Bush continued to work together on an independent basis. They raised the money for the children to go to summer camp in Toronto, Ohio. They bought a van, and organized trips to the Frick Museum, to the Brooklyn Museum, and out into the country. By 1970, when Holt, Rinehart and Winston brought out the young poets' first anthology, also called *The Voice of the Children*, the children had appeared on radio and television, and their work had been published in *McCall's, UHURU,* and the *New*

York Times, as well as in a number of anthologies. The Voice of the Children had truly been heard (and validated) by the adult world.

Anne Sexton

Apart from the fact that June Jordan and Anne Sexton were both poets working for the Collaborative, they could hardly have been more unlike. Sexton grew up in Massachusetts in a conventional middle-class family. She married young, and began to write poems as the result of a nervous breakdown. Despite her successes, she continued to think of herself primarily as a "patient," whose identity was in many ways predicated upon her sadness and madness. At the same time, she had a fierce hunger to reach beyond what she knew. "I need to learn," she wrote. "I am a stubborn person."

Perhaps because Herb Kohl seemed so entirely "other" to her, so deeply committed to education and social action, Sexton was drawn to him. She called him her brother, and signed her letters to him "Sister Anne." In the fall of 1966, she and Kohl both broke their hip (the same hip!) within two days of each other. "You sound more philosophical than I," Sexton lamented. "Send me some truth!!!!" Kohl did his best. He was genuinely fond of her, but it was clear from the beginning that he didn't have a lot of time to spare.

"Not only was I outside her pain, but I was obsessed with politics. I was obsessed with writing. I had thirty, forty, fifty children—my students—[to take care of] and I really didn't have time for Anne Sexton." Nonetheless, he sees now that "the way in which I didn't have time for her seemed to be valuable for her." She would call on the phone and it would be, "Herb, I'm in despair." He knew that she was desperate, and that such desperation could be dangerous. "But everyone I knew was in despair. I was functioning in poor communities where people were in despair because they were freezing at night, and people were hungry, so despair wasn't a big deal to me." For once the shrill voices of Anne Sexton's self-obsession ("My loss is greater than yours! / My pain is more valuable!") did not command total attention.

With Muriel Rukeyser too, whom she also met through the Collaborative, Sexton was forced to question some of the assumptions of her own anxious, pampered world. Rukeyser was no stranger to depression herself ("I have terrible periods. Depression is a mild name for it"), but unlike Sexton, who was always fidgeting with thoughts of suicide, Rukeyser never seriously considered it as an option. Rukeyser was the woman who had written in "Suicide Blues" of her severed head swimming around a ship, "Three times around and it wouldn't go down," the one who insisted, in the voice of the potted plant on her windowsill:

Flower flower flower flower
Today for the sake of all the dead
Burst into flower.

For Anne Sexton, Rukeyser's level of involvement, her compassion, her generosity were all something of a threat. At the same time, Sexton yearned to emulate her. "I don't want to be a 'safe poet' or a 'safe person,'" she wrote in her journal. "I don't want to be dead."

In the fall of 1967, Anne Sexton and her friend Bob Clawson started teaching at Wayland [Massachusetts] High School in "WASP North America." They were to work with twenty children for an hour a day, five days a week. Sexton, of course, was full of foreboding. "They will be people. I am afraid of people. Will I ever learn their names?"

Herb Kohl must have shared that trepidation, albeit from a distance. But in the end, Sexton's anxieties and self-doubt turned out to be useful for the students. Kohl says, "The kids could see her struggling with herself. It's like she was ripping off her skin in public." So what if she were Anne Sexton, a published author and a Pulitzer Prize winner? They treated her as one of themselves. "I can't believe you wrote those poems," student Steve Rizzo wrote to her. "You seem like us, ordinary. . . . If you could write, then we could write—anyone can write." Although there were certainly bad days, when Sexton felt she had nothing in her head, "nothing but a pounding heart and no curriculum," the teaching did come to give her joy. She read her own poems to the class, and gave unlikely assignments such as, "Pretend you are witnessing the crucifixion and write about it." She brought in a piece by Grace Paley, "The Sad Story of Six Boys About to be Drafted in Brooklyn," a Beatles song, and T. S. Eliot's "The Journey of the Magi," all of which excited prolonged discussion. (Having read the poem three times, the kids finally asked, "Who are the Magi?") She also kept her teaching journal with some diligence and wrote several new poems, including "The Papa and Mama Dance." The students didn't always understand her poems ("The Papa and Mama Dance" was in fact about incest), but nonetheless Sexton was triumphant. "I'm beginning to know them and they me. It's a small miracle in my life."

Another "small miracle" took place the following year, when Steve Rizzo borrowed Sexton's *To Bedlam and Part Way Back* and set three of the poems to music. Out of this came a chamber rock group: "Anne Sexton and Her Kind," which was to survive till 1971.

The class itself came to an end in the early summer of 1968. It had been, on the whole, a very valuable experience, even if some of the students would have appreciated a wider emotional range. As one put it bluntly in his class evaluation: "I would also enjoy having Miss Sexton read a poem with a happy ending, without death, incest, or related subjects." Sexton found this very funny. "None of my poems are happy—hardly any of them are." As Kohl says wryly, "Ambitions, hopes, and dreams were not her strong point." For that kind of help he turned to Muriel Rukeyser and Grace Paley.

Muriel Rukeyser

Muriel Rukeyser grew up in New York City. As a young woman, she had been dazzlingly successful, publishing her first book in the Yale Younger Poets series at the age of twenty-one. Her friend Jane Cooper remembers what an inspiration she was. "Just the idea of a young woman out in the world writing poems and making a living was amazing to me, because all the poets were men. She published five books before she was thirty. She was a *meteor.*"

The importance of having a "meteor" on one's horizon was something that Rukeyser herself recognized. "Who was your first living poet?" she used to ask her students at Sarah Lawrence. It would have pleased her to learn what her example meant to Grace Paley and Jane Cooper, especially since all three later became close friends. They used to read their work to each other over the telephone. Jane Cooper explains, "All of us who grew up before xeroxing are very good hearers!"

Rukeyser's most enduring relationships were with women, but she was never a separatist ("Whoever despises the penis despises the cunt / Whoever despises the cunt despises the life of the child"), and she and Kohl soon became good friends. By then, her early fame had fallen away, and she had lived through some difficult years, raising her son alone and out of wedlock, surviving the McCarthy era (as a communist sympathizer, if not a communist party member), and in July of 1964 enduring her first stroke. She had had to learn to speak again, and when Kohl met her in the spring of 1966, she had still not entirely recovered. "Her face was becoming unparalyzed. Some of her muscles sagged, and some didn't. She spoke slowly with a very deep voice." He found her extremely impressive, a "formidable person, an elemental force. She really believed that she could save the world."

That same strength and confidence operated in her teaching. Rukeyser was convinced, as she said in her poem "Rune," that "the word in the child needs me." At the same time it didn't matter where or how she started teaching, since for her "one's education has no edges, has no end, is not separated out and cannot be separated out in any way, and is full of strength because one refuses to have it separated out." Here, for example, is one of the exercises she used at the Community Resource Center in East Harlem. It is called "A Piece of Paper."

"I took a sheet of good typing paper and showed it to [the students]. 'Here it is,' I said, 'with whatever properties and possibilities it has.' I took the paper and in one gesture crumpled it small and threw it down in the middle of the table. They sat around looking at it in silence. 'Here it is now,' I said, 'with whatever possibilities and properties it has. Do something with it.'"

One student tore the paper in half. One set it on fire. "All right," Rukeyser told him. "That's a perfectly good response. It says it loud and clear. . . . We're heading toward words. What happens when we get to words?" And the student took another piece of paper and wrote in huge staggering letters, "help, HELP, H E L P!" A third student cut out a string of paper dolls and printed across their bodies, "People Need People."

For Rukeyser, none of these responses was "wrong." Each one drew words and possibilities out into the open: private, unexpected, sad, often "forbidden." One of her most famous exercises was to provide her students with the beginning, "I could not tell—" and see what then emerged. One of her students wrote about two children kissing in a dark corner, one white, one black. "I don't think the two of them pay any attention to each other in public," he added coolly. But that of course was part of the point. "Pay attention to what they tell you to forget," Rukeyser wrote in one of her poems. "Pay attention to what they tell you to forget. / Pay attention to what they tell you to forget."

Rukeyser has a poem called "A Simple Experiment" in which she writes of a magnet "shocked back" into "simple iron." It is possible, she says, to remagnetize that iron, to "stroke it and stroke it," until the molecules regain their "tending grace."

"Tending grace" is a good phrase for what she herself wanted to give, both as a teacher and a friend. Grace Paley says Rukeyser talked in harmonics. "It was like Sibelius, or the sea speaking. And people would try to extract grammatical sentences out of these waves of music that came towards them." Kohl describes her as "oceanic, dipped into the sources of language." It was as if she believed that words alone had power to heal. In the late sixties, during the riots in Harlem, Rukeyser wanted to go up to 125th Street and read her poems out loud in the street. Kohl persuaded her against it: "But every once in a while I have this dream of the whole world in riotous flames, and Muriel sitting, reading poetry with it all going on around her, and slowly the whole thing recedes. The words come out, the *presence* just comes out, with that conviction, and the flames draw back."

Grace Paley

Grace Paley was born in the South Bronx, the daughter of Russian Jewish immigrants. She published her first book of short stories in 1959, but she didn't know many other writers, didn't especially want to know them. There were far too many other things to think about. "First my father was sick that Friday, then the children were born, then I had those Tuesday-night meetings, then the war began." The words belong to a woman in one of her short stories, but they could easily be Paley's own. "I was so deeply involved in so many things," she says. "All of which really absorbed me totally."

If Rukeyser was the wise woman of the Collaborative, "the largest mind," the one who had gone to death's door and come back to speak of what she found there, Grace Paley was the reliable friend and comrade, the one who had been with T&W from the beginning. Jane Cooper remembers her from the time when T&W was still being talked and argued into existence, at the Sarah Lawrence Conference in February 1966. "Grace was my hero in that whole complicated session-after-session congress, when everybody was screeching at each other. Every time she would get up she would say something quite short and sensible, and it would be like, 'I think we should start in our own neighborhoods. My school is next to my apartment building. That's where I've been working.'"

Four months later, at the Huntting Conference, Paley helped draft the "Huntting Statement," which afterwards became a kind of manifesto for the Collaborative. This criticized the "milky texts and toneless curriculum" used in so many schools, and called for new principles, such as no grading, less emphasis on "correct" usage, and freedom for the kids "to invent the language by which they manage the world." The statement also argued that writing should not be estranged from the other arts, and that acting, drawing, and dancing could all be used to tell a story, and indeed, should be.

Once the funding came through, Paley worked for T&W in a number of New York City public schools. But she didn't do it very often. Resist was founded in 1967, the same year as T&W, and Paley was a committed anti-war activist. Besides, her children were in their teens and needed tending, and she had just started teaching two days a week at Sarah Lawrence.

Teaching college was new for her then, and she remembers trying to figure out "how to make smart kids dumb." It wasn't easy, but in time she was able to come up with her own methods and assignments: reading poems aloud around the table, because there were "tunes still missing" in the students' heads, teaching them to write "what they didn't know about what they knew." "Tell a story in the voice of someone with whom you are in conflict," she wrote in "Some Notes on Teaching." "Ask the oldest person you know to tell you a story told them by the oldest person they remember. And no personal journals, please, for about a year. Why? Boring to me. When you find only yourself interesting, you're boring."

When the papers came back to her, Paley's criticism was never framed in terms of "right or wrong," but rather, "true or false," a matter of moral accuracy, not logic or aesthetics. In "Some Notes on Teaching," she provided a list of the "lies" that had to be removed, among them, "the lie of injustice to characters, the lie of unnecessary adjectives, and the lie of the brilliant sentence you love the most." Then, lest her students get downhearted at the enormity of the task, she brought in her own first drafts to cheer them up. It was important to remember that everybody's work is clumsy and inaccurate at the beginning.

Meanwhile, back at the Collaborative, Herb Kohl was writing grant proposals and teaching his seminars and doing his best to keep T&W afloat. He didn't call Grace Paley often, because he knew how busy she was. But when he needed support she was the one he turned to.

She always had a story to tell him, most often something that would make him laugh. "And if you knew Grace, you'd know that the story was for you, and that it was appropriate, just listen it out." Paley was a realist; she never pretended that things weren't sometimes very difficult. But at the same time, "Life itself was more magical than the sadness of life. That was the spirit she infused for me, certainly. Being sad is no excuse!"

*   *   *

Grace Paley lives in Vermont now. June Jordan (and Herb Kohl) are out in California. Anne Sexton and Muriel Rukeyser are dead. But in the sprawling house that is Teachers & Writers Collaborative, there is no question that their influence endures. Poets, fiction writers, activists, and teachers: in the differences between them lies their collective strength.

A Note on Sources

This piece could not have been written without the kindness of the following people: Terri Bush, Barbara Christian, Jane Cooper, Florence Howe, June Jordan, Herb Kohl, Judy Kohl, Diane Middlebrook, Grace Paley, Robert Silvers, Tinka Topping, and Zelda Wirtschafter. Thank you very much. I have also drawn much useful information from *Journal of a Living Experiment*, edited, with commentary, by Phillip Lopate (New York: Teachers & Writers, 1979), and from *Anne Sexton: A Biography* by Diane Middlebrook (New York: Houghton Mifflin, 1991). Muriel Rukeyser's words on education are taken from "The Education of a Poet" in *The Writer on Her Work*, edited with an introduction by Janet Sternburg (New York: Norton, 1980). Grace Paley's "Notes on Teaching" are to be found in *The Point: Where Teaching and Writing Intersect*, edited by Nancy Larson Shapiro and Ron Padgett (New York: Teachers & Writers, 1983). The "description" of Grace Paley is taken from "Ruthie and Edie" in *Later the Same Day* (New York: Farrar, Straus, & Giroux, 1985), and later from "Wants" in *Little Disturbances of Man* (New York: Farrar, Straus, & Giroux, 1974). See also *Naming Our Destiny: New and Selected Poems* by June Jordan (New York: Thunder's Mouth Press, 1989); *The Voice of the Children*, writing collected by June Jordan and Terri Bush (New York: Holt, Rinehart and Winston, 1970); the *Collected Poems of Muriel Rukeyser* (New York: McGraw-Hill, 1978); *Selected Poems of Anne Sexton* (Boston: Houghton Mifflin, 1988); and *Teaching the Unteachable* by Herbert R. Kohl (New York: A New York Review Book, 1967).

Sheryl Noethe

Teaching Poetry on the River of No Return

In the fall of 1987, T&W sent poet Sheryl Noethe to Salmon, Idaho, population 3,308, for an extended residency. Sheryl arrived in September for planning and orientation. Beginning in November, she taught poetry writing to students at all levels for three months; in February she organized a big public reading; and in May she returned to distribute an anthology of her students' work. The next year, she was joined by poet Jack Collom. The two of them returned to Salmon for the next two years as well. In the final year of their residency, they co-authored Poetry Everywhere *(T&W). What follows are excerpts from Sheryl's letters and diaries from her first year in Salmon.—Editor*

September 18, 1987

In the rearview mirror I see horses and riders along the tops of the mountains. The clouds are red blankets shaken out by the sky. Buffaloes step out from within the boulders. Deer step lightly from the side of the road and watch me, poised for flight. I enter the city of Salmon and find my motel. The man in the office greets me like an old friend he's been waiting for. He tells me he didn't expect such a pretty lady and gives me the key to my room. It's charming, warm, homey, and has a little kitchen in it. I settle in and look out my window. The mountains are a thin blue paper cut-out against the deepening sky. The ridges at the very top fly like cranes, a sign of hope.

I drive out to the Cowboy Poetry Gathering at the fairgrounds and order biscuits and eggs. The cook is Chris Brady, who will introduce me to the people that I will be working with. The cowboys recite long, memorized rhyming poetry. I meet the women from the State Arts Council and the Salmon Arts Council. Everyone is friendly and glad to hear about the writing workshops. I drift through the gathering, meeting people. I am beginning to form an idea about what kind of people live here. I am alone but do not feel lonely. There are too many interesting things going on here.

On Monday I meet the Superintendent of Schools, Jim Smith. He takes me to meet the principal of the junior high school, George Artemis, who welcomes me and is delighted that I speak some Greek. Mr. Artemis introduces me to his wife and they invite me to dinner. We go on a tour of the school—big, airy, bright, calm. The teachers in the English department are all eager to have me come to their classes. Their enthusiasm propels me.

Tuesday at the Rotary Club the speaker doesn't show up, and they ask me to speak about Teachers & Writers in Idaho. I tell them about myself, the program, and the schools in New York. When I ask for questions, they ask me if I am married, and then if I am open to socializing. Not married, I reply, and glad to socialize. I get invited to go canoeing.

On Wednesday I meet the grade school teachers and all seven of them want me in their classrooms. Then Jim Smith takes me to the Chamber of Commerce meeting where we listen to a report on multiple road use, hunting and recreation versus conservation. This is an important topic here. I sit in on George Artemis's values class for eighth graders and then have dinner at his house. He sends me home with bags of apples, tomatoes, and plums from his garden.

Thursday I meet with the high school principal, Matt Weller. He describes how excellent his teachers are and says my major problem will be learning to say *no* due to time limits because every teacher will want each of their students to be in on the workshops. Then I go to the district potluck where I meet the teachers again and their families and eat heartily.

Friday I go canoeing and tip over in the glacial Salmon River. Survive.

Saturday I drive into Missoula, Montana, to shop and eat. Chris Brady and Holly Bevan, a local stringer for the newspaper, go too.

Monday I am on the radio. I talk for forty-five minutes, read my poems and children's poems from the South Bronx, and talk about schools, poetry, children, and how I fell into the river on Friday. Then I go to the Hospice and the women who run it are delighted to have me do poetry workshops with the volunteers. I am interviewed by two newspapers.

Tuesday I pass out the Teachers & Writers books that have arrived. The teachers are very pleased with the books. I set up my schedule with the junior high teachers and attend the Rotary slide show on hunger in the Sudan.

That evening I buy a lovely jeep.

Wednesday I go to the high school to arrange my schedule. One teacher wants me for all three of his classes because he doesn't feel comfortable having me in one and then doing the poetry workshop himself with the other two. We decide that I will do all three classes for each teacher, running the workshop for a month at a time, with the teachers receiving the full twelve-week workshop. On Thursday I meet with Jim Smith to make final plans. I will be in the junior high on Tuesdays and Wednesdays, working with three teachers each day, with an hour added where I will be in an office available to teachers and students. Mondays and Fridays I will work with seven teachers, four one day, three the next, at the Brooklyn grade school. On Thursdays I will see three teachers at the high school, doing a session of three classes a month, then switching to three different classes for the two following months. I will visit the Hospice in November and continue to read poetry on the "Voice of the Valley" radio program. I will also schedule some workshops for the Bridgeview Alternative School and for the Seventh Day Adventist School. These times will be arranged once I am installed in Salmon. I have made myself available to the library and will arrange for a regular writers' club, which I have advertised in the newspaper and over the radio.

I am looking forward eagerly to my life in Salmon and the benefits to my writing from the beauty, privacy, and solitude, and the remarkable people that live there.

October 30

I return to Salmon to continue my residency. The Superintendent of Schools and his two young daughters drive to the Missoula airport to get me. It's unseasonably warm and this near Halloween the streets and MacDonald's are full of witches and clowns, crying and eating hamburgers. We drive for about three hours and over Lost Trail Pass, out of Montana and into Idaho; in the front seat with the sun beating through the windshield I fall asleep and awaken entering Salmon. It is elk hunting season and the super has shot an elk and its head is sitting on the front porch of his cabin. The dog has torn out the elk's tongue, and there is blood in puddles. I look at the dimmed eyes of the giant beast. Jim Smith's daughter says, "Yuck," as she steps over a pool of blood to run upstairs and show me her two Cabbage Patch dolls. We drive into town with the want ads and look at a few apartments. Apartments, here, often mean mobile homes divided into two "studios" that rent at just over one hundred dollars. They are too tiny and bleak to spend a winter in. We drive to cabins and homes for rent and peek in the windows. I find one, an old stone house with lots of windows and a beautiful wood stove, that I imagine spending the winter in. The superintendent tells me if it was him he'd rent far from town, in an isolated cabin, and I tell him I desperately need an all-night grocery within walking distance to feel safe.

Then we go to an auction lot and talk to the men there about renting furniture while I'm here. They are agreeable. They invite me to the auction on Sunday. I begin to feel overwhelmed about things such as dishes, sheets, blankets, pots and spoons and telephones and desks and Jim Smith drives me to my motel so I can fall down and sleep.

October 31

I go to the bakery for coffee and rolls. The people there are all in costume. Clowns, mummies, Donald Ducks. One clown remembers me from the newspaper article and asks how the program is going and says he hopes I like it here.

I go and look inside the house that I want to rent. It is lovely and warm and big and empty and costs less than my room in NYC. A whole house. A wood stove. The woman who owns it offers to let me use her kitchenware and dining set and bed. It means a lot of work, hauling furniture and buying necessities, but after I examine more tiny mobile homes and an apartment complex I am more sure about the house. At the library one of the aides asks me how the poetry is going and says her daughter is in the fifth grade and will have me. I wonder how many people here know who I am. The man who showed me a tiny studio apartment heard me speak on the radio when I was here in September. We talk about the East. He shares the opinion of most of the people here: it's not a place to live.

The man who sold me my jeep calls and asks if I want to go flying in his single-engine four-seater airplane. Do I. It is at once the most exciting and scariest thing I have done in many years and we seem to hang on the cloudbanks, glide and float over the craggy Tetons. We see the forests burning and cannot land on Moose Creek like we planned.

November 2

I started at the grade school today. When I walked into my first class the children intoned in a breath, "She's here!" I had been afraid the children would be timid, shy, or too "nice" but instead they began asking me questions and wanting to hear my own poetry and telling me who the "good" writers are. They pulled out paper and sat poised over it waiting for me to stop talking and let them write. I assigned descriptive name acrostics and they busily and noisily set to. They wanted me to read their work and then wanted to read themselves. Class response was wonderful. It was consistently good in each of the four classes that I saw. I told the kids about buying a stick-shift jeep that I can't really drive. Their poems included jokes about my being a hazard on the streets.

> Shawn is a good trapper
> He traps muskrats
> And he traps coyotes, bobcat, fox, and beaver.
> When I reach down to get them they bite me
> Now I know to shoot them before I reach down to get them out of
> the trap.

★   ★   ★

> Being dumb isn't very smart
> and sometimes you can get hurt
> run and hide here she comes
> beautiful and weird awesome and cool! eeek! she's
> running me over by her
> acrostic jeep! Bye!

★   ★   ★

> Military Mike was a war kind of boy
> I held an automatic gun
> Killed his poster killed his thumb
> Everything in his room every
> Thing except his gun
>
> Sick that night
> Hyperventilating
> Every single morning
> Riding to school in a camouflaged jeep
> Motor broke down
> A temper tantrum grows
> Now he is dead on the mighty playground

November 3

Today was my first day at the junior high school. The children had been waiting anxiously for me for weeks because their teachers had gotten them excited. They were warm and friendly and curious and I read them a prose poem about boxing in the living room and they agreed humor is a great emotion to explore through poetry. I asked them to write name acrostics and use humor and honesty. They all wrote, and when I read the finished poems aloud they were delighted to hear each other's voices and jokes about themselves. The teachers were happy with what happened in class and said they couldn't wait until next week and neither could the kids. I wish there were more hours in the day.

> My friend has
> A dog
> That acts like a
> Table has fallen on him
>
> You have to watch out
> Even though this dog looks
> Neat, you might get
> Damp in the shoe.
> Every time you see this dog it would be wise to run!

★   ★   ★

> Kicking guns
> Excite everyone and aren't
> Very fun when they knock you down
> It isn't personal that it happens to me but
> Nobody likes it.
>
> Amber skies
> Move like a calm wind so
> Always watch when they come by.
> Run to see it.

★   ★   ★

> Just since I'm small I'm
> Under everybody
> So they all
> Tap me on the head
> It makes me very mad so I punch them in the
> Nose
>
> Bodily harm to
> One person makes him too
> Ornery
> To
> Stand!

★ ★ ★

My favorite things are soft, or pretty, or challenging
I love school and when I try, I
Can do quite well. I really like to be
Hugged or smiled at. I don't do many sports
Except I do enjoy cheerleading, volleyball, softball.
Laughter is contagious and I
Love to giggle and gossip.
Everyone teases me because I do well in school, and I often get upset.

Never before has acceptance meant so much
I have some really great friends
Could you ever believe the fun we
Have?
Older sistering is my specialty and I
Love my one brother a lot.
Sisters I am missing
Out on, but I really don't mind.
No one knows how sensitive I really am.

★ ★ ★

My name is Mykel if
You know me you will get a
Kick out of my jokes, but they are
Electrifying, you can't help
Liking them.

High above the sea
I see all the
Lovely sea
Leaning against the sky

November 11

The sixth graders are writing poems about my "colorful clothes" and
"funny shoes" and all the junior high kids are doing double-takes in
the hallways at nearly whatever I wear. However, the children in my
classes are loyal and they never are snide or mocking. They are quiet
about their opinions of my attire.

This morning I was out in my nightgown with a heavy coat on
over it trying to wrestle a paper bag down out of a tree on my driveway because I had no paper and was having no luck whatsoever with
starting a fire and a sixth grader came by on his bike. He said, "Hi,"

and I said, "Hi." He told me he had asked his parents if he could come over after school and chop wood for me. They said okay. I said, "Great. How about today after school?"

Sure enough, after school there he was on his bike. While he worked he instructed me about splitting wood:

- Don't even try to split a knot (where a branch grew).
- Split the grey logs with no bark, they're older and brittle.
- Never split logs drunk or you could hit your leg.
- Always have a full woodbox in the dead of winter.

He also told me which sixth grade boys already smoked cigarettes. We went inside and had club soda/orange juice drinks and he gave me a photograph of himself for my wallet. He told me that until I came to his class he didn't like poetry at all, but now he could see how it could be really fun. He said he didn't mind chopping wood with me because although it's hard work I was a pretty nice person. Then he grinned and became silent. I paid him five dollars, while he protested that he meant to do it free, and he promised me it would not go for candy. He said, "I'll spend all of it on school supplies." I said, "Well, what do you need?" He replied, "Paper." I asked him if he ate much candy. He said, "Oh, no."

Later that day I saw him circling my block on his bike. He had his little sister on the back. He invited me to dinner with his family and I gave him my phone number and said to have his mother call me. We agreed to chop together again when my woodbox got too low.

November 29

This week I and two new friends went up Panther Creek and climbed way up a mountain very slowly, encountering some drunk mountain men who joined us, and we found a natural hot spring, rumored to be the best one around, and one of the last ones left, and came over the mountain ridge to an area of running boiling water and a basin full of foggy sulfurous smoke rising, and then a pool of dark boiling water with billowing clouds of stinking steam seemingly straight from hell that obscured all sight and we had to wahoo to each other not to get lost. Then beneath a winter sky we stripped off our down jackets boots wool socks holofil liners hats scarves and dived into that murky pit of what appeared to be boiling rotten eggs BUT which turned out to be the grandest experience of my life. You lie and watch the frozen sky and snowfall while your body reddens like a lobster, and the sulfur makes you young again. The mountain men had jars of what is called Idaho tea and we sat in the water growing young and getting drunk and couldn't see each other and it was like out of Dante (etchings by Doré). I was with a nurse who drove out from Minneapolis and a military policewoman who grew up in these rough hills and knows the mountain men and everybody and every place.

The next day she took me up on Freeman Peak and taught me how to use a rifle. It turns out I am a deadeye and in some eighteen shots was entirely in the "kill zone" (the inner circle of the target) the whole time. I am not lying, only bragging. I would not shoot or eat meat but am now ready to protect free verse in every way. I have a roaring fire going in my wood stove that attests to my adaptability and fear of the Idaho night and its cold, cold blackness. When the fire burns low, I pop awake in my bed and start grabbing long underwear and mukluks and run for the front room where I toss logs into the stove in such a way that they do not suffocate the remaining embers but flare up and blaze fiercely until dawn, when I once again leap up from sleep and feed the fire.

At Thanksgiving dinner with a reclusive sharpshooter who teaches fifth grade, I got to listen to yet another heated discussion of wilderness and multiple road use and environmentalists (referred to as "wafflestompers" for their shoes) and managed again mostly to listen to all sides and not start volunteering the Absolute Truth on the spot. It's a touchy subject. Many people here would live much better if they logged the wilderness. As for the next generations of human beings and animals and forest. . . . There you are. They want to feed their families now. Anyway, I have also met some people from the Idaho Conservation League, which is frowned upon by most people here, and I am learning about things of which I formerly had no inkling. Yesterday I went to the Cheerleader's Bazaar at the high school and I ran into my fourth and fifth graders who rubbed their heads against my sleeve like deer and dragged their parents over to meet me and I ate fudge bars and drank coffee and purchased cowboy scarves and homemade goods. I live like a king. I am getting a little eccentric, but long hours of solitude beneath the awesome mountain ranges with my jeep parked outside the window have contributed to my dream life and peace of mind and heart. It is indeed the wild west. I have also met a fireman (whom I am taking home for Christmas) who pulls people out of the river and from burning houses and from weariness. But he's another story that will take much longer to tell.

I have collected sizeable amounts of kids' writing and it generally provokes the reader into delighted laughter. I'm developing a program for troubled junior high kids which involves word processing their writing and printing it out and having a bulletin board that highlights certain kids every week. I am learning word processing with the sixth graders! I am also attending the Hospice classes for volunteers on death and dying. I don't know when I'll do poetry with them, but I'm learning a lot from these women. I have rounded up about six women to take part in a writing group. The men are shy. Time however is going too fast. I may need years here.

January 15, 1988

Today I asked the class if they thought it would be better if poetry workshops were run on a voluntary, sign-up basis. They said yes, because that way the kids that wanted to write and concentrate would not be bothered or distracted by kids that were messing around. Then one boy raised his hand and said that he would never have signed up for poetry class, but now had come to look forward to it. If there had been a choice, he would not have taken poetry, but now knows how much he enjoys it. The class should be available to everyone so that they can learn to love writing. I asked them to raise their hands if they would not have taken poetry voluntarily, but now have learned how much they like to write. Most of the class raised their hands.

The principal, George Artemis, said that if he could change anything it would be that every student in his junior high would have poetry. He wants all eleven English slots to be involved in the workshop.

Jim Casterson, the junior high teacher who probably has done the most poetry work in his own classes, said that he thought the best legacy of T&W in Salmon would be the creation of a literary curriculum that all the teachers would use, one that would be mandatory along with grammar, etc. That curriculum would consist of a really great collection of poetry and other writing. He also suggested a resource person, a teacher in the school, to work at designing and implementing the poetry curriculum, and to visit the classrooms to see that it was being taught effectively. The other teachers at the school agreed that an established book list for teaching writing would be a big help, that they are pretty much on their own in finding examples of style and great poems to use.

One teacher's son broke his arm during school and had to go to the hospital. Later he told me the boy was upset while he waited to go into surgery because he was due to have the poetry workshop after lunch and would miss it because of the arm.

I got a love letter from a sixth grader who said that he is going to be a poet and just like me. Can I take him home? Can I keep him?

January 28

The fourth and fifth grade poetry reading approaches. We are making history. The young poets and I are floored by the idea. Mel Skeen, Brooklyn School principal, has offered to provide refreshments to everyone who attends and we have made and placed signs all over town, signs that emphasize the word FREE and have imaginative illustrations. We are some 112 readers and promised in the newspaper not to go over ninety minutes. Hah, we may go into the dawn. . . . Five fifth graders will be on the radio Monday, reading their poems as publicity for the reading. I can hear one poem right now, in a squeaky voice floating over the still valley, "I say JUMP and he sits. I say SIT and he jumps. I say OUT and he cries in plea. . . . " (our dog poems). There is also a whole series of haiku about my being scared in my house and quite a few acrostics where the acrostic word for the letter J just has to be JEEP, and then remarks about my eccentric rig. A close-knit and personal group. They are giving me these braided friendship bracelets and I am accumulating quite a scraggly armload of braided string. They count them tirelessly. They stop me in halls to show their friends the one they gave me.

A lady at the library told me her fourth grade boy, who likes trucks and sports and noise, comes home and talks about poetry to her. I told her boys that age are very tender and natural poets. I'm using Auden, Blake, and D. H. Lawrence. The high schoolers have finally warmed up to me: this week two different seniors dropped by with poems to give me. I accepted them at the door and sent them off. God, fourth graders are so easy. They drop by, have a glass of o.j. at my giant table in chairs that go way over their heads, and swing their legs and talk shop. They leave their bikes propped on the front step. Cute as all get-out. I am getting to know the little brothers and sisters that they tote around, too. I must know 600 kids here. I am endlessly greeting children, who hiss to parents, "IT'S THE POET," and the parents always smile.

February 4

Last night was the poetry reading. We held it in the City Center. I showed up at 6:30, half an hour early, to prepare. I set up the borrowed PA system and counted chairs. Kids started arriving in fancy

clothes with slicked-down hair, holding poems and folding and unfolding them. We went into an adjoining room to plan while the
parents drifted in. The teachers came too and stood with their classes.
I showed them how to talk into a microphone. I told them not to
rustle papers. Mel Skeen, the principal, walked into the room where
the teachers and I milled about with one hundred some students. He
looked at me and his eyes were round and his face rather pale. I wondered why he suddenly seemed so worried. He looked out into the
gathering room where we would read. There were people standing in
the aisles and along the walls and peeping in from the halls. Every chair
taken, people holding babies, families, grandparents. We counted between 250 and 300 people. It was the biggest gathering I've ever seen
or heard of in Salmon. Some parents, when they saw me coming in at
the head of a line of one hundred young writers, began muttering about
being there all night. I assured them nervousness makes for faster reading. There were eight classes in all, four fourth grades and four fifth.
The readers stood on the slightly raised platform and took turns at the
mike. The other kids sat on the floor around the platform. On we
went. They read about puppies, bunnies, love, their parents, broccoli;
they read haiku and acrostics and other poems; they were splotched
with red blushes in patterns over their faces and necks, they trembled,
they shook, but they each got up bravely and read like pros, introducing each poem as to name and technique. ("See," holding up the page,
"this spells my name.") They called the principal a punk rocker. They
wrote about When Sheryl Got Scared. Then they'd shuffle down and
the next class would fight their way to the mike and begin. People
laughed, clapped, sweated, it got hotter and hotter. But we all knew
we were a part of a grand design so we marched boldly forwards.
Amanda, who has brain damage and cannot get out her brilliance in
words, read her poems and people listened and could not understand,
but finally at the end of the third poem we heard "and my teacher
Mrs. Riggan, there she goes with a blue face, and Mrs. Crosby who is
as weird as the poet" and they loved Amanda. The kids acted like kings.
Sometimes they gesticulated or held out their arms. Sometimes they
pronounced the last words very mysteriously. It was like a Roman
procession in its formality and dignity. The young poets were serious
about their poetry and said, "Here's another for ya," and, "I wrote
this poem." Susanna Edgar recited:

> To walk in the woods
> is a gift to my father
> Oh! How he loves the wilderness

HAIKU
sort of.

So at 8:36 I shout, "Thanks for making history in Salmon!" and the principal runs up to me and says, "Hey, great, you made it!" (referring to the proposed ninety-minute length of reading: IMPOSSIBLE they'd all said) and some lady took an instant photo and gave it to me: it's me and Virgil Bosworth and Mr. Skeen and he's in a silver jogging suit and saying "You made it" and I'm pointing at my wrist and looking triumphant and my hair looks ridiculous.

Anyway, the reading was news, so I got to go back on the radio again today and say, "Yeah, you couldn't have squeezed another person in there with a shoehorn—it was the place to be." So I am on the radio now a lot and they play it again at noon and at five, I get to listen to my whispery old voice or else kids reading their wacky ideas with feeling, and I think about all those old guys grumping around in the barber shop listening to these kids or me.

Flora Arnstein

The Evolution of a Project

On a rainy day when my second graders had to remain indoors at recess I started to show one of the children how to make a house out of paper. Presently a group gathered around, and before I knew it the whole class was absorbed in making houses. Some of the children were not content with the limitations of my model—inventiveness came into play. "I'm going to put a porch on mine," says Emily. "Can I make a house on fire?" asks Eric and proceeds to cut out a jagged piece of orange paper and insert it into the roof. Doors and windows appear; one child is at work on miniature furnishings, chairs and tables.

It is only natural that with such an accumulation of houses we should find a place to put them. To the question, "How would you like to build a city?" there is enthusiastic response, so we scurry around the school to find an available table, which, installed in our room, we cover with heavy paper. Next morning at our daily conference we discuss what we want to have in our city: stores, schools, parks, gas stations . . . so many things that we write a list on the blackboard so as not to forget any.

But before we can build our city we must lay out the terrain, make some sort of a map or plan. On drawing paper each child outlines a map, and we pin them on the wallboard in order to be able to examine them and decide by vote which we prefer. The more mature children make more comprehensive plans, and it becomes evident to their teacher that this venture upon which they have embarked with such a joyous sense of fun will provide a wide range of educational experience in orienting the children to the city life around them. John's plan is selected by vote, and the next step is for each child to cut out a lot upon which he can place his house. This task includes learning to measure with a ruler, as well as becoming acquainted with certain terms, such as six inches by eight. Evidently some arithmetic will be included in this project.

The completion of the lots triggers another spurt of inventiveness. Trees, bushes, swings, teeters make their appearance; streets must be measured and laid out before the houses can be installed.

Around this time one of the mothers comes to visit the class. "I came," she tells me, "because Jimmy said 'School is fun—you don't have to learn anything.'" Another mother, calling for her child after school, says, "Andy told me that his teacher didn't do anything but 'get organized.'" Apparently there is a need to give the mothers some information concerning what is happening in our room. Children seldom report at home their doings in school, but in this instance since they mentioned their activity in connection with the building of their city, it is not surprising if some mothers wonder whether any learning is going on. The project method when employed without interpretation is bound to be misunderstood, and parents can easily believe that their children are "just playing." It is obvious to me that explanations are in order, so I send the mothers an invitation to a meeting one day after school.

I am agreeably surprised at the turnout and I proceed to outline the values inherent in our program. First I tell of our daily discussions to decide the next step in the evolution of our city. The practice of group discussion frequently is new to young children, and through engaging in it they learn procedures essential to group activity—how to listen without interrupting, how to make suggestions for bettering procedures, how to delegate activities, the proper checkups for following these; in short they learn the essentials of community action and how to work cooperatively.

I go on to list certain units of learning that are included in the making of the city. The children are introduced to the points of the compass. On the appropriate walls of our room we have placed large signs reading North, South, East, and West and we discuss the locations of certain landmarks in San Francisco, their relation to the school, and we orient our little city to the points of the compass. Thus a bit of geography is included in the project.

Along about this time we make our first sally forth into the neighboring world. Each of the children is given a card upon which is written a set of directions, such as "Go east on Washington Street," "Turn south on Maple," etc., and we start out to explore where these directions will lead us. In this manner abstract geography is given specific relevance. In addition some of the children who do not read too fluently are being afforded drills on words such as "street," "turn," etc.

Our next venture into the outside world is for the purpose of discovering how many street signs we can find, how the numbers run on houses, and any other observations we can make that may be pertinent to our little city. We return home full of ideas and proceed to make street signs such as "Wills Street," in honor of Tommy Wills who has been especially helpful in the measurement of our streets, "House for Rent," "Dangerous When Wet," and we install telephone poles, letter boxes, and as usual discuss every morning what we want to make next.

Now the teacher poses a question, "Where do you suppose we city people get our food from?" Donald brings to school a book on "Meat." We look at the pictures of cattle and sheep and decide to visit a butcher to find out more about the subject. I make a preliminary visit to my butcher to advise him of our projected arrival, but before we go we make a list of questions we would like to ask him. More cards appear with more detailed directions. This is going to be fun . . . the outing will be longer than the earlier one. We discuss procedures: how we will behave, how to take turns asking questions, not interrupt one another, not touch things.

On the day following our excursion we discuss whether the butcher has answered our questions satisfactorily. (This is a checkup on memory, which the children, of course, do not register as such.) They decide he has been very helpful, and it is suggested we write a letter to thank him for his courtesy. We compose it jointly (an exercise in English expression) and several children volunteer to copy the letter from the board. We vote who shall do the copying and Agnes is chosen.

Proceeding with our investigation of how a city is fed, we next turn our attention to milk. We experiment with containers: a gill, a pint, a quart bottle are brought to class to find out how many of each adds up to the other. We practically flood our room pouring water from one receptacle to another—for each of us must have a turn. Next day each child makes a picture record of what he or she has found out. Many weird bottles affirm that two pints make a quart . . . arithmetic.

And now we are ready for a visit to a dairy. Again we discuss procedures, for autos will be requisitioned on account of distance. The seating in the cars is decided on and arrangements agreeable to all are arrived at—that the boys go in different cars from the girls, and that each car have a leader who will direct the seating. All proceeds in an orderly fashion—incidentally the guide at the plant observes that he has never seen such well-behaved children.

The city project continues to grow. I bring miniature letter paper and envelopes to class, and presently an orgy of correspondence erupts. Each child wants to write to another in the city, so naturally a postman has to be elected to deliver the mail. The letters provide another learning process: the format of letters, the opening greeting to one's correspondent, how to close a letter, how to address an envelope. I gather up the letters afterwards, and note the misspelled words, which subsequently will appear on our spelling lists.

There is more to be learned, in particular how the various services of a city are administered. We solicit the fire department to send a member to explain to the children how the department operates, and to answer all our eager questions. Our city reflects our interest: numerous fire boxes are installed and tootsie-toy fire engines are brought from home. The police department likewise sends us an officer, and Merrytown (significantly named by the children) continues to offer new opportunities for learning.

Our preoccupation with our city, however, does not rule out other interests. We are not bound by preconceived limits. Jane brings to school a book on "paper," and we take time out to explore this field—how writing was recorded and messages sent before the invention of paper. Eric has decided to color an outline map of the United States—this because our butcher friend told us that some meat comes from Nevada, some from New Mexico and he wants to find out where these places are—more geography.

So much for the city project proper. Incidental learnings are explained to the mothers—some of which, in terms of group functioning, have already been mentioned. Rules relating to the running of our little community are formulated. We decide to have a mayor, designate a polling place, make ballots, and mark our choice for mayor with a cross. We live democratically to the extent that our understanding and experience permit.

To reassure the mothers that the city project does not comprise the whole of our educational experience, I explain that we also engage in daily drills in the "Three R's": practice in penmanship, in which we date each day's work to check our improvement; number drill, to expedite quick recall of combinations; and reading geared to the needs of each child. Some of the children read fluently, some have gotten off to a bad start; so we divide into groups, the better readers read to themselves or read plays aloud, each child taking a role. The others work with me, playing games with words, and because the games are fun they do not realize how quickly they learn new words. Many children who think they do not like to read are only discouraged—because it is more discouraging than some grownups know to have children around us who read better than we. Other reading activities include making books, pasting pictures in them and writing titles to the pictures, also compiling dictionaries and collecting magazine pictures showing things that begin with the appropriate alphabet letters.

Fortunately we know that a child need not be conscious of the learning process, in contradistinction to the old idea that unless a child were negative or unhappy he wasn't putting forth any real effort. As an example, one of our children elected to build a football stadium for Merrytown. The job was difficult and tedious for the not-too-skillful manipulation of a seven-year-old. Several times he was about to give up, but the encouragement of his peers induced him to hang on. Through doing so he was unlearning a habit of defeat under difficulty, and learning a new habit—an important adjunct to education.

Many parents are somewhat dubious about the interest approach to learning. They ask, "Will children always have to have fun in order to tackle a job? Life does not provide such situations; some day they will have to learn how to buckle down." The answer to these questions is no longer a matter of guesswork. We know that interest "lubricates" learning, releases and focuses a child's forces. But we know, too, that it only directs the innate, instinctive drive of every person to learn and grow. Adults, in their desire to see children achieve, sometimes lose sight of the potency of natural drives. We are all familiar with the little child's plea, as he or she pushes away the well-meant directing hand of an adult, "Let me do it!" This desire to accomplish for oneself is the child's greatest motivating force, and if we ally ourselves with it we find that "play" becomes unnecessary as motivation, once children arrive at the gratification of achievement that is the reward of their own efforts.

The mothers seem satisfied with the reassurance our meeting has provided them and respond later with enthusiasm to their children's invitation to visit their class one morning.

On this occasion, which has been planned at some length with the children, each child has an opportunity to expound on some aspect of the day's activities. An elected host announces each child's contribution. I sit in the audience and the children carry on by themselves. The mothers are impressed by the children's autonomy, and I too secretly rejoice at something I had hardly dared to hope for: the social responsibility of the children and the absence of friction that often occurs when immature children function on their own.

All in all the project method has received ample justification, and I have the courage to follow where it leads.

Notes on Contributors

FLORA ARNSTEIN was a pioneer in teaching children to write poetry, as described in her books *Children Write Poetry* and *Poetry in the Classroom*.

JANE AVRICH writes fiction and teaches English at Saint Ann's School in Brooklyn, N.Y.

JIM BERGER's plays "A Miracle Play" and "Icicles" were produced by Theater in a Box (New York). His poems have appeared in *Remington Review* and *Oink!*. He has taught in New York and Tanzania.

WESLEY BROWN is a playwright and fiction writer. Among his plays are *Love during Wartime* and *Boogie-Woogie and Booker T*. His novels include *Tragic Magic* and *Darktown Strutters*. He teaches at Rutgers University.

ACHILLE CHAVÉE (1906–1969) was a Belgian poet and aphorist. His works are available in French through Les Amis d'Achille Chavée, 83 rue A. Warocqué, B-7100 La Louvière, Belgium.

ARTHUR DORROS taught in the T&W program until he became a full-time author of children's books. His books include *Pretzels, Alligator Shoes, Abuela*, and *Animal Tracks*.

JOYCE DYER is assistant professor of English and director of writing at Hiram College in Hiram, Ohio. Formerly a teacher at Western Reserve Academy, she received the Ohio Teacher-Scholar award. Her study of Kate Chopin's novel *The Awakening* was published in the Twayne Masterwork Studies Series.

ED FRIEDMAN is a poet and the director of the Saint Mark's Poetry Project in New York. His books include *La Frontera, The Telephone Book, Mao & Matisse, Humans Work*, and *Lingomats*.

NAN FRY is a poet who has worked with the Maryland Poets-in-the-Schools program and is chairperson of the Academic Studies Department of the Corcoran School of Art in Washington, D.C.

MARGOT FORTUNATO GALT is a poet and teacher. T&W published her *Story in History*. She teaches at Hamline University and in the COMPAS writers-in-the-schools program in Minnesota.

ALLEN GINSBERG is the author of *Howl, Collected Poems*, and *Cosmopolitan Greetings*, among many others. He is the co-director of the Jack Kerouac School of Disembodied Poetics at Naropa Institute in Boulder, Colorado. He is Distinguished Professor at Brooklyn College.

JESSICA HAGEDORN is a poet whose *Pet Food & Apparitions* won the American Book Award from the Before Columbus Foundation. She is the editor of *Charlie Chan Is Dead: An Anthology of Contemporary Asian American Writing*. Her novel *Dogeaters* was nominated for the National Book Award.

ROBERT HERSHON is a poet, teacher, and publisher of Hanging Loose Books. His own books of poetry include *The Public Hug*, *How to Ride on the Woodlawn Express*, and *Into a Punchline*.

MARVIN HOFFMAN is a former director of T&W and co-founder of Houston Writers in the Schools. The author of *Vermont Diary* and *Reaching for the Light*, Hoffman teaches at Jones High School and Rice University, where he directs the School Writing Project.

BOB HOLMAN has published five books of poetry, including *Cupid's Cashbox* and *Panic★DJ*. He is the producer of award-winning poetry videos for WNYC-TV in New York and for PBS. Holman is also co-director and poetry slam host at the Nuyorican Poets Café in New York.

STEVE KATZ's works of fiction include *Wier & Pouce*, *Creamy and Delicious*, and *The Exagggerations of Peter Prince*. He teaches writing at the University of Colorado in Boulder.

WILLIAM KENNEDY's *Ironweed* won the Pulitzer Prize for fiction.

HERBERT KOHL's many books include *36 Children*; *Making Theater: Developing Plays with Young People*; *A Book of Puzzlements*; and *I Won't Learn from You*. He was founding director of T&W.

ELMORE LEONARD's bestselling crime novels include *Swag*, *Unknown Man No. 89*, *Glitz*, and *Rum Punch*.

KIM MACCONNEL is an artist who lives in New York and shows at the Holly Solomon Gallery. His work is in many public and private collections.

ANNE MARTIN has been a classroom teacher for over twenty-five years. She currently teaches kindergarten in Brookline, Massachusetts. Her books include *Reading Your Students*.

BERNADETTE MAYER's books include *The Bernadette Mayer Reader* and *The Art of Science Writing*. The recipient of a Poetry Fellowship from the National Endowment for the Arts, she teaches at The New School for Social Research in New York City.

CHRISTIAN McEWEN is a writer and editor of two anthologies of lesbian writing, *Naming the Waves* and *Out the Other Side*. She teaches at the New School for Social Research in New York City.

DAVE MORICE is a poet, artist, and teacher. His books include *Poetry Comics*, *How to Make Poetry Comics*, and *A Visit from Saint Alphabet*. He lives in Iowa City, Iowa.

SHERYL NOETHE is a poet and teacher of writing. Her books include *The Descent of Heaven over the Lake* and *Poetry Everywhere* (with Jack Collom). She has received a Poetry Fellowship from the National Endowment for the Arts. She lives in Missoula, Montana.

MAUREEN OWEN's most recent books of poetry include *Zombie Notes*, *Imaginary Income*, and *Untapped Maps*. She has taught writing workshops at the Saint Mark's Poetry Project in New York and at Saint Joseph's College in Hartford, Connecticut.

ROSALIND PACE is a poet and artist who works as a poet-in-the-schools. She has received a Duncan Lawrie prize in the Arvon International Poetry Competition. Pace is on the faculty of the Truro Center for the Arts at Castle Hill, Truro, Massachusetts. Her work at Poughkeepsie Day School was sponsored by Stella Chasteen.

RON PADGETT is a poet and the publications director of T&W. His books of poetry include *Great Balls of Fire*, *Triangles in the Afternoon*, and *The Big Something*. His volume of selected essays is called *Bloodwork*. He translated *The Complete Poems of Blaise Cendrars* and *The Poet Assassinated* by Guillaume Apollinaire.

JULIE PATTON's poems have appeared in *Transfer*. She is also a visual artist, with exhibitions in Cleveland and New York. Since 1984 she has taught imaginative writing in the T&W program and written for *Teachers & Writers* magazine.

FRANCES REINEHR has taught elementary school, conducted writing seminars, and developed curriculum in Lincoln, Nebraska, since 1968. She has twice received the Cooper Foundation Award for Excellence in Teaching.

MARCIA SIMON is a writer and child therapist. She is the author of *A Special Gift*, a novel for children that won a Peabody Award as an ABC-TV "Afterschool Special." She is on the faculty of the Truro Center for the Arts at Castle Hill, in Truro, Massachusetts. Her work at Poughkeepsie Day School was sponsored by Stella Chasteen.

ELIZABETH RADIN SIMONS is a folklorist and teacher who has taught writing and conducted teacher workshops all over the U.S. She is the author of *Student Worlds, Student Words*.

DANIEL JUDAH SKLAR is a playwright and teacher. His *Playmaking: Children Writing and Performing Their Own Plays* won the Distinguished Book Award from the American Alliance for Theatre & Education.

TONY TOWLE's books of poetry include *Autobiography, Some Musical Episodes,* and *North,* which won the Frank O'Hara Prize.

DAVID UNGER is a Guatemalan-born writer, translator, and teacher. In addition to being the U.S. coordinator of the Guadalajara International Book Fair, he is the editor of Nicanor Parra's *Antipoems: New and Selected.*

STEPHEN VINCENT's most recent book of poems is *Walking.* In the 1970s and 1980s he directed Momo's Press, publishing Victor Hernandez Cruz, Jessica Hagedorn, Hilton Obenzinger, and others. He is director of Book Studio, a book and CD-Rom packaging house.

ANNE WALDMAN is a poet and teacher. Her many books include *Skin Meat Bones, Iovis,* and *Makeup on Empty Space.* She is co-director of the Jack Kerouac School of Disembodied Poetics at Naropa Institute in Boulder, Colorado.

BILL ZAVATSKY is a poet, translator, and teacher. His books include *Theories of Rain* and *For Steve Royal,* and his translation of André Breton's *Earthlight,* a collection of poems, won the PEN/Book of the Month Club Translation Prize. He teaches high school English at Trinity School in New York City.

DID YOU KNOW

that every piece in this book
appeared originally
in *Teachers & Writers* magazine?

You don't have to wait for years for another collection such as this.
You can be in touch with the newest inspiring and useful ideas for
teaching writing—as they happen, in each new issue of
Teachers & Writers.
To subscribe, just send in the card that was inserted in this book.
Or, if the card has gone astray, contact us,
Teachers & Writers Collaborative,
5 Union Square West,
New York, NY 10003-3306
(212) 691-6590
for current subscription information.
Thank you.

OTHER T&W PUBLICATIONS YOU MIGHT ENJOY

The Teachers & Writers Handbook of Poetic Forms, edited by Ron Padgett. This T&W bestseller includes 74 entries on traditional and modern poetic forms by 19 poet-teachers. "A treasure"—*Kliatt.* "The definitions not only inform, they often provoke and inspire. A small wonder!"—*Poetry Project Newsletter.* "An entertaining reference work"—*Teaching English in the Two-Year College.* "A solid beginning reference source"—*Choice.*

Personal Fiction Writing by Meredith Sue Willis. A complete and practical guide for teachers of writing from elementary through college level. Contains more than 340 writing ideas. "A terrific resource for the classroom teacher as well as the novice writer"—*Harvard Educational Review.*

Playmaking: Children Writing and Performing Their Own Plays by Daniel Judah Sklar. A step-by-step account of teaching children to write, direct, and perform their own plays. Winner of the American Alliance for Theatre & Education's Distinguished Book Award. "Fascinating"—*Kliatt.*

The Story in History: Writing Your Way into the American Experience by Margot Fortunato Galt. Combines imaginative writing and American history. "One of the best idea books for teachers I have ever read"—*Kliatt.*

The List Poem: A Guide to Teaching & Writing Catalog Verse by Larry Fagin defines list poetry, traces its history, gives advice on teaching it, offers specific writing ideas, and presents more than 200 examples by children and adults. An *Instructor* Poetry Pick. "Outstanding"—*Kliatt.*

Poetry Everywhere: Teaching Poetry Writing in School and in the Community by Jack Collom & Sheryl Noethe. This big and "tremendously valuable resource work for teachers" (*Kliatt*) at all levels contains 60 writing exercises, extensive commentary, and 450 example poems.

The Writing Workshop, Vols. 1 & 2 by Alan Ziegler. A perfect combination of theory, practice, and specific assignments. "Invaluable to the writing teacher"—*Contemporary Education.* "Indispensable"—*Herbert R. Kohl.*

The Whole Word Catalogue, Vols. 1 & 2. T&W's bestselling guides to teaching imaginative writing. "*WWC 1* is probably the best practical guide for teachers who really want to stimulate their students to write"—*Learning.* "*WWC 2* is excellent. . . . It makes available approaches to the teaching of writing not found in other programs"—*Language Arts.*

For a complete free catalogue of T&W books, magazines, audiotapes, videotapes, and computer writing games, contact
Teachers & Writers Collaborative,
5 Union Square West, New York, NY 10003-3306, (212) 691-6590.